A
Korean
Nationalist
Entrepreneur

SUNY Series in Korean Studies
Sung Bae Park, editor

A
Korean
Nationalist
Entrepreneur

A *Life History of Kim Sŏngsu,*
1891–1955

Choong Soon Kim

STATE UNIVERSITY OF NEW YORK PRESS

Published by
State University of New York Press, Albany

For information, address the State University of New York Press,
State University Plaza, Albany, NY 12246

Production by David Ford
Marketing by Nancy Farrell

Library of Congress Cataloging-in-Publication Data

Kim, Choong Soon, 1938–
    A Korean nationalist entrepreneur : a life history of Kim Songsu,
1891–1955 / Choong Soon Kim.
        p.   cm. — (SUNY series in Korean studies)
    Includes bibliographical references (p. 211) and index.
    ISBN 0-7914-3721-3 (hc : alk. paper). — ISBN 0-7914-3722-1 (pbk. : alk.
paper)
        1. Kim, Sŏng-su, 1891–1955. 2. Statesmen—Korea (South)—Biography.
    3. Korea—History—Japanese occupation, 1910–1945.
    I. Kim, Sŏng-su, 1891–1955. II. Title. III. Series.
    DS917.92.K55K53   1998
    951.904′092
    [B]—DC21   97-35888
                                                            CIP

10   9   8   7   6   5   4   3   2   1

To the memory of my brother,
Choong Uk (1924–1967),
who led me to Chungang

CONTENTS

vii

ILLUSTRATIONS

ACKNOWLEDGMENTS

Well known by his pen name, Inch'on,[1] Kim Sŏngsu is a prominent figure in Korean modernization, and historians and social scientists at home and abroad continue to be interested in studying Kim and his work. There are several books written about Kim.[2] However, they are written in the Korean language. There is no single book written in English that treats Kim exclusively. I hope that this book addresses that absence, for in a way, I am long overdue in writing a book on Kim, since my interest in Kim and his work goes back nearly half a century.

In the early 1950s, I applied to Chungang, a high school founded by Kim and attended by my brother, who then went on to Koryŏ University, also founded by Kim. As a freshman, I met Kim for the first time on the front lawn of Chungang High School. Affected by the stroke he had had in 1951, Kim experienced difficulty moving around without the assistance of his wife; he seldom talked to anyone. Yet, wearing baggy, white, traditional Korean clothes, Kim struggled to kneel on the lawn and pull out weeds, one by one. (It was widely known that from his youth Kim had loved gardening.) Seeing his docile, humble appearance, I found it hard to believe that he was one of the most influential persons in modern Korean history. He seemed as modest as the grandfather of any ordinary Korean youngster.

When Kim died on February 18, 1955, I was still a Chungang student. With other classmates, I attended his funeral. Several of them were the descendants of Kim's friends, associates, and fellow nationalists, notably Chu

Yŏngil, grandson of Chu Sigyŏng, a linguist and cultural nationalist, Paik Soon (Paek Sun), son of Paek Kwansu, an intimate friend from childhood and close associate of Kim.[3] I was privileged to learn about Kim through the life histories of their families. (Incidentally, one of the former classmates and a personal friend, Yun Yŏ-ok, who attended the funeral with me, is currently principal of Chungang High School.) During the course of this study, Yun Yŏ-ok and I met often and recollected many memories of the past, including our first encounter with Kim. Also, all the newspaper clippings about Kim following his death, eventually proved a useful source for this book. I still remember the memorial poem for Kim written by my second cousin, Cho Chihun, who was then a professor at Koryŏ University. Therefore, I cherish the opportunity to write about Kim at last.

In preparing this book, I interviewed several Koreans who had been associates of Kim and had also witnessed or experienced many historical events. Han Man Nyun was one of the best informants because of his close ties to Kim Sŏngsu. Han's father, Han Kiak, a graduate of Chungang and Posŏng Junior College (Posŏng Chŏnmun Hakkyo), was one of the first reporters on *Tonga Ilbo*, which Kim founded in 1920. After serving as editor-in-chief of both *Sidae Ilbo* (in 1925) and *Chosŏn Ilbo* (in 1927), Han Kiak returned in 1930 to work for his old friend at Chungang.[4] Then, in 1932, when Kim took over the financially ailing Posŏng Junior College (which later became Koryŏ University, known to the English-speaking world as Korea University), Han Kiak served as the auditor of the board. Because of his father's work and close association with Kim, Han Man Nyun lived his teenage years near Chungang and met Kim frequently. Kim loved the boy and, upon the death of his father, personally gave him a scholarship for his college years in Posŏng.[5] Also, his father-in-law, Yu Chino, worked with Kim for nearly twenty-five years as a professor of law at Posŏng, drafted the first constitution of the Republic of Korea as recommended by Kim in 1948, and later served as president of Koryŏ University after Posŏng evolved into a comprehensive university.

Other helpful associates were Ch'ae Munsik, Kim Sŏn'gi, Song Ch'an'gyu, Pae Sŏp, Yi Ch'ŏlsŭng, Yi Sangdon, and Yun T'aekchung, to whom I am grateful for granting me lengthy interviews. Many surviving members of Kim's family graciously answered numerous questions. I am thankful to Inch'on Kinyŏmhoe for granting me permission to cite Kim Sŏngsu's biography extensively. Kim Jaeho and Kim Jaeyoul were effective guides and wonderful assistants in arranging my interviews with several elderly Koreans who had close ties to Kim Sŏngsu.

I would like to express my appreciation to two prominent historians, Koh Byong-ik and Lee Ki-baik. They encouraged me to undertake this project and guided me along the way. Koh advised me to compare Kim's role in Korean modernization with that of Chang Chien of China. Lee advised me to examine cultural nationalism as a valuable concept in interpreting Kim's work in Colonial Korea. Most of all, I am indebted to Lee's impartial view of Korean history.

My appreciation extends to several anthropologists and sociologists in the United States and Korea. Nancy Abelmann, Chun Kyung-Soo, Roy Richard Grinker, Han Seung-mi, Roger L. Janelli, Seung-Kyung Kim, Lee Kwang-Kyu, Lee Mun Woong, Wang Hahn-Sok, Dawnhee Yim, and Yoon Hyungsook gave me counsel, support, and encouragement. Han Kyung Koo read the entire manuscript. I am thankful to Carol Wallace Orr for her editorial advice. I am appreciative of *Tonga Ilbo*'s permission to reproduce the photographs and for its courtesy.

I am indebted to Robert Siegel and Sung Bae Park for inviting me to submit my project to the State University of New York Press for the SUNY series in Korean studies. Zina Lawrence at SUNY Press gave me enthusiastic support and guided the long process of evaluation. I am thankful to Lani Blackman for meticulous copyediting. David Ford has been a wonderful production editor, shepherding the entire bookmaking process. My appreciation also extends to the anonymous readers for their thorough evaluations, kind remarks, and constructive criticism that has improved this book.

This book is an unexpected outcome of two senior Fulbright awards, one in 1988–1989 for research, and another in 1993–1994 for research and lecturing, both of which allowed me to stay in Korea for prolonged periods of time. I owe special gratitude to the support provided by two consecutive faculty research grants from the University of Tennessee at Martin, and the assistance given by the faculty and staff of the Department of Sociology and Anthropology, University of Tennessee at Martin. Larry C. Ingram has been unfailing in giving editorial advice on many occasions.

I undertook the initial writing at Yonsei University, Seoul, Korea, during my tenure as a senior Fulbright scholar (1993–1994) affiliated with the Sociology Department. My gratitude extends to many members of the Yonsei University faculty for their hospitality. Cho Haejeong, Chun Incho, Hahm Chaibong, Jon Byong-Je, Lee Sangsup, Lee Sung-il, Nam Kisim, Park Youngsik, Song Bok, Song Do Young, and Yun Chin were all gracious hosts, wonderful supporters, and invaluable guides. Lew Seok-Choon, a graduate of Chungang High School, kindly loaned me his office in the Inmungwan at Yonsei University for ten months during his sabbatical. Without the assistance of the capable Cho Kyungjin, my job would have been much more difficult. Lee Jeong-Hyun and Kang Hammchan were instrumental in the preparation of a guide for romanization.

I owe special gratitude to my family. My wife, Sang, as she often has done before, bore a heavy burden during the writing of this book. While I was abroad working on the book with Sang's support, our sons, John and Drew, remained in the United States for a year without benefit of parental comfort. Later, they read the first draft of the manuscript and provided valuable comments and suggestions. Without the understanding and encouragement of my family, I could not have written this book. I am forever grateful.

Finally, I have to say a few words about my translations from the Korean and about Korean and Japanese names. Although I have tried to preserve the meaning of the original Korean, I have paraphrased for English-speaking readers rather than provided literal translations. I accept responsibility for any awkward transcriptions resulting from my effort to retain the original Korean nuances. I have romanized the names of persons, institutions, and organizations according to the McCune-Reischauer system with the exception of the few Korean names that have established romanizations of their own. In cases of familiar names, such as Seoul and Tokyo, I have adopted the standard English spellings without diacritical marks.

Also, following customary Chinese, Japanese, and Korean usage, and contrary to American usage, when dealing with native Koreans, I give the family names of people first, without placing a comma before their personal names, except for Syngman Rhee (Yi Sŭngman). The official name of South Korea is the Republic of Korea (ROK), and that of North Korea, the Democratic People's Republic of Korea (DPRK). Throughout this book I use the informal designation Korea. North Korea is specified when necessary to avoid any possible confusion.

INTRODUCTION

This book delineates the life of a moderate Korean nationalist and entrepreneur, Kim Sŏngsu (1891–1955), and his projects for Korean modernization during the colonial era in the early twentieth century.

During the Japanese domination, Kim led the moderate nationalist movement that eschewed overt resistance to Japanese imperialism and advocated self-strengthening programs to lay the foundation for future Korean independence. Unlike radical nationalists who advocated social revolution and overt resistance to Japanese colonialism, the moderate nationalist movement included an emphasis on education, the establishment of modern industries, and the publishing of newspapers and magazines to promote education for the populace.

Michael Edson Robinson, a historian, in his book, *Cultural Nationalism in Colonial Korea: 1920–1925,* labels the ideological aim of the moderate and gradualist movement as cultural nationalism, and classifies Kim as a leader of the cultural nationalists.[1]

Kim Sŏngsu's various projects encompassed the cultural nationalists' agenda: in 1915, Kim took over and developed a post-elementary school, Chungang, and in 1932, he established Posŏng Junior College, which later became Koryŏ (Korea) University; in 1919, he founded Korea's first modern textile firm, Kyŏngsŏng Spinning and Weaving Company; in 1920, he established one of Korea's major newspapers, *Tonga Ilbo.* In 1946, after Korea's liberation from Japan, Kim became a pivotal figure in the conservative Korean Democratic

1

Party (KDP), which became the main opposition party in Korea in the 1950s. He eventually became vice president in 1951 under Syngman Rhee (Yi Sŭngman). As Carter J. Eckert, in his book, *Offspring of Empire,* recognizes, Kim's "own history has been so closely intertwined with some of the deepest currents of modern Korean history itself"[2] that his story is indeed modern Korean history.

Despite the importance of their work during the period of Japanese domination and modernization, the cultural nationalists and their contributions have not been fully evaluated by scholars interested in modern Korean history. While some scholars praise the accomplishments of the cultural nationalists, others, especially students and revisionists, castigate their work. Considering the paucity of literature written in English on the work of the cultural nationalists, my main objective in this book is to contribute to the understanding, particularly in the West, of the Korean cultural nationalism movement led by Kim Sŏngsu and his close associates.

To describe this movement, I use a "life history method" that focuses on Kim Sŏngsu.[3] In anthropology, life histories are "useful for examining the patterning of general values, foci of cultural interests, and perceptions of social and natural relationships."[4] In addition to providing a narrative that includes encapsulated stories, the focus on Kim here sheds light on the Japanese colonial policies that affected Korean education, on native industries and nascent capitalism, on Korean vernacular newspapers, and on other cultural movements, some of which are excluded from the standard history text books.

Perhaps some non-anthropologists may be skeptical about the validity and reliability of life-history materials. Nonetheless, "To the objection that life-history data frequently cannot be checked against objective observations of real behavior," as Pertti J. Pelto indicates, "very frequently a chief anthropological concern is the patterning of peoples' beliefs and conceptualizations of past events, rather than the truth or falseness of these accounts."[5] Indeed, my objective is to relate the sentiments of many Koreans, who had endured the Japanese brutality during enemy occupation. In this sense, this book is an *emic* interpretation of Japanese colonial history in Korea, and also an ethno-history.

Indeed, the sixty-three-year life of Kim Sŏngsu spans the history of the rapidly changing, modern Korea after the Treaty of Kanghwa in 1876. Kim was born in 1891, on the brink of the collapse of the Chosŏn dynasty (1392–1910) of Korea. When Kim was seven years old, King Kojong (1864–1907) proclaimed the land an empire to be called the Great Han Empire (Taehan Cheguk), which in actuality made Korea a de facto Japanese colony. Thus, Kim's ambitious modernization projects were founded under Japanese colonial rule. When the Korean peninsula finally gained independence from Japan in 1945, Kim played a significant role in the establishment of a new republic that adopted the principles of democracy despite the threat of the communists and their sympathizers. In his later years, he dedicated his life to fighting the increasingly autocratic rule of Syngman Rhee, president of the first republic.

Because Kim's modernization projects involved education, industrialization, and the media, some native intellectuals metaphorically relate them to the teachings of great Korean pedagogues and patriots. Cho Chihun claims that Kim's programs closely paralleled the "three-front-battle (*samjŏnnon*)" advocated by Son Pyŏnghŭi.[6] (Son was the third ranking leader of the Eastern Learning (Tonghak) religious movement of Korea, an independence activist, and the chair of the thirty-three representatives who signed the Declaration of Independence in the March First Movement in 1919.) The three-front-battle strategy included emphasis on education, establishment of industry, and publishing of newspapers and magazines to promote learning to the Korean populace.

Kang Chujin maintains that Kim's endeavors replicated those of An Ch'angho, who was a moderate nationalist, an educator, and a key member of the Korean Provisional Government (Taehan Min'guk Imsi Chŏngbu) during the period of Japanese colonial rule.[7] An founded both the Hŭngsadan (Society for the Fostering of Activists), a fraternity of nationalist intellectuals, and the Taesŏng School in P'yŏngyang. As a member of the New People's Association (Sinminhoe) that was formed in 1907, An and his associates promoted Korean industry by establishing a ceramics factory and Korean education by establishing schools.[8]

Some historians, such as Koh Byong-ik (Ko Pyŏngik), suggest that Kim Sŏngsu shared many similarities with the late Ch'ing reformer, Chang Chien (1853–1925), of Kiangsu. In order to save his country, Chang Chien became a pioneer industrialist, utilizing the skilled labor and long-staple cotton produced in his home district of Nantung, Kiangsu.[9] According to John K. Fairbank, Edwin O. Reischauer, and Albert M. Craig in their book, *East Asia: The Modern Transformation:*

> Chang Chien used Western technical advice and production methods but handled his labor force like a Confucian Robert Owen, paternally concerned with their "joys and sorrows alike" as well as their living quarters and education. Prospering, he built three more mills and branched out into cotton-growing, steamship transport, and consumer industries—flour, oil, and salt production—and also became a philanthropist, eventually making Nantung a model district with schools and technical colleges, roads, parks, homes for the orphaned and aged, even a new jail. Having thus made the transition from

scholar-gentry to entrepreneur, Chang Chien became head of
the Kiangsu Education Association, a promoter of railways,
and in 1909 president of Kiangsu Provincial Assembly, where
he pushed for constitutional government.[10]

Although there are some remarkable similarities between Chang's projects and
those of Kim, it is highly unlikely that Kim knew about Chang's programs, and
used them as his role models. The truth is actually just an interesting parallel development somewhat like the independent invention of many cultural items
that were invented in many parts of the world simultaneously.

Others believe that Kim Sŏngsu might have been influenced by Mohandas (Mahatma, "great soul") Gandhi, India's major nationalist leader, and his
swaraj (self-rule) movement. Gandhi's insistence on nonviolence, self-sufficiency, and national unity, appealed to Kim and his associates. In fact, in December 1923, a group of moderate nationalists led by Kim were planning to
organize a political club (Yŏnjŏnghoe) for gradual nationalist development
within the colonial political framework, emulating Gandhi's *swaraj* movement
in the 1920s. The movement was aborted when opposition arose from a radical
faction. Although the Yŏnjŏnghoe movement fell short, Kim's respect for
Gandhi's vision continued, and mutual admiration developed. In reply to Kim's
earlier letter, dated November 26, 1927, Gandhi wrote Kim and advised him to
use "nonviolence" as a means toward Korea's independence.[11] There is every evidence that Kim respected and sympathized with Gandhi, yet there is no concrete
evidence that Kim's modernization projects, other than in their use of the principle of nonviolence, were influenced by Gandhi. In fact, Kim's programs were
already put in place when he learned of Gandhi's *swaraj* movement.

Still others, such as Carter J. Eckert, imply that Kim's modernization programs might have been influenced by Ōkuma Shigenobu, a Meiji patriot and
statesman and founder of Waseda University, Kim's alma mater.[12] It is highly
likely that Ōkuma's influence on Kim had been profound, because Kim respected Ōkuma and his accomplishments in behalf of Japan. Because he had never
personally met Ōkuma and had only seen him in public gatherings at the university auditorium, Kim himself denied that Ōkuma directly influenced him.[13]
Direct and intimate personal contact is not a necessary condition for influencing someone's thoughts or ideas, however. For example, although I never met
Kim personally, only saw him at a distance at school gatherings, as a student at
Chungang, I learned about him, respected his work, and was influenced by his
work.

Because of the various scholarly opinions about historical influences on
Kim, it is no easy task to trace the origins of Kim's ideas for Korean modern-

ization, mainly because he assimilated a variety of cultural values from a rapidly changing Korean society. He drew his moral values in part from the dynastic era. Then, during the colonial period, he was forced to become a realist in dealing with the colonial authorities because the entire peninsula took on the role of a huge prison. Even after Korea became independent, Kim's struggles as a champion of anti-communism and anti-autocratic rule continued. In addition, one cannot dismiss the probability that Kim actually conceived his notions about Korean modernization from his parents and his in-laws. A plethora of role models surrounded him as he was growing up. And, without a doubt, his overseas study and worldwide travels would have reinforced and otherwise affected his earlier thought. Thus, the origins of Kim's ethical complexity and enculturation are difficult to trace, and may not stem from a single source.

An Overview of Korean History

A review of recent Korean history reveals the magnitude of its complexity and distinctive qualities. An irony is its ethnonym, *Chosŏn*, the Korean version of the Chinese phrase *chao-hsien*, which may be roughly translated as "morning calm and freshness." The ethnonym *Chosŏn* has been used twice in Korean history; during the first tribal state (2333 B.C.–194 B.C.) and again during the Chosŏn dynasty (1392–1910). From this ethnonym, Korea has acquired the epithet by which it is still known today, "the land of the morning calm." North Koreans, even at the present, use the ethnonym beside the official name of the Democratic People's Republic of Korea (DPRK). Despite the ethnonym, however, those familiar with Korea's geopolitical history may wonder if the country has ever been "calm." Historical evidence indicates that, instead of experiencing tranquility, Koreans have often been awakened by the clattering of horses' hooves or the artillery fire of foreign intruders. The peninsula has seemingly been "the land of broken calm," as the subtitle of Shannon McCune's book on Korea indicates.[14]

Geopolitically, Korea is in the middle of the Far East. The long northern border of the Korean peninsula is linked with the vast expanse of Manchuria, an area almost forty-three times Korea's size. Comparison of Korea with the Russo-Siberian land mass, with which it shares an eleven-mile border, is almost ludicrous. Across the Eastern Sea lies the island nation of Japan, an area almost seventy percent larger than Korea. The channel between Korea and Japan is so narrow that on a clear day one can see Tsushima Island of Japan from Pusan, on the southeastern tip of Korea. As a consequence, the peninsula has always been vulnerable to attacks from neighboring states.[15] In addition to invasion and domination by Chinese dynasties over the centuries,[16] there have been continual intrusions from nomadic northern tribes such as the Yen, Khitan, Jurchen, and Mongols.[17]

The rise and fall of Chinese dynasties had a profound impact on the security of Korea. Furthermore, two full-scale Japanese invasions of Korea by Hideyoshi Toyotomi in the sixteenth century, which devastated the Chosŏn dynasty of Korea,[18] and the invasion of the Manchu state of the Late Ch'ing into Chosŏn in the seventeenth century were debilitating.

As the history of Korea reveals, in spite of foreign invasions and colonization by its much larger and stronger neighbors, the Korean peninsula had been united since the seventh century; except in rare and temporary instances, it has remained undivided, protected on its northern border by two great rivers, the Yalu and the Tumen. Korea has maintained its identity and continuity. According to Gregory Henderson, in his book, *Korea: The Politics of the Vortex*, "smallness of dimension, stability of boundaries, ethnic and religious homogeneity, and *exceptional historical continuity mark Korea*" [emphasis added].[19]

Unlike the common view that the history of Korea is the story of adversities, the judgment of some historians, notably Lee Ki-baik, is that, except for two invasions by Hideyoshi in the sixteenth century and Ch'ing Emperor T'ai Tsung in the seventeenth century, the Chosŏn dynasty was able to maintain peaceful relations with other nations for five hundred years. Lee observes that in the period comparable to Chosŏn, China was ruled by foreign forces for three hundred years, France had to experience a war for a hundred years, and Germany had a war for thirty years.[20]

Beginning in the early nineteenth century, however, Koreans had to deal with yet another threat from the West. In direct response to Western intrusion, Yi Haung of the Chosŏn dynasty of Korea, better known in Korean history as the Taewŏn'gun, adopted a policy of isolationism. (The country became known as the Hermit Kingdom during this period.) Nevertheless, it would be a mistake for anyone to believe that Korea was unaware of the existence of the West and its potential impact on the peninsula. Before and after the Hideyoshi invasions in the sixteenth century and thereafter in the seventeenth century, Chosŏn began to understand the West, especially through Catholicism, called Western Learning (*Sŏhak*). Practical Learning (*Sirhak*),[21] in the seventeenth and the eighteenth centuries, led to "enlightenment thought (*kaehwa sasang*)"[22] that aimed to reform Chosŏn dynasty institutions. Enlightenment thought served as a guiding metaphor for future modernization.

In the name of modernization, Korea was forced in 1876 to sign a treaty with Japan known as the "Treaty of Kanghwa." The most important feature of the treaty was the provision for opening Korean ports. Although the treaty was unfair, it brought Korea for the first time onto the international stage. Beginning in the mid-nineteenth century, foreigners, competing for Korean trade, clashed on Korean soil, leading to the Russo-Japanese War of 1904–1905. Victory in this conflict provided Japan with a firm base for taking sole control of the Korean peninsula. Japan moved immediately to establish a protectorate over Korea, and in 1905 forced the ministry of foreign affairs to sign the Protectorate Treaty (*Ŭlsa nŭngyak*). Five years later, Japan annexed Korea and maintained it as its colony until 1945.

During the period of turmoil in the late nineteenth century, especially after the Treaty of Kanghwa in 1876, Korea faced two major challenges: first, to deal with the imminent threat of foreign forces, particularly from Japan; and second, to bring about domestic reform and modernization in order to retain its sovereignty. From the collapse of the Chosŏn dynasty to the Treaty of Kanghwa and up to the annexation, there were various reform movements under the influence of the enlightenment thought. It was an attempt to find solutions to the pressing problems of nineteenth-century Korea by applying the results of their work in new directions. Enlightenment thought stressed national self-strengthening through education and the development of Korean commerce and industry; it exerted a powerful influence on officialdom, including *yangban* (or nobility)[23] and the royal in-law family. Nevertheless, the ambitious effort to copy Japan's Meiji Restoration and to make the Korean nation independent failed in reality because of factional strife within the reform movement, the interference of Chinese troops, and an unrealistic hope of winning Japanese support for the progressive plans. As the coup d'état of 1884 (*kapsin chŏngbyŏn*) by the progressives failed, the power of the progressives came to an end.

Nevertheless, various reforms, revolts, and rebellious movements followed one after another, among them the Reform (*kabo kyŏngjang*), Peasant rebellion (Tonghak) of 1894, the Righteous armies (*ŭibyŏng*) and Independence Club (Tongnip Hyŏphoe) movements of 1895. Those actions were aimed at retaining Korea's sovereignty and resisting foreign threat, at curing the domestic illness that resulted from incompatible class structure, subsistence level economic structure, and an inept government unable to deal with domestic problems.

The reform of 1894 was a sweeping one, affecting virtually every aspect of the administration, of the economy, and of sociocultural activities. There was an effort to eliminate class distinctions between *yangban* and commoners, and to introduce the concept of equality and dignity for all. The reform package was so broad and extensive that it included a new standardization of weights and measures, adoption of a new calendar, and an order to cut the Korean male's traditional topknot (*sangt'u*). Martina Deuchler, in her book, *Confucian Gentlemen and Barbarian Envoys,* calls the drastic *Kabo* reform "the starting point of

Korea's modernization because those reforms introduced genuine modern features into Korea." [24] However, the package did not include strengthening military manpower, which was essential then to the security of a state confronting foreign threats. Most of all, since the reforms were planned under Japanese domination not only were they ineffective, but they also had the unintended consequence of accelerating the penetration into Korea of Japan's developing capitalist economy. Also, some of the reform programs, such as ordering the cutting of the topknot, brought furious opposition from conservative Koreans. However, the reforms as a whole significantly advanced Korea's modernization, although they failed to guarantee Korea's sovereignty.

In a direct response to Japanese domination, in 1895 *yangban* officialdom and the Confucian literati mobilized the peasantry and formed guerrilla bands called "Righteous armies" throughout the country. Some bands included hundreds and thousands of fighters, but, until they absorbed the government soldiers disbanded by the Japanese in 1907, they possessed neither military training nor military discipline. The bands were for the most part equipped only with the spirit to fight the Japanese. Using guerrilla tactics, some bands were successful in attacking Japanese garrisons. In 1907, ten thousand mobilized guerrilla forces from all over the country attacked the Residency-General headquarters, and the advance units were able to penetrate to positions less than ten miles from Seoul's East Gate (Tongdaemun). Yet, they had too many deficiencies in manpower and weaponry to defeat the Japanese forces in Korea. The activities of the Righteous armies reached a peak in 1908 and declined thereafter, and after annexation, the soldiers became independence fighters. The Righteous armies demonstrated the most courageous anti-Japanese fighting in Korean history, yet, because they composed mostly Confucian literati, they undertook no efforts toward domestic reform. Rather, they represented a movement against Western thought, especially Catholicism, and in favor of retaining the status quo. Theirs was a noble action to demonstrate patriotism, never intended to be a national movement for modernization.

Unlike the Righteous armies, the Peasant rebellion undertook two major tasks, domestic reform, and fighting against Japan to retain sovereignty. After the execution of its founder, Ch'oe Cheu, in 1864, the Peasant rebellion went underground, but, by 1894, it had expanded and was well enough organized to express the peasantry's deep hostility toward the *yangban* class. The rebels led a resistance against the inroads of foreign powers, hoisting banners and calling for a crusade to expel the Japanese and Westerners. The Peasant rebellion erupted into a revolutionary peasant struggle, employing large-scale military operations. Started in Kobu county, Chŏlla province, by Chŏn Pongjun and his fellow peasants, the Peasant rebellion raged against the county magistrate's abuse of power and corruption. Peasants from all the surrounding areas joined forces with the Righteous armies, swelling their ranks to over ten thousand men, and controlling parts of Chŏlla and Ch'ungch'ŏng provinces after crushing government troops. Eventually, the movement spread to other provinces. As Japan intervened militarily, the Righteous armies fought the Japanese face-to-face. However, professional Japanese troops, armed with superior weapons and training, defeated the ill-equipped peasant army. Yet, the aims of the Righteous armies reflected a recurrent demand in Korean history.[25]

The founding of the Independence Club in 1896 by Sŏ Chaep'il (Philip Jaisohn), who had exiled himself to America, and by other new intelligentsia, who were influenced by Western thought, certainly signaled the arrival of the Westernization movement. The Club's activities were aimed toward three goals: first, safeguarding the nation's independence in the face of external aggression; second, by means of a popular rights movement, bringing about wider participation in the political process; and third, promoting a self-strengthening movement.

Unlike earlier programs and movements, the Club not only dealt with both the nation's independence and domestic reform, but it also pursued the rights of individuals and civil liberty. The goals of the Club "were to establish schools in each village to provide a new-style of education; to build textile and paper mills and ironworks, thus furthering the country's commercialization and industrialization; and to ensure the nation's security by developing a modern national defense capacity."[26] In 1896, to express the views of Independence Club members, Sŏ founded *The Independent*, a thrice-weekly newspaper that eventually evolved into a daily. It was the first genuinely modern newspaper written in the Korean *han'gŭl* alphabet.[27]

As the activities and goals of the Independent Club gained popularity among the general public, those in power feared that the Club's latent goal was to abolish the monarchy, and their threats to destroy the Club drove Sŏ Chaep'il back to the United States. Eventually, the ailing dynasty arrested the leaders of the Club and then called in troops to clear the street demonstrators, who were protesting against the arrest of their leaders. Although the Club came abruptly to an end, its purposes and actions had made a profound impact on Korean history as a whole and modernization in particular. Even after 1910, when Korea became a Japanese colony (via a provision of the Japanese protectorate in 1905), many Koreans, known and unknown, committed themselves to carrying out the programs of the Independence Club with the intent of laying the foundation for an independent Korea. The most notable among them were An Ch'angho, Son Pyŏnghŭi, and Kim Sŏngsu, to name just a few. Kim was one of the most successful in actually practicing the principal points included in the goals of the Independent Club, and the institutions he established then are still functioning well today.

Modernization as a Transformative Process

Modernization is a frequently used term in contemporary social science literature, yet it is a difficult concept to define. As John K. Fairbank and his associates have indicated, "[modernization] means little except as it is specifically defined and concretely applied."[28]

In an effort to characterize modernization, Émile Durkheim, Henry Sumner Maine, Robert Redfield, Ferdinand Tönnies, and Max Weber attempted to define "modern" in contrast to "traditional" by dichotomizing and polarizing the two concepts.[29] Some may think of "modern" in terms of present-day industrialization and technology, with its jet travel, space exploration, and nuclear power.[30] Marion J. Levy, Jr., defines modern society as a place where the "members use inanimate sources of energy and/or use tools to multiply the effects of their efforts."[31] Still others define modernization as synonymous with Westernization or "Europeanization."[32]

Modernization is, however, not synonymous with Westernization. Although the impact of the Western world on Eastern modernization has been profound in the past few centuries, such was not always the case. In fact, Asia's influence on Western modernization dominated at one time. According to Fairbank and his associates, "In 1500 an observer might more logically have looked forward to the 'Asianization' of Europe. . . . The great series of inventions emanating from China—paper, printing, the wheel barrow, the crossbow, canal lock-gates, the sternpost rudder, the compass, gunpowder, porcelain . . . to none of these early influences were there comparable movements in the opposite direction."[33] Korea, as an influence on modernization, is no exception. As Richard M. Steers and his colleagues point out, "In the year 1234 Koreans developed the first movable metal type for printing, 200 years before the Germans 'invented' it. In 1442 Koreans developed the pluviometer, or rain gauge, 200 years before the Italians 'invented' it, and employed farming methods unknown in the West. And in 1592, in response to a Japanese invasion, Koreans developed and built the world's first iron-clad ships, again 200 years before they were 'invented' by the Americans."[34]

Modernization, then, is a phenomenon in both the West and the East. Fairbank and his associates assert:

> The difference is that modernization has been more gradual
> and evolutionary in the West, going on over a longer period
> and much of it indeed arising from within Western civiliza-
> tion. In East Asia the shorter duration of modernization and
> the external origin of many of the stimuli for it have resulted
> in a more precipitous rate of change and a tendency toward
> modifications of traditional culture and society that are sud-
> den and revolutionary rather than slow and evolutionary.[35]

Modernization in the East, including Korea, includes adoption of Western technology and Western forms of organization, but not of essential Western values, such as the importance of the individual, which have at best played a secondary role. The transformation of Korea can be better described as modernization
than as westernization.

In her book, Martina Deuchler states: "'modernization' is generally understood as action that consists of several transformative processes: commercialization, industrialization, secularization, a diffusion of education, and expansion of popular involvement in the political process."[36] S. N. Eisenstadt, in
his book, *Modernization: Protest and Change,* defines modernization as "the
process of change towards those types of social, economic, and political systems
that have developed in western Europe and North America from the seventeenth century to the nineteenth and have then spread to other European countries and in the nineteenth and twentieth centuries to the South America, Asian,
and African countries."[37] This modernization includes not only rapid economic
development through industrialization, the use of scientific technology, the
mechanization of transportation, and the scientific improvement of agriculture,
but also broad political and social change. The political and social change must
include an ideology that upholds the rights of individuals and civil liberties.
Modernization is neither a simple change within tradition, nor is it a simple
self-defensive reflex in response to Western stimuli; instead, modernization
must include some significant transformation of traditional values as the result
of contact with other cultures—especially with the West.

According to this definition, Korean modernization did not take place before the nineteenth century, although Korea recognized the West in the sixteenth and seventeenth centuries. The enlightened thought of the seventeenth and
eighteenth centuries did not contain the criteria for modernization because it
did not include transformation, but only added new parts to the traditional body.
Perhaps the genuine effort toward modernization in Korea that was initiated by
Koreans themselves started in the late nineteenth century with the *Kabo* reform
in 1894.[38]

In discussing Korean modernization, Norman Jacobs, in his book, *The Korean Road to Modernization and Development,* points out that in Asia modernization "usually is termed *westernization.*"[39] This observation may be true in the case of Japanese modernization, but it may be incorrect in Korean modernization. While Japanese modernization has emulated that of the West, especially via Meiji Restoration in the late 1860s, Korean modernization has tended to model after the Japanese one. King Kojong, who was forced by the Japanese to sign the Treaty of Kanghwa and the most humiliating Protectorate Treaty, for instance, assembled a secret inspection team to study the contemporary Japanese civilization in light of modernization, and dispatched the group to Japan at the end of February 1881.

Also, on the one hand, because Japanese modernization was initiated spontaneously, willingly, and positively without foreign domination as were the cases in China and Korea, its impact was profound. On the other hand, even if many Koreans, ranging from king to the commoners, were aware of the necessity of modernization, they were reluctant, hesitant, and even ashamed of emulating the Japanese model of modernization, because they were under Japanese domination as well as the pressure from the West. In this respect, Korean modernization would be equivalent to and parallel with that of the Chinese, including the Taiwanese, but it is different from that of the Japanese. Nonetheless, in haphazard fashion, modernization in Korea escalated under Japan's domination and eventual colonization.

Kim Sŏngsu was one of those moderate nationalists—cultural nationalists— who sought Korean independence and well-being as a nation through modernization, even if it meant dealing with the Japanese within the limits of the colonial system.

Kim Sŏngsu's Modernization via Cultural Nationalism

Kim Sŏngsu's Career

Kim Sŏngsu was born fifteen years after the signing of the Treaty of Kanghwa, when foreign pressure was building to open Korean ports under the pretext of Korean modernization. Although he was born to one of the wealthiest landlords in Korea at the time, the period was the most unfortunate in modern Korean history. When the Reform of 1894 was introduced and the Righteous armies rose up, he was four years old. When the ambitious modernization effort was initiated by the Independence Club in 1896, he was barely six years old. When the Protectorate Treaty was signed in 1905, he was a teenager. At the tender age of eighteen, he went with Song Chinu, his alter-ego for life, to Tokyo to study, and, as a student at the preparatory course for Waseda University, he observed the official Japanese annexation in 1910.

When he went home after graduation from Waseda University in 1914, Korea was a Japanese colony. As a colonial subject, who was educated in an elite university in Japan, however, Kim had a few options. Like some other sons of wealthy Korean families, he could have chosen a comfortable life doing nothing at all; he could have worked in the colonial government, so long as he was willing to work for the Japanese; or he could have joined the Korean independence fighters in Manchuria. Instead, he chose to remain in Korea and initiate some tangible projects for Korean modernization, trusting that strengthening the nation could be accomplished through education, especially education for the future elite. Kim eventually established not only schools but also a textile firm and a national newspaper that encouraged learning among the masses.

When Kim took over the financially ailing Kiho Hakkyo in order to create the Chungang School in 1915, he was only twenty-five. When he founded Kyŏngsŏng Spinning and Weaving Company in 1919, he was twenty-nine, as he was when he played a role in plotting the greatest anti-Japanese independence movement, the "March First Movement." The following year, he started *Tonga Ilbo*, a daily newspaper. When he took over the ill-managed and financially ailing Posŏng Junior College in 1932, he was just forty-two.

When Korea became independent from Japan after World War II, Kim insisted that the Korean Provisional Government in Shanghai be the legitimate governing body of the peninsula.[40] When the nation was drifting in the midst of struggles between the left and the right after 1945 until the first republic was born in 1948, he supported the right and played an active role in forming the Republic of Korea. As the Syngman Rhee government began to drift toward authoritarian rule, occasioned by the Korean War (1950–1953) and a sagging economy, Kim became a major critic. In 1951, he was elected vice president by the Korean National Assembly, where he served only one year and thirteen days before resigning on May 29, 1952, denouncing Rhee's abuse of power and dictatorship.

During the colonial years, Korea produced many independence fighters. Some threw hand grenades and detonated bombs to assassinate high-ranking Japanese officials. In fact, Itō Hirobumi, the chief Japanese architect of the Protectorate Treaty, was assassinated in 1909 by a Korean patriot, An Chunggŭn. Many nationalists chose direct armed confrontation and fought face-to-face against the Japanese in Manchuria, the Maritime Provinces, and elsewhere.

Others appealed to world opinion through various international organizations and networks while residing overseas. Still, the great majority of Koreans remained in the colony, and used whatever means were available to contribute to Korea's eventual independence. Kim was one of those who chose to remain in the colony and carry out nationalistic activities.

Because this book tells the story of Korean modernization through the life of a visionary Korean, who devoted his career to various modernization projects via cultural nationalism, it will be appropriate to elaborate further on the concept of cultural nationalism that is used in this book.

Cultural Nationalism

Korean nationalism as an ideological movement and as a major source of anti-Japanese movement had been running high ever since the Japanese domination began in the late nineteenth century and since 1910 in particular. The March First Movement strengthened the impetus toward nationalism.[41] Although the ultimate destiny of the Korean nationalist movement was based on the single issue of eventually regaining Korean independence, the movement was unsuccessful in harnessing all the programs and all the nationalist energies into "a drive to unseat the Japanese."[42] Instead, the Korean nationalists were sharply divided into two factions: radical nationalists who advocated social revolution and overt resistance to Japanese imperialism; and moderate nationalists who advocated gradual solutions to the problem of independence. They were labelled "cultural nationalists."[43]

Under the Japanese domination, many Korean nationalists could hardly be called political nationalists who "seek to achieve a representative state for their community and to secure citizenship rights for its members, thereby giving collective experience a political reality,"[44] because of the colonial rules and regulations. Thus, many Koreans became cultural nationalists whose aims were "to regenerate the national community by creating, preserving or strengthening a people's cultural identity when it is felt to be lacking, inadequate or threatened."[45] In fact, cultural nationalists were realists, believing that, although political independence was presently unobtainable, as evidenced in the outcome of the March First Movement, social, cultural, and economic self-strengthening was certainly an acceptable secondary goal. Although the March First Movement failed to obtain Korean independence, it brought about a true renaissance to cultural nationalism.

Cultural nationalists' solutions to the problem of independence were moderate and gradual; they "advocated education and enlightenment to nurture new values and skills while shaping mass nationalist sentiment to lay the basis for future independence."[46] Governor-General Saitō's *nissen yūwa* (harmony between Japan and Korea) policy gave cultural nationalists room to maneuver. However, moderates of cultural nationalist persuasion seized this opportunity to act within the prescribed limits. Kim and his associates thought that the problem was not just a shortsighted goal of throwing out the Japanese at all costs; it was rather the transformation of the nation by developing fundamental strength based on the Western model. Kim Sŏngsu and his colleagues devoted their energies toward such endeavors, and Kim was successful in this effort. Michael Edson Robinson relates, "The personal, educational, and professional enmeshment of Kim [Sŏngsu] . . . illustrates the close world of the Korean intelligentsia of the 1920s. It also helps to illumine the origins and progression of political factions."[47] Indeed, Kim was a Korean intelligentsia in the development of cultural nationalism in Korea, but he was also an "intellectual" in Korean cultural nationalism according to Kosaku Yoshino's definition on intellectuals in cultural nationalism, for intellectuals (or thinking elites) are those who formulate ideas and ideals of the nation's cultural identity.[48]

Critique of Cultural Nationalism

The cultural nationalist movement faced a serious challenge from radical nationalism, which attacked the premise of cultural nationalism—a solution to the long-term problems of Korean independence. Robinson summed up the sentiment of the radical nationalists:

> Heavily influenced by their study of Marx and other Socialist writers, radicals attacked the fundamental precepts of the cultural nationalist program. They questioned the utility of national reform within the colonial system, arguing that without political independence talk of national development was meaningless. Furthermore, they questioned the basic motives of the cultural nationalist leadership's advocacy of cultural and economic development. Under Japanese colonial rule, did not such movements serve only the interests of the middle and upper class Korean elite? Such criticism diluted the mass appeal of cultural nationalism and, furthermore, spilt nationalist leaders over issues of class versus national interests as well as tactics for independence.[49]

Such factional divisions and disputes were precisely what the Japanese wanted to see for their strategy of "divide and conquer." (Carter J. Eckert supports such an interpretation.[50]) Consequently, instead of directing their efforts toward the Japanese colonialists, the nationalists were diverted by infighting. Both factions were deeply wounded by their ideological disputes. Even after the half century since Korea's independence from Japanese occupation, many Koreans remained jaded by the insidious strategy of the Japanese colonialists. Kim's modernization projects and his way of handling the Japanese colonialists was criticized in the same way that cultural nationalism was criticized by the radicals. The revisionist critique of Kim by some students, especially by students at Koryŏ University, was severe at times.

If armed confrontation and face-to-face fighting were the "only" means to achieve independence, certainly Kim cannot be considered an independence fighter. Kim neither engaged in armed confrontation against the Japanese nor spent a day in a Japanese prison, although his wife, Yi Aju (1899–1967), was sentenced to six months' imprisonment for her active participation in the March First Movement. Although at times he was humiliated by them, Kim had to work with the Japanese colonialists to accomplish his various projects, and thus he spent endless hours with Japanese officials. According to Kang Tongjin, the actual number of meetings between Kim and his associates and Governor-General Saitō Makoto, from 1919 to 1926, were: Kim, fourteen; Song Chinu, fifteen; Chang Tŏksu, twelve; Yi Sanghyŏp, eight.[51] These contacts with the Japanese authorities made Kim and his associates vulnerable to charges of collaboration with the Japanese.

Korean scholars and intellectuals hold differing views about these collaboration charges. Kim Hakjoon (Hakchun), for one, maintains that such contacts with Saitō were clearly the result of Japanese political and administrative pressure. If things were going smoothly, he says, what reasons would Kim and his associates have to meet Saitō?[52] Yu Chino believes that it was impossible for a person responsible for running two schools, a newspaper, and a textile firm to avoid contact with Japanese officials under the colonial rules, unless one went overseas, was hidden from the public, or gave up all those projects altogether.[53]

Because Robinson has summarized cultural nationalism and the criticism of it in his well-received book, *Cultural Nationalism in Colonial Korea, 1920-1925*,[54] I do not recapitulate the debates in this book. Nor do I try to depict Kim as a legendary warrior against the Japanese colonialists. Instead, this book describes what Kim actually accomplished for Korean modernization, what stirred him to initiate such projects, and how he pursued those projects under particular sociopolitical circumstances.

Because this book uses the life history of Kim Sŏngsu to understand Korean modernization and cultural nationalism, the focus of chapter 1 is on Kim's background and the long journey that led him to modernization. The remaining chapters deal with Kim's various projects. These different projects happen to be the same as the chronological order. These include the establishment of Chungang School (chapter 2), Kyŏngsŏng Spinning and Weaving Company (chapter 3), *Tonga Ilbo* (chapter 4), and Koryŏ University (chapter 5). In chapter 6, I discuss Kim's involvement in Korean politics in order to illustrate the political vortex of post-World War II Korea. Finally, in chapter 7, in addition to summarizing his role in Korean modernization, I talk about Kim as a person and the ways in which he is remembered by Koreans.

CHAPTER ONE

A Long Journey from Premodern to Modern

E ven though Kim Sŏngsu's life was not long, it was an astonishing journey. Geographically, he ventured from the tiny village of Inch'on, in the southwestern corner of north Chŏlla province, to Tokyo, Japan. Over time, he made a journey from premodern to modern, experiencing the collapse of the last dynasty of Korea, enlightenment movements, Japanese colonization, eventual Korean independence, and the birth of a new republic modeled on Western liberal democracies. Indeed, Kim weathered the sweeping changes of modern Korean history.

The Son of Enterprising Landlords

Kim Sŏngsu was born in Inch'on-ri *(figs. 1.1 & 1.8)* on October 11, 1891 (September 9 in the lunar calendar), as the first son of Kim Kyŏngjung (1863–1945, Chisan in pen name) and Lady Ko.¹ The Kims belonged to the lineage of Pibyŏn-nanggong of the Ulsan Kim clan, a well-respected *yangban* (nobility) lineage that produced the noted neo-Confucian scholar Kim Inhu (1510–1560), a contemporary and disciple of Yi Hwang (1501–1570). Yi, better known by his pen name, T'oegye, was regarded as Korea's foremost neo-Confucian thinker.²

19

Despite being categorized as *yangban,* the Kim lineage was not wealthy.[3] Kim Sŏngsu's family fortune originated when Kim's great-grandfather, Myŏnghwan, who was a humble Confucian scholar, was able to arrange for his third son, Yohyŏp (1833–1909; *fig.1.2*), to marry the daughter of a wealthy landlord, Chŏng Keryang, from Inch'on-ri of Kobu (now Koch'ang) county.

As the third son in a family that strictly followed primogeniture rule, whereby the firstborn son was given more of the parents' property than any other, Yohyŏp was free to choose his residence.[4] At the same time, Chŏng, the father of his intended, wanted his only daughter to live near her natal home. Thus, when he married Chŏng (1831–1911; *fig.1.3*), Yohyŏp moved to Inch'on-ri, a village near the Gulf of Chulp'o.[5] Yohyŏp established a new nuclear family in this village that was dominated by members of the Yŏnil Chŏng clan. Yohyŏp's father-in-law, often called *mansŏkkun* (meaning a very large landowner, but its literal meaning is a person whose total annual rice harvest is 10,000 *sŏk* [1 *sŏk* equals 5.1 bushels]), allocated some rice paddies to the newlywed couple.

Although there are no known records regarding the exact amount of land, the allocation could have been the modest beginning of Yohyŏp's becoming a rich landowner, however, there is an indication that he acquired land and wealth largely because of his wife's exceptional frugality and strict household management. It is said that she was so parsimonious about heating the house in winter that a chamber pot (*yogang*) in her bedroom was frozen for most of the winter.[6] Nevertheless, Yohyŏp's accumulation of wealth was gradual, and was not noticeable until his middle years.

Meanwhile, children were born—Kijung (1859–1933, Wŏnp'a or Tongbok in pen name; *fig.1.4*) in 1859 and Kyŏngjung (1863–1945, Chinsan in pen name; *fig.1.5*) four years later. To accommodate the growing family, Yohyŏp undertook the project of expanding his living area; he became a landlord before he was thirty years of age.

When I saw Yohyŏp's first dwelling, a well-preserved, tiny, thatch-roofed house, I was incredulous, for how could someone who had started with a small plot of farmland and a simple home acquire such wealth in his lifetime. When he died, in 1909, Yohyŏp left his two sons a considerable inheritance. He willed Kijung land producing approximately 1,000 *sŏk* of rice per year and Kyŏngjung, his second son, about one-fifth that amount. The two brothers acquired more wealth after their relocation to Chulp'o by capitalizing on the opportunity to export rice. Owing largely to the rice exporting, they became very successful and enterprising landlords.

By 1861, the first building of the current Kim family compound had been built. Further construction included the addition of main reception quarters in

1879, minor living quarters in 1881, a gatehouse to the main reception quarters in 1893, and minor reception quarters in 1903. This expansion became a compound of connected domiciles that allowed Kijung's family and Kyŏngjung's families to have its own *sarang* (detached reception area) and *an* (family quarters), storage buildings, servants' quarters, and private entrance.

Kim Sŏngsu was born to Kyŏngjung and his wife in this family compound and was adopted in 1893 by his heirless uncle, Kijung. In fact, in Korea, to uphold the patrilineal descent rule, when families were heirless, either having only daughters or no children at all, they sometimes tried polygynous arrangements, although such instances were limited. Most often they adopted a male, but the range of choices for the adopted male heirs from agnate (persons related by patrilineal descent) and the most preferred ones were nephews. (Despite a revision of the South Korean civil code in 1977 that permitted adoption of someone with a different surname and the entry of the husband's name into his wife's family register, Koreans still adhere to a strict agnatic principle.) In the case of Sŏngsu, the adoption did not take Sŏngsu far from his biological parents; Sŏngsu simply moved to an adjacent building. The adoption gave Sŏngsu access to the wealth of both families, allowing him later in life to undertake various modernization projects.

The Kim family compound dominates the countryside in Inch'on-ri region, yet it is surprisingly modest, considering their accumulated wealth. Although my family wealth is nowhere near that of the Kims, my own family estate in Haejŏri, a village in northeast Kyŏngsang province, seems larger, more grand, and more luxurious than that of the Kims. The Kims must indeed have been frugal when it came to housing.

In addition to becoming a landlord, Yohyŏp became a ranking officer in the government. He occupied various government posts, including *ch'ambong* (royal tomb official), *ŭigŭmbu* (state tribunal), *kunsu* (county magistrate), *chungch'uwŏn* (counsel of the minister without portfolio), and *pisŏwŏn* (royal secretary).

The real emergence of the Kims as landlords took place when Kijung relocated to Chulp'o in 1907, followed by Kyŏngjung after Yohyŏp's death in 1909. Several family tales concern the move, one of them a ghost story. The family compound in Inch'on-ri, they say, was haunted, and some burnt remnants of the ghost can still be seen under the overhang of the house. A fortune-teller advised the family members that, if they relocated across the bay, they would be free of the ghost.[7]

Their genuine motivations for relocating were, however, sociopolitical as well as economical.[8] It appeared to be that their primary concerns were safety and security. The most imminent threats were the "fire brigands" (*hwajŏk*), frustrated peasants who were tired of *yangban* misrule. Riding on horseback and armed with muskets, they roamed the countryside, attacking *yangban* landlords and shattering the public peace on all sides. The Kims had been attacked several times by the fire brigands, and because of the Japanese garrison, Chulp'o was safer than it was in Inch'on-ri from the fire brigands' attacks. Nevertheless, it was not absolutely safe from Ŭibyŏng attacks. In fact, on September 2, 1908, Ŭibyŏng came to Chulp'o, attacked a pro-Japanese organization of a branch of the Korea Association (Taehan Hyŏphoe Chihoe), and killed Kim Yŏngin, general affairs director of the organization.[9] At any event, the relocated Kims built a modest thatch-roofed house *(fig.1.9)* for the two families.

Another reason for the Kims' relocation was economic. (Nowadays, due to the accumulation of eroded soil deposits, and because of the lowering sea level, Chulp'o is a small fishing village.) Until the ports of Mokp'o and Kunsan were built, however, Chulp'o was a major commercial port. From Chulp'o, rice harvested in the fields of the Honam Plain was exported to Japan, and many Japanese merchants came there to buy. Kijung and Kyŏngjung were able to capitalize on the locale of Chulp'o to expand their landholding and wealth. According to Carter J. Eckert, "About 5 percent of the Kunsan export trade in rice was passing through Chulp'o, and most of this rice was coming from Koch'ang County, where the Kims had their original holdings."[10]

After their relocation to Chulp'o, the Kims did not keep records of the capital increase. The only available records on Kijung's family were *tojobu* (estate records) from 1918 to 1924, and Kim Yongsŏp used these records to give us a detailed account of the Kijung family's landholding and yearly harvests for six years. By 1920, the Kims had become large landlords, harvesting an annual total of 20,000 *sŏk* of rice.[11] Of the two brothers, Kyŏngjung was the more business-oriented, just as Yŏnsu *(fig.1.6)* was more business-minded than Sŏngsu. In 1918, for instance, Kijung owned 750 *chŏngbo* (about 1,800 acres) of land, while Kyŏngjung owned in the neighborhood of 1,300 *chŏngbo* (about 3,185 acres),[12] even though Kijung originally inherited five times more land than Kyŏngjung.

The Son of

Patriotic Enlightenment

Being born into a rich family was not Kim Sŏngsu's only privilege. He was also privileged to have two fathers, natural and adoptive, and a father-in-law, all of whom were, in addition to well-known landlords, scholars and leaders of the enlightenment movement. Their roles in the movement made them different from most other landlords. By then, according to Kim Yongsŏp, the Korean landlords were classified into three categories: first, those who wanted to retain their privileged economic status by maintaining the existing socioeconomic structure; second, those who would give away their land to their tenants or donate their land to various public organizations, recognizing the social injustice in land ownership (this class includes Yun Kisŏ, Pak Sŏkhyŏn, and Yi Hŭijik); and third, those who would not give up their landownership, but instead joined the patriotic enlightenment movement, which accepted the ideas of Western civilization concerning national self-strengthening and modernization, and those aimed for eventual independence from Japan. Kim Yongsŏp characterizes Kijung and Kyŏngjung as belonging to the third category.[13]

In addition to being landlords, Kijung and Kyŏngjung served in the government. Kijung passed the civil service examination and in 1888 received a *chinsa* (literary licentiate) degree, which made him eligible for admission to the national academy and afforded him promising career opportunities in an official government post. Two years later, Kijung became the magistrate of Tongbok (now Chinsan) county. Both brothers served in several positions in the protectorate government, including royal tomb official (*ch'ambong*), and county magistrate (*kunsu*). When Japanese interference and arrogance reached their height, and as the protectorate period evolved toward annexation, Kyŏngjung resigned his post as Chinsan (now Kŭmsan) county magistrate in 1905.

After leaving the government, they returned to Chulp'o and joined other landlords of the region in playing leading roles in the patriotic enlightenment movement. Both Kijung and Kyŏngjung were sympathetic to the goals of the Enlightenment Party (Kaehwadang), which looked to Meiji Japan as a model for Korean national development.[14] To both Kijung and Kyŏngjung, the patriotic enlightenment movement meant national self-strengthening through education and economic growth, which was the theme of the Enlightenment Party in the 1880s.[15] The brothers joined the Chŏlla Educational Association (Honam Hakhoe), a provincial scholarly organization in the province of Chŏlla. In the period of deepening national crisis under Japanese domination, scholars made an effort to inform and educate the people, "to foster awareness of the meaning of independence and to disseminate the new Western learning broadly throughout the society."[16] Kyŏngjung became a trustee and also a major financial backer of the vital learned society, which published the *Honam Hakpo,* a monthly journal. Then, in 1908, in order to further the goal of self-strengthening through education, Kijung founded Yŏngsin Hakkyo (Yŏngsin School) in Chulp'o.

Kyŏngjung was an exceptional Confucian scholar, writer, and historian. His scholarly orientation and pattern of thought were reflected in his two major works, an essay entitled "Odoimmun" (An introduction to our way), and the seventeen-volume *Chosŏnsa* (*History of Korea*), published in 1934. "Odoimmun," written in response to the increasing influence of Western thought (via Catholicism) on Korea, called for preserving and revitalizing neo-Confucianism. The essay introduced the neo-Confucian basic philosophy and way of study and related them to existing traditional Korean thought. *Chosŏnsa*, written in Chinese ideograms, was a voluminous and detailed Korean history that took many years to complete. Kyŏngjung's view of history was based on neo-Confucian ideology. He wrote the volumes in order to preserve the history of Korea under the Japanese occupation.

Despite the Kims' stand as faithful advocates of neo-Confucianism, they took an active role in Korean modernization on the eve of the collapse of the Chosŏn dynasty. While others raised or joined Righteous armies to fight against the Japanese directly, the Kims chose other means. They were active in education, establishing the Yŏngsin School as a means of strengthening the nation according to the major tenets of the Enlightenment Party. At the same time, they were active in scholarly organizations in order to promote awareness of the meaning of independence and to foster new learning throughout the society. Kim Yongsŏp characterized the Kims as the landlords, industrial capitalists, and reformists for modernization.[17] This view may be accurate in part, but it failed to note the strong influence of neo-Confucianism on the movement.

To Enlighten Himself

Until he was seven years old, Sŏngsu's parents taught him the basic Chinese ideograms and the etiquette required of *yangban*; then they hired a teacher to school him at home, inviting Sŏngsu's peers in the village to study together with him. It was a de facto *sŏdang* (a traditional tutorial school). Sŏngsu was taught the Confucian classics and ethics and Oriental philosophy intensively in his most sensitive and formative years.[18]

Then, following traditional custom, in 1903, Sŏngsu married at the age of twelve (thirteen by Korean age-reckoning, because in Korea, at birth one is already one year old). He married Ko Kwangsŏk (1886–1919), who was five years older and the daughter of Ko Chŏngju (1863–1934), a member of the Changhŭng Ko clan, an enlightenment movement sympathizer and progressive landlord-bureaucrat of Ch'angp'ŏng county (currently Tamyang) in south Chŏlla province. Like Kijung and Kyŏngjung, Ko Chŏngju had passed the high civil service examination (*munkwa*), after which he had become an official in the prestigious Royal Library (*Kyujanggak*) in Seoul. Ko also resigned his position at about the same time as Kijung and Kyŏngjung, for he, too, was an enlightenment movement sympathizer. When he returned to his hometown, he established Ch'anghǔng Ǔisuk (or Ch'angp'ǒng School) to teach a new kind of learning that included subjects, such as, English, Japanese, and math, in addition to Chinese.

The credentials, background, and opinions on the enlightenment movement of Sŏngsu's father-in-law were almost identical to those of his two fathers. Perhaps Sŏngsu's ideas on education were influenced first by his father-in-law, because Ko Chŏngju founded Ch'anghǔng Ǔisuk before Sŏngsu's father founded his school in Chulp'o. It is particularly noteworthy that Sŏngsu himself attended Ch'anghǔng Ǔisuk in 1906. His father-in-law invited a teacher from Seoul to teach English to his son-in-law and his own son, anticipating that English would be essential if they were to go to Shanghai or Tokyo for further study. During his stay in Ch'anghǔng Ǔisuk, Sŏngsu became acquainted with Song Chinu *(fig.1.7),* who later was thought to be Sŏngsu's most intimate friend. Until his assassination in 1945, Song was Sŏngsu's most trustworthy comrade. When Sŏngsu returned from Ch'anghǔng Ǔisuk, Kijung asked him, "What was your accomplishment in Ch'angp'ǒng [Ch'anghǔng Ǔisuk]?" Sŏngsu answered that he made a friend, Song Chinu, from Tamyang county, and added that his indomitable spirit and ambition were too good to be left unnoticed in the countryside.[19] Sŏngsu was confident of Song's potential to be a great nationalist leader.

Song Chinu, however, was not satisfied with life at Ch'angp'yǒng School. He remarked that the place was like a small pond, an allusion to the saying that a frog in a small well was unaware of the gigantic ocean.[20] He returned to his hometown, and Kim Sŏngsu sorely missed him. A few months later, after Song's departure, Sŏngsu also returned home, where he confined himself to the house, doing nothing in particular. It was a very troubling and uncertain time for both Sŏngsu, at the age of fifteen, and for Korea, a country now under Japanese domination.

In 1907, when Sŏngsu was sixteen, he asked his father's permission to go to Naesosa, a Buddhist temple built in the early seventh century during the reign of Mu Wang (600–641 A.D.) of the Paekche dynasty (18 B.C.–660 A.D.), to study and enjoy the aesthetic scenery of the temple. The temple was located less than twelve kilometers from Chulp'o. His father approved, and Sŏngsu journeyed to Naesosa with Paek Kwansu, who was from the nearby town of Hǔngdŏk. After learning that Sŏngsu and Kwansu were in Naesosa, Song Chinu joined them. They studied together, and enjoyed talking about political topics of the time.

In the meantime, the Japanese protectorate was nearing annexation. In 1907, a new cabinet led by Yi Wanyong was formed under Japanese direction. Kojong lost the throne by a Japanese trick, and Sunjong became emperor in

July 1907, with the reign title of Yunghŭi (Abundant Prosperity). Nevertheless, Japan dissolved the remaining Korean army units by August 1, 1907. In response to the deeper Japanese penetration, resistance movements to preserve Korea's independence sprang up. The Righteous armies grew rapidly and confronted the Japanese forces militarily. Koch'ang, Chŏngŭp, and Changsŏng of Chŏlla province were their strongholds. The parents of Kim, Song, and Paek worried that Naesosa could be vulnerable to battles between the Righteous armies and the Japanese, and so ordered the boys to come home. Before their return, the teenagers discussed their future plans. Paek wanted to go to Seoul. Song insisted on studying in Japan. Kim broached a practical problem: whatever they wanted to do would require parental permission. They promised each other to stay together.

Sŏngsu told his parents about his wish to study in Japan, but permission was not granted. They worried about the uncertainty of Korea's future. The most vehement opposition came from his wife. She knew that her brother, Ko Kwangjun, who had once studied with Sŏngsu at Ch'angp'yŏng School for English Studies and who had gone to Shanghai to study, had not returned after several years. She threatened her husband that, if he went to Japan, she would go back to her natal home. In the meantime, no word came either from Song or Paek.

Wildly frustrated, Sŏngsu learned from a postal clerk in Hŭngdŏk that there was a place in Kunsan where one could learn English. With permission from his parents, Sŏngsu went there to a hospital run by a Christian missionary. When the hospital told Sŏngsu that in order to learn English he had to make a commitment to Christianity, Sŏngsu disappointed, returned home. He still kept his topknot. It would be unthinkable for anyone so indoctrinated in Confucianism to become a Christian. And, he knew that it would be almost impossible to obtain his parents' approval.

In April 1908, Sŏngsu learned that there would be a public lecture in Hup'o, near Chulp'o. The lecture would be sponsored by the Korea Association (Taehan Hyŏphoe), a political and social organization created to carry out the goals of the patriotic enlightenment movement, which sought to establish a foundation for the recovery of Korean sovereignty through the development of native industries and widely available educational opportunities.

From a lecture delivered by Han Sŭngi, who taught English and physics at Kŭmho Hakkyo (Kŭmho School) in Kunsan, Sŏngsu learned about civil rights, the concept of equality, and the idea that sovereign power should belong to the people, not the king. He also learned that all those concepts were included in the Reform of 1894. Sŏngsu paid a visit to Han and asked many questions regarding the contents of his lecture. Sŏngsu told Han that he wanted to learn

English. Han subsequently arranged for Sŏngsu to enter at the Kŭmho School, which offered a variety of subjects. Besides English instruction, the curriculum included Korean language, math, history, geography, physics, chemistry, music, and physical education. Evening classes taught Japanese and textile arts. In May 1908, when Sŏngsu enrolled at Kŭmho School, he was introduced to the world of modern education.[21]

The schooling at Kŭmho was more intensive and extensive than he had previously experienced in the Ch'angp'yŏng School for English Studies. While broadening his education at the Kŭmho School, Sŏngsu still wanted to study in Japan. At that time, the summer of 1908, he met Hong Myŏnghŭi, who was three years older and a middle-school student in Tokyo. Hong told Sŏngsu about the prosperity of Japan and its educational system and facilities; Sŏngsu could not wait any longer. But then, Song Chinu visited Sŏngsu and tried to convince Sŏngsu to study with him at Hansŏng Institute for Teacher Training (Hansŏng Kyowŏn Yangsŏngso) in Seoul. Instead, Sŏngsu induced Song to go with him to Tokyo.

While waiting for his official permit (*tohangjŭng*) to go overseas, Sŏngsu asked Pak Ilbyŏng, then a Japanese language teacher at Kŭmho School, to seek in his behalf the necessary parental approval. Sŏngsu's parents, although strong advocates of modern education and sympathizers with the enlightenment movement, failed to find merit in Sŏngsu's request. Knowing of Sŏngsu's plan in advance, his parents rushed a messenger to Kunsan with a letter telling Sŏngsu that his mother was deathly ill; they asked him to return home at once. Sŏngsu, however, found out from the messenger that it was not true. As soon as he received the official permit to sail to Japan, he cut off his long-kept topknot as a symbolic gesture that he had become a modern man. Instead of returning home as his parents wished, Sŏngsu wrote a long letter, seeking an apology from his parents; he enclosed a photograph that showed him without his topknot. Sŏngsu and Song Chinu invited Paek Kwansu to join them in going to Tokyo, but Paek declined; he could not obtain parental permission.

In October 1908, at the port of Kunsan, seventeen-year-old Kim Sŏngsu and Song Chinu stepped abroad a steamship for Japan. Soon Sŏngsu's parents changed their mind about his journey; they praised his courage. More than his parents, Sŏngsu's wife was hurt by his departure, but apologetic letters from her husband helped Ko Kwangsŏk to learn to live with his absence.

When Sŏngsu arrived in Japan, the Japanese language that he had learned in Kunsan was not adequate for communication with the natives. So, from the Japanese port of Simonoseki to Tokyo, Sŏngsu wrote Chinese ideograms (*kanji* in Japanese)[22] to communicate. With the help of Hong Myŏnghŭi, Kim Sŏngsu and Song Chinu settled in Tokyo. Both enrolled at Seisoku English School, which served as a preparatory school for middle-school entrance. They learned English and math in school and Japanese from a private tutor. In April 1909, both transferred to Kinjō Middle School as fifth graders. Then, in April 1910, the year Korea was formally annexed to Japan, both entered Waseda University's preparatory program. When Korea became an official Japanese colony on August 29, 1910, Song decided to return to Korea, for he could not stay and study in the national capital of the invaders. Together with Ko Kwangjun, Sŏngsu's brother-in-law, who had gone to Shanghai earlier and was then in Tokyo, Song left Tokyo, despite Sŏngsu's efforts to dissuade him; Sŏngsu argued that Song's actions would not help Korea's future.

Song's drastic departure revealed the remarkable difference between the two friends, although they were exceptionally close. Song, who was one year older than Kim, was more emotional, while Kim was rather calm and quiet.[23] Such differences were manifest in their works. While Kim worked behind the scenes as an intellectual in making plans and providing capital for various projects, Song led the people and carried out the projects. Kim might be called a "thinking elite" (or intellectual) in accordance with Yoshino's definition, and Song could be named an "intelligentsia," for he responded to certain ideas and ideals.[24] Nevertheless, since both Kim and Song had been one and the same person intellectually, spiritually, and even physically in various projects, both were intellectuals as well as intelligentsia. Any analytical distinction between two is futile.

Kim Sŏngsu remained in Tokyo while Song went back to Korea. Having completed his preparatory program, Kim went on to Waseda University's regular program and majored in political economy. Six months later, Song Chinu, deciding that Kim was right, returned to Tokyo, this time coming with Sŏngsu's younger brother, Yŏnsu. Song entered Meiji University instead of Waseda, and majored in law. Previously, during his stay in Tokyo before his return to Korea, Song was uncomfortable receiving financial help from Kim. This time, upon his return to Tokyo, Song had no uneasy feelings about his financial dependency. Sŏngsu's parents knew that they were paying for Song Chinu's expenses as well. They felt the need to help because Song's family financial condition was deteriorating.

Yŏnsu began his education in Japan as a fifteen-year-old teenager. He was brilliant enough to be admitted to the prestigious Asabu Middle School and later to one of the most selective high schools, the Third High School [Dai San Kōtō Gakkō]. He was accepted at Kyoto Imperial University, where he majored in economics. Sŏngsu stayed in Japan six years, and, when he graduated from Waseda University in 1914, he was twenty-three. Yŏonsu remained in Japan three years longer than Sŏngsu—for a full decade.[25]

The Impact of

Japanese Education

Kim Sŏngsu's thoughts about Korean modernization were greatly influenced by his study in Japan. Kim's biography edited by Ko Chaeuk delineated Kim's first encounter with Japan vividly.[26] Kim was impressed by Japan from the first day. He was amazed by Japan's prosperity. As he traveled from Simonoseki to Tokyo, Kim viewed from the train window, Japan's thick forests, well-divided rice paddies, clean-looking countryside, and well-planned cities. His feelings were a mixture of amazement and dismay. He was astonished by Tokyo's skyline, its flourishing marketplaces, its school facilities, and public buildings. He was incredulous that Korean Righteous armies were able to fight against the Japanese with only knives and bamboo sticks. During his late adolescence, Kim was at a perceptive age, and it is not hard to understand why Kim used Japan as a model for Korean modernization.

Kim was not the only Korean who admired Japan and tended to emulate the Japanese model. In fact, although King Kojong was the most humiliated Chosŏn king by the Japanese in its 500 years dynastic era, he dispatched his delegates to Japan to study Japanese modernization. Despite his humiliation, in the mind of the king, Japan was still his frame of reference for modernization.

No one can assess exactly how and to what extent Kim was affected by his stay in Japan, but, without any doubt, it was the most significant period for Kim in preparing for his future modernization projects for Korea. Kim himself said that his education at Waseda was the most meaningful and memorable experience of his adolescence.[27] One of his major accomplishments was the cultivation of relationships with a new generation of prominent and capable Koreans. Besides maintaining his friendship with Song Chinu, Kim made friends with many promising young Korean intellectuals during his years in Japan.

Chang Tŏksu from Chaeryŏng of Hwanghae province was one of these friends. Kim met him at the Waseda preparatory program. Chang possessed many talents required of a leader, and he was known as an eloquent orator. During his years at Waseda, he had won first place in the national Japanese oratorical contest, and he had played the role of prime minister at the moot national assembly at Waseda. Despite his capability and potential, Chang came from a poor family and had difficulty supporting himself. Knowing Chang's financial situation, Kim helped him, dealing with Chang as if he were his younger brother.[28] Later, Chang worked with Kim, as Song did.

In addition to these friends, Kim Sŏngsu's warmth touched many other Koreans who studied in Japan. The list resembles a *Who's Who* in prominent Korean society at the time. Among his acquaintances were: Hyŏn Sangyun, Ch'oe Tusŏn, and Yang Wŏnmo at Waseda University, Pak Yonghŭi, Yu Ŏkkyŏm, and Kim Uyŏng at Tokyo Imperial University; Cho Mansik, Kim Pyŏngno, Hyŏn Chunho, Cho Soang, and Chŏng Nosik at Meiji University; and Kim Toyŏn at Keio University. Kim Sŏngsu's network of friends in Tokyo also included Yŏ Unhyŏng, An Chaehong, Paek Namhun, Sin Ikhŭi, Ch'oe Namsŏn, and Yi Kanghyŏn. Among all these comrades, Song Chinu, Chang Tŏksu, Hyŏn Sangyun, Kim Chunyŏn, Yang Wŏnmo, Ch'oe Tusŏn, and Yi Kanghyŏn would become lifelong friends and work closely with Kim in his schools, newspapers, and textile industries.[29] In more than one way, Kim Sŏngsu was a rich person. The support, dedication, and loyalty of Kim's friends were just as important as the financial backing from his family funds. Without such devoted and talented friends, Kim's projects would never have been successful.

In his final year in Waseda, Kim began to think about his future. He realized that, if he were to launch any project that promised to contribute to Korean modernization, most of the financing would have to come from his family wealth, which was controlled by his fathers. As enlightened thinkers, both of his fathers were keenly aware of the necessity for Korean modernization, but they had never witnessed the type of progress and modernization developed in Japan. Thus, Kim invited both of his fathers to see Japan for themselves.

In October 1913, a few months before Kim's graduation and during Waseda's thirtieth anniversary celebration, Kim's fathers spent twenty days in Tokyo. In addition to taking them to see the ancient Japanese ruins, Kim guided them through prosperous Japanese cities and educational institutions. Kim's fathers were particularly impressed by the grand anniversary events at Waseda. Dressed in their traditional Korean overcoats (*turumagi*) and hats (*kat*), which were in stark contrast to the Japanese traditional dress, they were truly impressed with Japan's modernization.[30]

The evening before his fathers were to depart for Korea, Sŏngsu talked to them about his aspirations to dedicate his time and energy to education in Korea. He explained to them that Japan's progress within such a short period of time stemmed from education, and added, "Not because we like the Japanese, if we want to be free from Japanese bondage, we have to catch up to the Japanese educational system." Kijung replied, "We have a long way to go."[31] Sŏngsu told him that it could be done, and Song Chinu agreed: "When we first came to Japan, we saw that the good components (cultural elements) came from either the Asian continent or the West, not from Japan's own invention or innovation. Then we came to understand that Japan's success was the result of its education and solidarity as a nation."[32] Sŏngsu emphasized the importance of private school education.

The conversation eventually led to a discussion of Sŏngsu's plans after his graduation. Kijung, Sŏngsu's adoptive father, asked Sŏngsu whether he would be interested in running an educational institution or not. Sŏngsu replied that he wanted to devote his career for education, if he would be allowed to do so.[33] Doubting that Sŏngsu would be interested in running Yŏngsin School, the small country school that he had established, Kijung asked him what kind of school he wanted to run. Sŏngsu replied that he wanted to start with a middle school in Seoul.[34]

Because he himself had founded a school, Kijung seemed pleased with his adopted son's commitment to education; yet, he was worried about Sŏngsu's inexperience, particularly in Seoul. Kyŏngjung, who was not satisfied with Sŏngsu's career plan, interrupted the conversation, and told his older brother not to take a young man's words seriously.[35] In the eyes of a father, a son—even on the eve of college graduation—is an immature youngster. Although Kijung endorsed Sŏngsu's career plan, Kyŏngjung rejected it. Kyŏngjung spoke emphatically to both Kijung and Sŏngsu: "It would not be easy even for a country to run an educational system." Kyŏngjung told Sŏngsu, regardless of what his adoptive father had said, as long as he would live, he would not allow Sŏngsu to run an educational institution.[36] In the face of Kyŏngjung's adamant opposition, Sŏngsu had to relinquish his dream. Nevertheless, his commitment to education remained, and besides, Sŏngsu sensed that at least he could get some support from his adopted father.

When Sŏngsu left Korea for Japan in 1908, he was a teenager and Korea was a Japanese protectorate. When he returned to Korea in July 1914, as a mature gentleman with a university degree, Sŏngsu found that his homeland had already become an official Japanese colony. When Sŏngsu journeyed to Japan, he had been accompanied by Song Chinu, but when he returned to Korea, he was alone. Song Chinu had become sick and had come home early for treatment. It was a rather quiet homecoming for Sŏngsu, but his ambitious project for fostering private education in Korea was about to materialize.

1.1. Scenes of Inch'on-ri

1.2. Kim Yohyŏp

1.3. Kim Yohyŏp's wife, Madam Chŏng

1.4. Kim Kijung

1.5. Kim Kyŏngjung

1.6. Kim Sŏngsu *(seated)* with his younger brother, Yŏnsu, in Tokyo

1.7. Kim Sŏngsu *(right)* with Song Chinu

1.8. The Kim family compound in Inch'on-ri
(above and opposite, top)

1.9. Part of the Kim family compound in Chulp'o

CHAPTER TWO

Education as a Means for Korean Modernization

Historically, Korea placed an enormous emphasis on education as a means for modernization, independence, and power. Even before Japanese domination many Koreans recognized the importance of education. In 1895, for instance, King Kojong handed down an edict on education for the nation's future, emphasizing its importance. In Korea, there was a popular song that emphasized the importance of education: "Knowledge is power, you ought to learn to survive . . ." Every elderly Korean will remember this song.

During the period of Japanese domination in the early 1900s, education was further emphasized, trusting that education should lay the foundation for future Korean independence. Many Korean nationalist intellectuals, who once had been active in political movements, dedicated themselves to educational endeavors, because open political activity became difficult, if not impossible. Kim Sŏngsu's adoptive father, Kijung, who established the Yŏngsin School in 1908, was one of these nationalist intellectuals. In fact, "In the scant few years before Korea fell completely under Japanese colonial domination, the number of private schools that were founded reached some 3,000, being particularly numerous in the northern half of the country." [1]

Nevertheless, around 1914, when Kim Sŏngsu planned to run a private school, the growth of private schools was at a standstill, if not declining, mainly because of Japanese control and financial difficulties, except a few under the auspices of American missionary organizations.[2] In addition to disseminating the new learning, many private schools in those day served as hotbeds for the nationalist movement. Naturally, Japan frowned on these private schools. Japan felt the necessity to control Korean education, particularly private educational institutions during the Residency-General period. After the annexation, Japan's educational policy changed; Japan directed its efforts toward an elementary and vocational level education, which would be good enough to perform menial tasks in the Japanese language, and for the Japanese. It prohibited elite education.

Founding Chungang School

(Chungang Hakkyo)

After his return to Chulp'o in July 1914, Kim Sŏngsu contemplated a way to start a post-elementary private school. He visited Song Chinu, who was extremely ill, and brought along a well-known medical doctor. Although he was sick, Song's spirits were high; he criticized the colonial policy of Governor-General Terauchi Masatake. Song needled Kim for not doing anything, for not going to Seoul to fight against Japanese policy.[3] Among many other things, he argued that Japanese educational policy against Koreans under the leadership of Governor-General Terauchi Masatake, as manifested in a new Korean educational act promulgated in 1911, was discriminatory. Japanese nationals in the public schools run by the Government-General were compulsorily enrolled for six years of elementary school and five years of middle school, while Koreans had four years of common school (pot'ong hakkyo), equivalent to an elementary school, and four years of high common school (kodŭng pot'ong hakkyo), equivalent to a middle school, so that Koreans were not able to compete with the Japanese.

Thinking that Chulp'o was too removed from the center of educational activities, Kim Sŏngsu decided to go to Seoul to see the reality of Korean education, particularly the status and role of private education. In the fall of 1914, he left for Seoul intending to initiate a private post-elementary school.

Kim Sŏngsu found that private schools in Seoul were stagnating. Discriminatory laws and financial difficulties acted as major hindrances to the development of private schools. Well-to-do Seoulites were sending their children to the Japanese-run public schools instead of the Korean private schools, because they realized that the Japanese schools had better facilities and offered richer curricula than their private counterparts. Kim was disappointed by this trend, yet could not simply blame it on anti-nationalism. He realized that insisting on Korean nationalism through private education alone was an insufficient incentive to attract students. He believed that private schools needed facilities as good as those of public schools.

Initially, he contacted his former friends in Tokyo, including Ch'oe Namsŏn and An Chaehong, and gathered information regarding the condition of Korean education. With the assistance of these friends, in spring 1915, he completed a proposal to establish a private school with the name Paeksan Hakkyo (Paeksan School). He sent a middleman to the educational director of the Government-General, Sekiya Teizaburō, to gauge his response to the proposal. Sekiya did not want to grant permission for Koreans to establish a private school. Annoyed that Kim dared to name the school before even meeting with him to discuss the proposal, Sekiya vented his anger at the middleman; he used the name of the school as a pretext for his refusal. He reproached the middleman that the name Paeksan had to be an abbreviation of Paektusan (the tallest mountain in Korea, located in North Korea and often a symbol of all Korea). Because of such a deceptive name, Sekiya told the middleman that unless Kim Sŏngsu renamed the school Mount Fuji (symbolizing Japan), he would not approve.[4] Sekiya rejected Kim's proposal.

So Kim Sŏngsu's first step toward starting a school was turned down outright by the colonial government, but this rejection was merely the beginning for Kim of an endless struggle with the Japanese. It was also the beginning of a series of confrontations with Japanese colonialists. The rejection of his proposal offered Kim his first opportunity to test his determination against Japanese policy.

Word traveled in Seoul that Kim Sŏngsu's plan to establish a new school had been rejected by the Government-General. Several private schools, having financial difficulties asked Kim to donate money, but Kim was determined to establish his own school. However, the Central Educational Association (Chungang Hakhoe) not only asked Kim for his money, but also for his leadership.

Sponsored by Chungang Hakkyo (Chungang School), the Central Educational Association combined several educational associations. Scholars formed such educational associations (*hakhoe*) for the purpose of informing and educating people during the period when the national crisis with Japan was escalating. When it became impossible to carry on political activities openly and lawfully, scholarly and educational movements flourished. In essence, their hidden agenda was a nationalistic perspective that "led them to strive to foster awareness of the meaning of independence and to disseminate the new Western learning broadly throughout the society."[5] Some of the groups were formed around scholars in particular provincial areas, among them Yi Kap's North and West Educational Association (Sŏbuk Hakhoe), Yi Kwangjong's Kyŏnggi-Ch'ungch'ŏng Educational Association (Kiho Hŭnghakhoe), Yi Ch'ae's Chŏlla Educational Association (Honam Hakhoe), Yu Kilchun's Society for the Fostering of Activists (Hŭngsadan), Kim Yunsik's Korea Educational Association (Taedong Hakhoe), Chang Chiyŏn's Kyŏngsang Educational Association (Yŏngnam Hakhoe), and Namgung Ŏk's Kangwŏn Educational Association (Kwandong Hakhoe).

Some of these educational associations established schools. The Kyŏnggi-Ch'ungch'ŏng association's Kiho Hakkyo, founded in 1908, was an example. A large traditional Korean house served as the school building. The financial crises common to these schools after the annexation in 1910 forced many of them to consolidate for survival. Accordingly, the educational associations that sponsored the schools were also consolidated. In December 1910, the Honam, Yŏngnam, and Kwandong educational associations consolidated to become the Chungang Educational Association, and the Kiho School became the Chungang School. Thus, the Chungang School, not founded by any single individual but by the support of nationwide educational associations, can be considered a people's school (*minnip hakkyo*).[6]

Kim Sŏngsu was not a stranger to the Chungang School, because his father-in-law, Ko Chŏngju, was a charter member of Honam Educational Association, and his natural father, Kyŏngjung, was a major financial supporter of the official publication of the association. Also, the founder of the Chŏlla Educational Association, Yi Ch'ae, was once principal of the Yŏngsin School, founded by Kim's adoptive father, Kijung.

The financial condition of the Chungang School, even after consolidation, continued to worsen. In 1913, Yu Kilchun donated his personal money to save the school, but it was insufficient, and the financial woes became worse after Yu's death. The school even looked toward the Catholic Church for some aid, but was unsuccessful. By 1915, when Namgung Hun was the seventh principal of the Chungang School, the financial condition of the school sunk so low that most of the teachers went unpaid, and the school was on the verge of collapse. It was at this time that the Chungang Educational Association asked Kim Sŏngsu to take over the school.[7]

In order to assess the state of the Chungang School, Kim Sŏngsu met the president of the Chungang Educational Association, Kim Yunsik, and many elders, including Yi Sangjae, Yu Kŭn, Yu Chint'ae, Pak Sŭngbong, Yu Sŏngjun, and Yi Ukkyu. After surveying the relationship between the school and the association, the management of the school, and the state of the school's finances, Kim concluded that the association's poor management of school funds had caused more damage than had Japanese control. It appeared that the leaders of the association were more interested in managing the association than in managing the school. In spite of his findings, the leaders of the association wanted Kim Sŏngsu to run the school; they offered to invest more money. Kim refused the initial offer from the association, knowing that the existing structural relationship between the school and the association would nullify any additional investment, no matter how sizable. He wanted to run the school independent of the association's poor managerial skills.

Most of the scholars who formed the educational associations were highly motivated yet premodern in their managerial techniques. They needed a young person like Kim Sŏngsu, who had acquired modern managerial skills from his modern education. Yet, elders in the association were uncomfortable about handing over the school to a twenty-four-year old, untested, and unknown person. Kim told the association that he wanted to save the school, but he did not have any solution that would save both the school and the association. Thus, Kim finally told the association that he had to give up the idea of taking over the school.[8] In response to Kim's ultimatum, the elders of the association finally agreed to hand over the school to the young man, realizing there was no alternative. As soon as Kim and the Chungang School reached an agreement, Kim hurried back to Chulp'o to report the negotiation to his parents and to ask for their financial backing.

Fasting for Parental Support for the Chungang School

Kim Kijung and Kyŏngjung were initially surprised to hear their son's plan to take over the Chungang School for the Chungang Educational Association. This was no small accomplishment for a young man. Yet, they began to worry about his inexperience in a job that would be difficult even for a seasoned, experienced, and distinguished scholar. Most of all, Kim's parents were reluctant to mortgage large parts of the family assets to subsidize the school. For them, it was a great risk, particularly in light of Sŏngsu's inexperience.

Sŏngsu's persistence with his plan was persuasive enough to his adopted father, Kijung, who had himself established a school. Kijung's approval was based on neither Sŏngsu's plan nor logic: Kijung realized that he could not change his son's determination, and also that he did not want to discourage a young man with such a noble cause. Kijung approved Sŏngsu's request, and told his adopted son to do his best for a fruitful result.[9] Kijung handed down 300 *turak* (about 479 acres) of land to his adopted son. (The size of *turak* varies by region and locale. *Turak* originally referred to the land area where one *tu* [eighteen liters] of seeds could be planted, so the density of the planting of the seeds makes the size of the land variable. Roughly, one *turak* equals 195.43 *p'yŏng*, and 1,224 *p'yŏng* make an acre.)

Although Kijung's understanding and support touched Sŏngsu to the point of tears, he knew that his adopted father's donation was insufficient to take over and run the school effectively. His natural father's support was also necessary. His natural father, however, was not persuaded by either his son or his older brother. Kyŏngjung could not believe that the Seoul dignitaries had dared to delegate such a big endeavor to an inexperienced young man. He thought that there must be an ulterior motive, a scheme to embezzle money from his son. Learning of Kyŏngjung's suspicions, the Chungang Educational Association sent an official delegate to Kyŏngjung to assure him that it was not a scam. Kyŏngjung was convinced, yet he still believed that it was a reckless undertaking for a youngster. Sŏngsu felt bitter about his natural father's tenacious refusal to support him. He reproached Kyŏngjung: "People say that you are a God-fearing rich man. . . . If so, you ought to spend your wealth in accordance with God's will." [10] Kyŏngjung cried out, "You are impertinent! Are you telling me that you are speaking for God?" [11] Sŏngsu tried to explain that he was not speaking for God, but he meant to say that his intention was congruent with the intention of God. [12] His father remained adamant, and Sŏngsu responded to his father's disapproval by fasting.

While he was fasting, Sŏngsu was thinking that, if he defaulted on his plan, he would end up letting down influential Korean dignitaries. Ultimately, no one would trust him, even in other venues. His integrity as a young leader was in jeopardy. Seeing him fasting, Kyŏngjung felt sorry for his natural son. Reassessing the situation, he concluded that perhaps his son was more mature than he had thought. Furthermore, he admired his son, for, while some sons of wealthy families were drinking and gambling in an attempt to overcome their depression under Japanese oppression, his son was devoted to education. Finally, Kyŏngjung told his son that he could go ahead and promised to give him support for his educational project. Sŏngsu told others later that he actually fasted only one and a half days; the second night his mother gave him a meal. Kijung knew about the deception, but Kyŏngjung was unaware of it. [13] Kijung and Kyŏngjung were to serve as the founders of a new school.

After winning the support of his fathers, he ran into another obstacle, gaining permission from the Government-General. The educational department of the Government-General was reluctant to approve the proposal. Kim's biography related the difficulties and the humiliation that he experienced during his visit to the educational department of the Government-General. The *His-*

torical Documents on Korea-Japan Relations (September 23, 1919) of the Korean Provisional Government described the episode: Kim Sŏngsu's appointment with Sekiya Teizaburō, director of the educational department, was at 9:00 A.M. Kim Sŏngsu arrived promptly at 8:45 and waited more than four hours. At 1:20 P.M., Kim was led to Sekiya's office. Even after Kim entered the office and stood before him for more than ten minutes, Sekiya, pretending that he was busy examining papers, did not look at Kim. It was sheer humiliation for Kim. Finally, Sekiya raised his head and asked Kim Sŏngsu why he wanted to take over the Chungang School. Kim answered that he wished to educate young people. But because Sekiya's office did not allow establishing any new private school, Kim told Sekiya that he wanted to take over a school that was on the verge of closing due to financial problems. Sekiya asked Kim why he wanted to educate young people. Kim replied that Koreans wanted to live well like other people (by means of improved education). Sekiya then insulted Kim by saying that it sounded like fool's talk, and angrily shouted that the Korean Government-General educates Korean people. Sekiya suggested Kim invest the money in a business.[14] Thus, Kim's first visit accomplished nothing but humiliation. If Kim wanted to avoid such humiliation in the future, he would have to give up his dream for education and his plan for the Chungang School.

But Kim was tenacious and lucky. At that time, two Waseda University law professors, Nagai Ryutarō and Tanaka Hozumi, both of whom were influential in the Japanese government, visited Korea. Using his Waseda alumni network, Kim asked their help. They agreed, and Kim's takeover of the Chungang School became official on April 27, 1915.[15]

Throughout the ordeal, Kim Sŏngsu, unknown, untested, and inexperienced, demonstrated several characteristics that would inform others of his philosophy of work and his style in dealing with his project. Kim appeared to be gentle, kind, and easygoing, but he showed strong willpower in pursuing his objectives. He was a classic example of the idealized Korean personality called *woeyu naegang,* meaning docile in appearance, but firm in heart and spirit. Kim also demonstrated his potential to become a great manager. Recognizing that the financial problems of the school were due to poor management, he planned to apply modern management techniques to running the school. Kim knew that noble aspirations for Korean education alone were not sufficient to make the school a success. In pursuing his project, Kim was a cold realist. But he was also selfless, in that if he had cared about his own pride and honor, he would not have endured the humiliation and disrespect of the director in the Government-General. His family was rich enough that he could have lived comfortably without dealing with the Japanese colonialists.

Chungang Becomes a
Modern School

The school Kim Sŏngsu took over was small, barely 80 *p'yŏng* (or 0.065 acres), and remodeled from a traditional Korean dwelling. Since its establishment in 1908 up until Kim Sŏngsu took it over, only three hundred students had graduated from the school.

After Kim Sŏngsu took over, he offered Yu Kŭn the position of principal, and An Chaehong that of vice-principal. Yu was an elderly Korean scholar, journalist, and educator in the late Chosŏn dynasty. Together with Chang Chiyŏn and Namgung Ŏk, Yu founded *Hwangsŏng Sinmun* (*Capital Gazette*), and occupied the position of chief-editor and later president of the newspaper. *Hwangsŏng Sinmun* served as the voice of the Confucianist reform element within the Independence Club. Before the annexation, Yu served as the principal of Hwimun Ŭisuk (the Hwimun School) and of the Kesan School. In July 1915, Song Chinu, who finally graduated from Meiji University after his illness, joined Kim Sŏngsu. Song Chinu's arrival encouraged Kim. Kim delegated most internal school affairs to Song, and simply remained as a teacher of English and economics while planning to build a new, larger school building in a different location. Expansion of Chungang was inevitable, because, in March 1915, the Japanese announced a new private educational act that was more restrictive than that of 1911.[16] Among many other restrictions, the act extended the three-year term for *kodŭng pot'ong hakkyo* (middle school) to four years. Chungang had to expand its facilities.

In March 1917, when Yu Kŭn resigned from his post as the principal, Kim Sŏngsu became the principal of the school, and Song Chinu became the vice-principal. Accordingly, in June 1917, Kim Sŏngsu bought 4,300 *p'yŏng* (about 3.52 acres) of land in Kedong, Chongnogu.[17] Now in the center of Seoul, Kedong was at that time a remote and quiet place. Song Chinu once told Kim that if he built the school in such a remote corner of the city, it might be a hindrance to the growth and prosperity of the school, because students had to walk very far from the main street. Kim responded to Song that Seoul was growing, and very soon, houses would be built in front of the school gate.[18]

Students may have had to walk a distance, yet, as a former student of Chungang, I always thought it was one of the rarest locales in Seoul for a school. The mountains behind the school provided aesthetic pleasure, wonderful fresh air, and a view of the city all the way to Mount Namsan. Kim's words to Song were visionary. Houses have indeed been built up to the front gate, and Chungang has become a focal point of Seoul, particularly north of the Han River. Construction began soon after the land purchase was closed. On December 1, 1917, Chungang relocated from Hwadong *(fig.2.1)* to the modern school at Kedong *(fig.2.2)*. When the building was completed, Kim hired many distinguished teachers with university degrees, including Ch'oe Kyudong, Yi Chunghwa, Yi Kwangjong, Yi Kyuyŏng, and Kwŏn Tŏkkyu. Distinguished young teachers such as Pyŏn Yŏngt'ae, Yu Kyŏngsang, Yu T'aero, Cho Ch'ŏlho, Ko Hŭidong, Na Wŏnjong, and Pak Haedon also joined Chungang's teaching staff. Many of Kim's friends in Tokyo joined Song Chinu administration, including Ch'oe Tusŏn, Hyŏn Sangyun, and Yi Kanghyŏn.

The educational department of the Government-General, particularly Sekiya, was surprised at Kim's remarkable accomplishment. Sekiya, who once humiliated Kim Sŏngsu by asking him whether he had his father's permission to propose such a project, began addressing Kim Sŏngsu as *Kin sensei* (address for a senior or a teacher) as opposed to *Kin kun* (address for a junior youth). The Government-General recognized that the Chungang School, especially with Kim and his staff, could not be dismissed.[19]

As the school became modern in every respect, Kim Sŏngsu, as the principal and the founder of the newly expanded Chungang, drafted the educational mission of the school *(kyoji)*. The bywords were *ungwŏn* (grandeur and far-reaching pursuits), *yonggyŏn* (bravery and firmness), and *sŏngsin* (sincerity, faith, and trust). He elaborated on each of these three basic mottoes. The mission of the school was to teach students to broaden their horizons and seek new frontiers; to pursue an ideal and discipline a strong body to achieve that ideal; and to maintain their integrity, probity *(ŭiri)*, and morality in serving the public. Kim's own writings on *sinŭi ilgwan* (trust all the time and all the way) survive in the form of hanging scrolls *(chokcha)* and reflect part of his philosophy and world view.

Because Kim himself wrote very little on his ideas about nationalism, some Korean writers believe that the mission statement on Chungang education is an important document of his thoughts on the subject.[20] In his later years, Kim hired others to transcribe his thoughts, but that mission statement was written by Kim himself. This being the case, we know that Kim's vision consisted of educating young Koreans to look beyond given conditions, to prepare mentally and physically for the future, and to become useful leaders for the country. In later years, his notion of educating the future elite was clearly manifested in Posŏng Junior College.

In March 1918, as the Chungang School developed into a prestigious institution, Kim stepped down from his post and named Song Chinu as principal.

Kim rarely headed up of the institutions that he established, unless it was absolutely necessary. He referred to this preference in his inaugural address as the president of the *Tonga Ilbo* (October 23, 1924) by saying, "As a part of my nature, I rather like to assist somebody from the sidelines in doing certain work, but I do not enjoy running the work directly."[21] In fact, Kim was the principal of the Chungang School for less than two years, from March 1917 to March 1918, and from September 1931 to May 1932. Nevertheless, the educational mission of the school remained unchanged.

Chungang as a Way to Foster Nationalism

It was well known among Koreans that the purpose of Chungang was not only to offer modern education but also to foster Korean nationalism. For example, Chungang required students to wear black uniforms of Korean-made cotton, whereas students at other schools wore Japanese-made clothes. When I was a student at Chungang, the principal, Sim Hyŏngp'il, used to tell us, "As far as academic excellence alone is concerned, perhaps Kyŏnggi (formerly Keijō Daiichi Kōtō Futue Gakkō, a public school that was established by the Japanese primarily for Japanese, although some Koreans attended) is better than we are. Yet, we have a better track record on nationalism and anti-Japanese movements than that of Kyŏnggi. Ours cannot be matched by any other school's."

Parenthetically, Kim Sŏngsu's second son, Sanggi, was accepted by Kyŏnggi while Kim Sŏngsu was on a lengthy overseas visit (1929–1931). When Kim discovered this, he asked his son to transfer to Chungang. One of Kim's close friends told him that Kyŏnggi had better facilities and people rated the school above Chungang, thus suggested Kim let his son to stay in Kyŏnggi. Kim Sŏngsu responded seriously to his friend, and insisted that a Korean should initially receive a Korean education. To have a national education, Kim urged that one had to attend a private school. Sanggi finished up the term at Kyŏnggi. However, he transferred to Chungang at the end of the school year.[22]

Several episodes demonstrated Chungang's intention of displaying the spirit of nationalism and defying Japanese rules. As a customary event on New Years, the Government-General ordered every school to give the students Japanese rice cakes designed with the chrysanthemum insignia, a symbol of the Japanese Imperial court. Instead of the Japanese rice cakes, Kim Sŏngsu distributed Korean rice cakes (*injŏlmi*) covered with powdered sesame and peas wrapped in Korean paper (*hanji*), made in his home. Yun T'aekchung, who graduated from both Chungang and Posŏng Junior College, and who associated closely with Kim Sŏngsu, recalled the memory of Kim's rice cakes:

> We Chungang students received *injŏlmi* not only in January, but also on June 1, Chungang's anniversary. Frankly, they were not as sweet as those Japanese rice cakes. Some students complained that the *injŏlmi* spoiled easily because of the powdered peas. Some wanted to have the Japanese rice cakes instead. Inch'on [Kim Sŏngsu] used to say, "There is a reason for the *injŏlmi* wrapped up in *hanji*." Most students took them and ate them without knowing much of their meaning.[23]

Another element of Chungang's education that fostered nationalism was Korean language instruction, which was allowed in schools as an elective until 1939, when the Japanese prohibited the use of Korean in the classroom. Defying the prohibition, Chungang kept the Korean language in its curriculum. Kwŏn Tŏkkyu, the Korean language teacher, continued his courses in Korean, and the English teachers, Pyŏn Yŏngt'ae (who later became minister of foreign affairs under Syngman Rhee) and Yu Kyŏngsang used Korean in their English classes until liberation in 1945. Cho Ch'ŏlho and Pak Ch'angha, both physical education teachers, also used Korean in their classes. Because of the extensive use of Korean in Chungang instruction, Japanese language competency among Chungang students was poor; they faced difficulties when they took the entrance examination for advanced studies.[24]

Chungang's spirit alone, however, could not withstand the ever-increasing Japanese pressure. Originally, the badge worn on students' caps, as Chungang Kodŭng Pot'ong Hakkyo evolved into Chungang Middle School in 1921, depicted the Chinese ideogram for "middle" encircled by the *mugunghwa* (rose of Sharon), the Korean national flower. In December 1938, the internal affairs department of the office of Kyŏnggi province ordered the Chongno police station to confiscate Chungang's cap-badges. Laurels replaced the *mugunghwa* until the liberation, when the *mugunghwa* cap-badge was restored.[25]

Chungang as the Center of the March First Movement

Among many Chungang educational missions to promote nationalism and anti-Japanese colonialism, from minor symbols to major events, the role of

Chungang in the March First Movement (Samil Undong) was the most significant. When Japanese colonial efforts intensified, a large number of Koreans participated in a nationwide anti-Japanese demonstration on March 1, 1919, declaring
Korean independence from Japan. The doctrine of self-determinism put forward by Woodrow Wilson as an integral part of the post-World War I peace set-
tlement indirectly provided the ignition. The March First Movement was known
as a movement that was coordinated through various religious organizations:
Ch'ŏndogyo (Religion of the Heavenly Way), Christian, Buddhist, and others.
Ch'ŏndogyo evolved from Tonghak (Eastern Learning), and originated in 1860
with Ch'oe Cheu, who claimed to have received a vision from heaven that instructed him to establish a religion based on faith in God and man to alleviate
the sufferings of the people. Its doctrine drew inspiration from other religions,
both indigenous and foreign. Its members staged a rebellion against the ruling
Chosŏn dynasty in 1894, and then participated in the independence movement
during the Japanese occupation of 1910 to 1945.

The central figures in the movement were thirty-three men who signed the
Korean Declaration of Independence as representatives of the whole Korean
people; they were led by Son Pyŏnghŭi for Ch'ŏndogyo, Yi Sŭnghun for the
Christian groups, and Han Yongun for the Buddhists. Some historians, such as
Yi Hyŏnhŭi, knowing the contributions made by others, said that the represen-
tatives numbered forty-eight, and perhaps the number should be even higher.[26]

A declaration of independence was originally scheduled to be signed on
March 3, 1919, the date of funeral rites for King Kojong, but the representatives
decided to act two days earlier. On March 1, the thirty-three representatives
met at the T'aehwagwan restaurant and formally promulgated a Declaration of
Independence proclaiming that Korea had become an independent nation. The
opening line of the declaration read, "We herewith proclaim the independence
of Korea and the liberty of the Korean people." The declaration proclaimed to
the world that Korea had the right to exist as a free and independent nation,
and that it had been annexed to Japan by outside forces and against its will.
Students gathered in Pagoda Park in Seoul and marched through the streets.
Passions spread quickly throughout the city. The greatest mass movement of Korean people in all their history was a direct manifestation of a nationwide effort
to regain Korea's lost independence against Japanese authoritarian military rule
(*budan seiji*).

Most people familiar with the movement either are unaware of or have
overlooked the role of Chungang School and people who were associated with
Chungang, namely, Kim Sŏngsu, Song Chinu (principal of the school at the
time), and Hyŏn Sangyun (a Chungang instructor then). Their role in the preparation of the March First Movement was integral and indispensable. Chin Tŏkkyu

sums up the role of Chungang in the movement as "the result of Kim Sŏngsu's educational endeavor."[27]

In this book, I do not claim that the March First Movement was planned solely by the Chungang team. Nor do I intend to take credit away from the religious organizations that formed the backbone of the movement. The movements influenced by Wilson's self-determinism were plotted secretly by several organizations. However, the Chungang team was one of them. The role played by the Chungang team was to coordinate the students in Tokyo and the various religious leaders in Korea. In drafting the contents of the Korean Declaration of Independence the Chungang team played a significant role as well.

Movements toward a declaration of Korea's independence were initially started by the overseas Korean independence fighters, for they had gained access to Wilson's doctrine of self-determination of the nations. In January 1919, Korean patriots in Shanghai organized the New Korea Youth Association (Sinhan Ch'ŏngnyŏndang) and sent Kim Kyusik as its representative to the peace conference in Paris to make an appeal for Korean independence. The organization sent representatives to Korea, Japan, Manchuria, Siberia, and other areas to seek potential independence activists. Chang Tŏksu and Sŏnu Hyŏk were dispatched to Korea. Chang was arrested by Japanese authorities in Inch'ŏn, but Sŏnu was able to contact Christian leaders in north P'yŏngan province, including Yi Sŭnghun. In Tokyo, Korean students formed the Korean Youth Independence Corps (Chosŏn Ch'ŏngnyŏn Tongniptan), which adopted a series of resolutions and issued a declaration for Korea's independence on February 8, 1919.

While such movements were developing among the patriots exiled overseas, between December 1918 and January 1919, independence movements were formed in Korea: the Chungang team, including Kim Sŏngsu, Song Chinu, and Hyŏn Sangyun; the Ch'ŏndogyo team, including Son Pyŏnghŭi, Kwŏn Tongjin, O Sech'ang, and Ch'oe Rin; and other teams that had close contact with American missionaries via the YMCA and Severance Medical College (the current medical college of Yonsei University), including Pak Hŭido, Yi Kapsŏng, young college students at Posŏng Junior College, Yŏnhŭi Junior College (formerly Chosŏn Christian College and currently Yonsei University), and Seoul Medical College.

The Chungang team members began to discuss their plan in December 1918, in Chungang's *sukchiksil* (night-duty room). Since Chungang's relocation, the *sukchiksil (fig. 2.3)* had served a dual purpose as a night-duty room and a lounge for staff, and Song Chinu and Hyŏn Sangyun stayed there. Before Kim Sŏngsu acquired his own house in Seoul, he lived in a boardinghouse; when he joined Song Chinu and Hyŏn Sangyun many nights in the *sukchiksil* to discuss strategy, meals were delivered from his boarding house. The *sukchiksil* was not only the place where the Chungang team discussed their plans, but also the place where they coordinated their activities with other organizations. (The *sukchiksil* was later remodeled and rebuilt and designated as the room where the March First Movement was born. Also, a memorial slab was erected on the site of the original site of the *sukchiksil* to commemorate the historical event.)

As they heard the news that Syngman Rhee from the United States and Kim Kyusik from China were going to attend the peace conference in Paris in January 1919, Kim Sŏngsu, Song Chinu, and Hyŏn Sangyun had discussions almost daily at the *sukchiksil,* and escalated their plan for an independence movement in Korea. They agreed to join with the Ch'ŏndogyo team because it had an underground organization. In January 1919, the Chungang team asked Hyŏn Sangyun to contact his former teacher Ch'oe Rin, who was the principal of Posŏng School (then owned and run by the Ch'ŏndogyo). Wholeheartedly agreeing with the notion of organizing an independence movement, Ch'oe kept close contact with the Chungang team, and also discussed the plan with O Sech'ang and Kwŏn Tongjin of Ch'ŏndogyo; he obtained their approval.[28] Ch'oe waited for the final decision from Son Pyŏnghŭi, the head of Ch'ŏndogyo.[29]

Also in January 1919, a secret messenger from the Korean student organization in Tokyo, Song Kebaek, came to Seoul, and one night he showed Hyŏn Sangyun the Declaration of Independence drafted by the students in Tokyo. Hyŏn was the senior (*sŏnbae*)[30] of Song at Waseda University. Being deeply moved by the draft of the students' declaration of independence, Hyŏn and Song notified Kim Sŏngsu, and showed the draft to Ch'oe Namsŏn. Ch'oe was inspired enough to volunteer to write the domestic version of the declaration for the movement in Korea. (In fact, Ch'oe also wrote the Declaration of Independence for the March First Movement.) The draft of the students' declaration of independence was delivered to Son Pyŏnghŭi via Ch'oe Rin. Son was impressed by the draft, and asked Ch'oe Rin, "How can we just sit and simply watch [the development of the movement] while the young people are actively organizing a movement [*undong*] for the nation [*minjok*]?"[31] Son told Ch'oe to pursue the plan for the movement. It was the middle of January 1919 when this initial phase of the March First Movement was completed. The Chungang team had played an instrumental role in the development of the movement, as had Ch'oe Rin, as Frank Baldwin asserts in his dissertation entitled "The March First Movement: Korean Challenge and Japanese Response."[32]

Although Kim Sŏngsu, Song Chinu, Ch'oe Rin, Hyŏn Sangyun, and Ch'oe Namsŏn frequently met in the Chungang *sukchiksil,* they also held secret meetings at the residences of Kim Sŏngsu and Ch'oe Rin. Yi Pyŏnghŏn from Ch'ŏndogyo, who delivered Ch'oe Rin's message to Kim Sŏngsu's residence in the presence of Song Chinu, Ch'oe Namsŏn, and Hyŏn Sangyun, recalls Kim

Sŏngsu's caution: "For every matter, if there is a beginning, there will be an end. In order to accomplish the goal, you have to do your best. Be cautious, trustful, and keep the faith."[33]

The Chungang team together with Ch'oe Rin invited some high-ranking officers to serve as the representatives of the movement, but they declined. They then thought in terms of Christian leaders, particularly Yi Sŭnghun, the founder of Osan School, a Presbyterian elder, and one of the most respected and influential leaders of the time. They decided to invite Yi to Seoul for a discussion. Ch'oe Namsŏn wrote a letter to Yi that was finally delivered to him after having gone through four persons. On receiving the letter, Yi promptly came to Kim Sŏngsu's home in Seoul, and after learning of all the progress, he promptly agreed to join the movement. With the formation of a coalition of Ch'ŏndogyo and Christian leaders, the movement evolved into the second phase. Kim Sŏngsu contributed several thousand *yen* to Yi Sŭnghun for organizing activities.[34] The exact amount is unknown.

In the meantime, Yi Sŭnghun was cooperating closely with fellow Christian leaders, such as Ham T'aeyŏng (who later served as vice president in the Syngman Rhee government) and Yi Kapsŏng. On February 21, 1919, Ch'oe Namsŏn arranged to meet Ch'oe Rin of Ch'ŏndogyo to form a united front, and on February 24, Yi Sŭnghun, Ham T'aeyŏng, and Ch'oe Rin met Son Pyŏnghŭi; they also reached an agreement to join in a united front for the movement. This was the movement's final phase. To launch the March First Movement, as indicated in Yi Chongil's memo of September 30, 1910, Ch'ŏndogyo planned a reenactment of the Peasant rebellion (Tonghak) of 1910, when Korea became a Japanese colony. Ch'ŏndogyo also contributed 5,000 *yen* to Yi Sŭnghun.[35] In order to expand the movement to all the religious organizations in Korea, Ch'oe Rin, Yi Sŭnghun, and Ham T'aeyŏng sought the participation of Buddhist organizations via Han Yongun and Paek Yongsŏng. The Buddhist organizations approved.[36] In addition Buddhists, Confucianists,[37] students,[38] and women[39] joined the planning of the movement.

Because Yi Chongil's office in Posŏngsa was near Chungang School, he was able to visit Chungang's *sukchiksil* often to discuss the independence movement. Yi might have influenced the young Chungang team to coordinate their planning with the Ch'ŏndogyo leaders.[40] His visits were intensive in 1918, and continued until February 2, 1919. According to Yi's memo of February 20, 1919, Kim Sŏngsu also visited the church of Ch'ŏndogyo to talk about the movement.[41] Although Yi played a key role in bringing the Chungang team and Ch'ŏndogyo together, Kim Sŏngsu's initiative provided the impetus. Kim Sŏngsu was the one who insisted that an overseas independence movement was needed, yet, he also understood that, in order to demonstrate the will of Koreans directly to the Japanese authorities, the movement had to enlist twenty million Koreans.[42]

Despite the role played by the Chungang team in plotting the March First Movement, Kim Sŏngsu, Song Chinu, and Hyŏn Sangyun were not among the thirty-three representatives who signed the Declaration of Independence. Song Chinu and Hyŏn Sangyun, however, were included in the list of forty-eight as were Ham T'aeyŏng and other key participants in the planning of the movement. Both Song and Hyŏn were arrested by the Japanese authorities and held in jail for a year before they were freed due to a lack of evidence.

Kim Sŏngsu's biography explained that the Chungang team was excluded from the list of the thirty-three representatives because most of the participants believed that the religious organizations should be seen as the prominent organizers of the movement.[43] Ch'oe Hyŏngyŏn adds that, if the movement was to continue, some of its key members needed to stay out of jail.[44] Commenting specifically on the absence of Kim Sŏngsu from both lists, Ch'oe points out that, if Kim's involvement had been uncovered, there would have been no strong organizers, supporters, and financial backers outside the jail. Most of all, if Kim Sŏngsu's involvement had been known, Chungang School would have been forced to close. In fact, there had been a precedent closing. When An Ch'angho was arrested in the "incident of 105 persons,"[45] the Japanese authorities closed his Taesŏng School in P'yŏngyang in 1912. Song Chinu and Hyŏn Sangyun, who worried about a possible closing of Chungang, insisted that Kim Sŏngsu stay away from Seoul during preparations for the movement. Kim Sŏngsu eventually went to Chulp'o at the end of February.[46]

Kim Sŏngsu was criticized for his absence from the scene during the March First Movement. It was believed that he avoided the crisis because he feared possible imprisonment; however, Kim's supporters asserted that it was the Chungang team that insisted on his absence. The team believed that the movement would take a symbolic stance against the policies of the Government-General, and awaken Koreans to future independence. If the movement alone were intended to end Japanese rule instantly, there would be no need to save Kim Sŏngsu for the future. Unlike other young radicals, however, the Chungang team did not believe that the movement would bring about Korea's independence immediately; thus, they could not afford Kim's imprisonment.[47] Kim Sŏngsu was basically an organizer and financial backer, not an action-oriented revolutionary.

As revealed in the planning stage of the March First Movement, above and beyond its role of disseminating the new learning, Chungang School was renowned as a hotbed of nationalism. For instance, on June 10, 1926, seven years after the March First Movement, on the day of the state funeral of King

Sunjong (1907–1910), the last king of Chosŏn dynasty, students launched an anti-Japanese demonstration shouting "Long live Korean independence (*Taehan tongnip manse*)!" This demonstration was known as the "June Tenth Anti-Japanese Movement" (*Yuksip Manse Sagŏn*). About forty Chungang students, led by Yi Sŏnho, participated in the demonstration. Out of eleven students, who led the demonstration and were convicted and imprisoned from one to three years, four were Chungang students. Yu Myŏnghŭi, who received the longest sentence, was a Chungang student.[48] Chungang students played a major part in this movement. Consequently, Kim Sŏngsu had to face police inquiries at the Chongno police station, for the names of Kim, Ch'oe Namsŏn, and Ch'oe Rin were used in a student manifesto (*kyŏngmun*).[49]

The March First Movement notwithstanding, Kim Sŏngsu's first ground-breaking project for Korean modernization, establishing a private educational institution, was successful. It was a test of his strength and endurance, of friendship, of cooperation from his friends and associates, and of his ability to overcome difficulties working within Japanese rule in the colony. Most of all, he learned that education was a major means to lay the foundation for an independent Korea. He firmly believed that Korean modernization could not be accomplished without emphasizing education.

2.1. The old Chungang School in Hwadong

2.2. The new Chungang School buildings in Kedong

2.3. Chungang's *sukchiksil* (renovated)

CHAPTER THREE

Establishment of an Enterprise for Korean Modernization

The outbreak of the March First Movement quickly spread throughout the nation and gathered enormous momentum. Japan was stunned by the enormity of the movement, in which more than two million Koreans took part in more than 1,500 demonstrations.[1] The demonstrations quickly spread to various overseas areas, including, Manchuria, the Russian Maritime Territory, and other places.

The movement was so vast in its scale and intensity that the Japanese authorities were caught by surprise. In response to the movement, Japan mobilized its military forces. Army and navy contingents fired indiscriminately into the crowds of peaceful demonstrators and set fire to schools, churches, and private dwellings. Han Woo-keun (Ugǔn), a historian, notes: "Although accurate statistics are not available, it is generally agreed that about seven thousand people were killed and fifteen thousand wounded. Seven hundred and fifteen private houses, forty-seven churches and two school buildings were destroyed by fire. About 46,000 were arrested, of whom around 10,000, including 186 women, were tried and convicted."[2] These reports were issued by the Japanese authorities. Actual numbers in all these categories could have been exceeded in the official reports.

Although the rally was intended to be entirely peaceful, the demonstration exhibited the brutality of the Japanese occupation and the length to which Koreans were willing to go to reach independence. The Western powers, however, were not moved to act, for they held Japan in high esteem as a victorious ally in World War I. Many thoughtful Koreans, including Kim Sŏngsu and his colleagues, recognized that a fighting spirit alone would not suffice. Bare fists, determination, and will were no match for cold bullets and cruel acts of suppression. They understood that the fight had to be a long lasting one.

For Kim Sŏngsu, the March First Movement stood as a turning point in advocating and pursuing the goals set by the Independence Club. While Kim's close associates, Song Chinu and Hyŏn Sangyun, were in police custody awaiting trial for their roles as members of the Chungang team in the March First Movement, they never mentioned Kim Sŏngsu's role to the Japanese authorities in order to safeguard him.[3]

After the March First Movement took root, Kim faced a personal tragedy. His wife, Ko Kwangsŏk, died after giving birth to twin sons on October 27, 1919. Fifteen months later, Kim married Yi Aju, who had been a demonstrator in the March First Movement. Kim first met Yi in August 1919, when he attended a court hearing of Chŏngsin Girls School students who took part in the March First Movement. As a fourth-year student, who was the school leader for the demonstration, Yi was sentenced to a six-month prison term for her alleged role in the demonstration. Kim was impressed by Yi Aju, especially for her tenacious stand during the court hearing. While Yi was serving her prison term, she had surgery for parotitis at the Severance Hospital, where Kim paid her a visit. Later, via a matchmaker, the thirty-one-year-old widower married the twenty-three-year-old Yi on January 30, 1921.

Although the March First Movement failed to achieve its ultimate goal— to obtain Korea's independence—it did accomplish many things. Despite the enormous casualties, the movement displayed the pride of the nation, highlighted the inhumane treatment of Koreans by the Japanese occupiers, and demonstrated the potential power of Koreans against their aggressors. The Korean people's political consciousness reached a new stage of awareness. The demonstrations showed that nationalist passions among Koreans at every level could be mobilized for anti-Japanese activities.

The establishment of the Provisional Government in Shanghai in April 1919 was a by-product of the March First Movement. The independence fighters in Manchuria and the Russian Maritime Territory were regrouped under a single banner of the General Headquarters of the Restoration Army (Kwangbokkun Ch'ongyŏng) in Antung prefecture in Manchuria. The Provisional Government was able not only to dispatch its envoys to international conferences and to put out its principal publication, *Tongnip Sinmun* (*Independence News*), but also to continue informing the independence movement both within Korea and in the outside world.

Obvious changes occurred in Japan's colonial policy in Korea, which was now carried out by the enlightened administration (*bunka*). At this time, Japan announced a conciliatory move that it was abandoning reliance on its gendarmerie police forces to maintain control in Korea in favor of a so-called enlightened administration (*munhwa chŏngch'i*). Japan even abolished the wearing of uniforms and swords by civilian officials, although all those gestures were superficial; Admiral Saitō Makoto was appointed the new governor-general. Eventually Saitō was proclaimed the so-called enlightened administration.

Up to this time, not one single civil official was appointed to the post of governor-general. The previous requirement that governors-general be appointed from the ranks of active-duty generals or admirals was suspended so that civilian officials could take their place in the colonial government; the gendarmerie police system was abandoned, although the number of Japanese policemen in Korea was actually increased[4]; the Korean educational system was to be expanded and its standards raised to the same level as that of the Japanese; and press controls were relaxed to permit the publication of Korean newspapers in the Korean language, *han'gŭl*. This policy allowed Kim Sŏngsu to establish the *Tonga Ilbo*. The *Chosŏn Ilbo* and *Sidae Ilbo* were also established.

Admiral Saitō Makoto, urbane, well-traveled, and fluent in English, brought with him Mizuno Rentarō, a former home minister, as director-general of political affairs. Saitō skillfully manipulated colonial policy by replacing the naked coercion of the former policy with softer but more effective policies of cooperation under the label of "harmony between Japan and Korea (*nissen yūwa*)." Ironically, perhaps the March First Movement allowed Japan to increase its exploitation of the Korean economy, which came to resemble a classic colonial economy. Huge quantities of Korean rice had to be shipped to Japan to overcome a severe shortage, and Korea became a market for the output of Japanese industry, particularly clothing, yarn, and thread.[5]

Nevertheless, there was a persistent growth of native Korean capital investment. Kim Sŏngsu's Seoul Textile Company was an example. "Established in 1919," as Lee Ki-baik claims, "it was a purely Korean enterprise launched with Korean capital . . . announced a policy of hiring only Koreans and it maintained this special characteristic of a native Korean enterprise throughout its history."[6]

Establishment of the Kyŏngsŏng Spinning and Weaving Company (Kyŏngbang)

Realizing that clothing, yarn, and thread were the major goods imported from Japan, Kim thought that, if there were going to be an industrial movement, it had to begin with textiles. Yi Kanghyŏn, an old friend of Kim Sŏngsu during his Tokyo years, majored in cotton textiles at Tokyo Higher Industrial School, taught physics and math at Chungang School, and was instrumental in Kim's establishing a cotton textile industry.

Taking over the Kyŏngsŏng Cord Company
(Kyŏngsŏng Chingnyu)

Even before he established the Kyŏngsŏng Spinning and Weaving Company (Kyŏngbang), in 1917 Kim Sŏngsu took over the financially ailing Kyŏngsŏng Cord Company (Kyŏngsŏng Chingnyu Chusik Hoesa). Since Kim required Chungang students to wear Korean-made cotton as their school uniform, he felt the need to develop high quality Korean-made textiles.

Founded in 1910 as an unlimited partnership, the Kyŏngsŏng Cord Company was converted in 1911 to a joint-stock company of eighteen shareholders, making it the first joint-stock textile company in Korean history.[7] Yun Ch'iso, father of the former president of South Korea, Yun Posŏn, was the president.[8] Although the factory employed as many as 150 workers in 1915, it was a premodern factory in many ways, relying heavily on old-fashioned manual labor. It produced mainly cords and belts that were used to tie down Korean men's traditional trousers (paji) at the ankles, as well as other traditional clothing accessories. The company also produced socks, gloves, and a few other items of clothing. As traditional Korean clothing was on the decline, however, the future prospects of the company appeared gloomy. By 1915, the company faced a crisis, and in 1917, by the time Kim Sŏngsu took over, it faced bankruptcy.[9]

Kim Sŏngsu turned the cord company around. He halted the production of chingnyu (cords and belts woven from cotton yarn), and began producing cotton cloth. Supplies of Korean-made textiles were then short because the old-fashioned textiles, handmade for domestic consumption, were on the decline; cotton textiles from England and Japan, and silk from China, had gained market prominence. In 1910, the year that Kyŏngsŏng Cord Company was founded, imported textiles came heavily from Japan (63 percent) and from England (37 percent). In 1914, when World War I broke out, Japanese imported cotton textiles dominated 97 percent of the Korean market, and this figure increased to 99.4 percent in 1918.[10]

Kim Sŏngsu thought the cord company must produce cotton cloth in response to the overwhelming Japanese market dominance. He changed the name of the company to the Chungang Commercial and Industrial Company (Chungang Sanggong Chusik Hoesa), and with a remodeled factory and forty new Toyoda looms, it produced cotton clothing starting in 1918. Although the company improved greatly as it compared with that of the pre-Kim Sŏngsu takeover, it was not yet a genuine modern factory compared with that of the Japanese-owned establishments. It represented even less than 50 percent improvement when compared with a newly established, Japanese-owned textile firm in Pusan, the Chōsen Spinning and Weaving Company (Chōsen Bōshoku or Chōbō). Established in 1917, the same year that Kim Sŏngsu took over the Kyŏngsŏng Cord Company, the Chōbō was capitalized at 5 million *yen*; but, in as much as it did not start to produce cotton clothing until 1919, the Chungang Commercial and Industrial Company should be considered the first modern Korean textile company to produce cloth.[11]

Even after Kim Sŏngsu established the Kyŏngsŏng Spinning and Weaving Company, the Chungang Commercial and Industrial Company remained a separate company. In 1944, it merged with the Kyŏngsŏng Spinning and Weaving Company. Its total capital at the time of merger was estimated at 1 million *yen*.[12]

Even though Kim Sŏngsu took over the near bankrupt Kyŏngsŏng Cord Company, he never had a concrete plan to expand the company. The increasingly popular cotton broadcloth required a separate and full-scale facility similar to the Japanese-owned Chōbō being built in Pusan. Kyŏngbang was an outgrowth of the Kyŏngsŏng Cord Company, and was a purely Korean enterprise launched with Korean capital. As Eckert points out, it was "the first Korean-owned (and Korean-managed) large-scale industrial enterprise" in the history of Korea.[13]

Kim Sŏngsu's establishing Kyŏngbang took place in the midst of two major challenges that colonial Korea had faced: one was the increasing importation of cotton cloth from overseas, especially from Japan; this importation threatened to wipe out Korean-made cotton textiles; and, another was the challenge of Chōbō, the Japanese facility, which was scheduled to begin large-scale production in 1919. To counter the increasing domination of the textile industry in Korea, the moderate nationalist leaders agreed that a Korean-owned textile industry with Korean capital and technology must be founded. Such a sentiment was fueled by memories of the March First Movement.

Also, the change in Japanese colonial practices after the March First Movement, particularly the introduction of the so-called *bunka* (cultural or enlightened) policies, encouraged native Korean businesses to grow. Before then, and ever since the annexation in 1910, any investment either Korean or Japanese private investment was restricted because of the so-called 1910 Company Law, which required that all new companies had to be officially licensed by the Government-General. However, recognizing the fact that a growing number of Koreans had been disaffected by the colonial policy and the regulations that governed native Korean entrepreneurship before and after the March First Movement, the Japanese authorities were inclined to repeal the law.[14] Although the law was not officially repealed until April 1920, Kim Sŏngsu was able to take advantage of the lax enforcement of it to establish Kyŏngbang. The repeal of the Company Law in 1920 allowed the growth of Korean firms from 554 in 1920 to 1,763 in 1929.[15]

Both the *bunka* policies and the relaxation of the Company Law promoted the establishment of a cotton-textile industry in Korea. Development of the industry was also encouraged by that part of Japanese colonial policy that allowed the production of raw materials, rice farming, silk manufacture, livestock raising, and cotton farming. In 1910, when Korea was annexed, cotton farms occupied about 3,000 *chŏngbo* (1 *chŏngbo* equals 2.45 acres), but increased to 94,000 *chŏngbo* by 1918, with an anticipated increase to 250,000 *chŏngbo* in 1919.[16] The prospect of a domestic cotton supply looked ever more promising for the emerging textile firms.

No one would disagree that the socioeconomic and political factors I have mentioned thus far were incentive enough for a nationalist entrepreneur to establish a Korean-owned textile company. Nevertheless, regarding Kim Sŏngsu's specific motives for establishing Kyŏngbang, there is some disagreement. Some critics question whether Kim's motivation came solely from his nationalism.[17] As Kim himself indicated to Song Ch'an'gyu, profit-making must be a factor in a business enterprise, otherwise, a business would be a charity. No one can deny that profit-making was a part of Kim and his family's motives in founding Kyŏngbang. Nevertheless, it would be unfair to say that profit-making was Kim's only motive. Even in establishing a business enterprise, Kim elected a manufacturing industry that was essential for Korean modernization and that would increase employment. If profit-making had been his sole purpose, Kim could have invested his family holdings in banking and other lucrative fields as some other wealthy Korean businessmen did.[18] Also, it must be pointed out that Kyŏngbang was not a company that generated any profit until it was taken over by Kim's younger brother, Yŏnsu, a genius in business management in his time, who became managing director (*ch'wich'eyŏk*). Profits grew after 1925,[19] and Kyŏngbang prospered when Kim Yŏnsu became its president in 1935.[20] It could be argued, however, that Kim Sŏngsu spent more of his family assets than he increased them.[21]

The Birth of Kyŏngbang

In as much as a detailed description of Kyŏngbang is available in the well-documented English edition of Carter J. Eckert's *Offspring of Empire* (1991), and Daniel L. McNamara's *The Colonial Origins of Korean Enterprise* (1990),[22] this book covers only the company's formative period, from 1919, when Kim Sŏngsu established the company, until 1925, when Kim Yŏnsu assumed its management. Kim Sŏngsu founded Kyŏngbang and managed it through the difficulties of its development; Kim Yŏnsu, drawing on his innate business talent and his training in economics, later expanded the company into a modern business enterprise.

Kyŏngbang had its genesis in mid-August 1919, when Kim Sŏngsu and his family members and other associates began an operation to produce and supply increasingly popular cotton broadcloth using modern facilities. The original owners of the firm were Kim Sŏngsu, his adoptive father, and his natural father. Later, the ownership expanded to include Pak Yŏnghyo, Pak Yonghŭi, Pyŏn Kwangho, Chang Tuhyŏn, Chang Ch'unjae, Yi Sŏngjun, Ch'oe Chun, Yun Sangŭn, Cho Kehyŏn, Yi Iru, and others, most of whom were large landlords and wealthy merchants.[23] Kim Sŏngsu and his associates applied to the bureau of industry of the Government-General for permission to establish Kyŏngbang. Since this was the time before formal repeal of the Company Law, permission was initially delayed under trivial pretexts. After several months of delay, permission was granted on October 5, 1919. On that day, the first general stockholders' meeting of the Kyŏngsŏng Spinning and Weaving Company, Ltd. was held in the T'aehwagwan, a branch location of the Myŏngwŏlgwan restaurant in Seoul.[24]

Whereas Kyŏngsŏng Cord Company was founded in 1910 as an unlimited partnership (*hammyŏng hoesa*) and later converted into a joint-stock company (*chusik hoesa*), Kyŏngbang was a joint-stock company from the beginning, the idea being to open the ownership to as many Koreans as possible. Kim Sŏngsu's biography as well as Korean scholarship in general recognize that the concept of "one share per person" (*irin ilju*) is in keeping with the spirit of nationalism.[25] Even before he applied for permission from the Government-General to establish the company, Kim Sŏngsu traveled all over the country inducing people to participate in the stock sharing. The company's authorized capital had been fixed at one million *yen,* and the first paid-in capital had to be 250,000 *yen,* one quarter of the total. The price of stock per share was 12.5 *yen,* which was equivalent to two *kama* (120 kilograms) worth of rice.

Despite Kim Sŏngsu's extensive travel to seek out subscribers for the Kyŏngbang shares, the first sale brought in only a quarter of the necessary one million *yen.* The low response to the stock offering stemmed from several causes, one of them being that the price of the stock was higher than most ordinary persons could afford.[26] At the same time, the price seemed reasonable to those who had money, but these people were eager for investments that promised higher rates of return, such as usury and real estate speculation, especially real estate involving rice paddies. Also, many native Korean scholars speculate that most Koreans were unaccustomed to the concept of a joint-stock company.[27] Even if the concept of the joint-stock company had been introduced in the nineteenth century and publicized in *Hansŏng Sunbo,*[28] considering the low circulation of such a newspaper, it is highly unlikely that the concept had infiltrated the Korean populace. And, even if the concept had been understood, it would have been by only a few wealthy people, mostly landlords and merchants, who were, in fact, the majority shareholders of Kyŏngbang.

Nevertheless, Kim Sŏngsu's efforts to attract shareholders beyond a few wealthy Koreans throughout the country was moderately successful. The total number of shareholders reached 188; the total number of shareholders who held fewer than 500 shares was 180 (95.7 percent), and the number of shares held by those 180 was 12,680 (63.5 percent), out of 20,000 total shares. Out of 20,000 shares, 3,790 were held by the original owners. Despite Kim's widespread effort, the great majority of the remaining stocks was held largely by landlords and wealthy merchants. Among the family members of Kim Sŏngsu, his adoptive father bought 800 shares, his natural father purchased 2,000 shares, and Kim Sŏngsu had 200 shares.[29]

Kyŏngbang shareholders elected Pak Yŏnghyo, who held 200 Kyŏngbang shares, as its first president, a position he occupied until 1935. Kim Sŏngsu was one of the five managing directors. There is some criticism regarding Pak's background and his pro-Japanese stance. As the critics point out, although Pak was an early enlightenment leader, no one can deny his close association with the Japanese.[30] Even if Kyŏngbang was founded in the name of nationalism, as Kim Sŏngsu's biography points out, the shareholders had a utilitarian reason for wanting Pak as the president. As the founders had had trouble dealing with the colonial authorities when they needed permission to establish the company, the shareholders surmised that managing a Korean-owned company under the colonial government would be difficult and that Pak Yŏnghyo's Japan connection might ease such difficulty.[31] Most of all, in 1919 Kim Sŏngsu was a mere twenty-eight years old, only about four years out of college. At that age, some were still in college or graduate school and worrying about their grades. Because of Kim's youth and inexperience, the Kyŏngbang shareholders wanted to have a president like Pak who was visible politically and could deal with the Japanese authorities.

Regardless of Pak's Japanese connections, the company displayed a strong nationalistic sentiment to promote a Korean-owned and Korean-operated industrial enterprise. Standard Korean scholarship stresses Kyŏngbang as the prime example of national capital.[32] Even in its employment practices, Kyŏngbang had a policy of hiring only Koreans. This does not necessarily mean that there were no Japanese employees at all at Kyŏngbang. In fact, Kyŏngbang's technical experts were not all Korean, some were Japanese. A limited use of Japanese experts at that time was essential, considering the low-level of Korean technology as well as the restricted opportunities for education. Similarly, Japanese investment in Kyŏngbang was not completely prohibited. As Eckert points out: "By 1945 Japanese constituted over 13.6 percent of the total number of stockholders, and their combined stock represented 5.6 percent of the total 260,000 shares,"[33] surely an insignificant number in terms of the total Kyŏngbang shares. Some exceptions to the principle of nationalism were unavoidable, given limited capital and technology and strict colonial rule. Nevertheless, owners and managers kept their commitment to prefer Korean investors and to employ Koreans whenever possible.

It should be added that Kim Sŏngsu's travels all over the country to attract a large number of shareholders were not absolutely necessary. His family then was rich enough to make the company a strictly family enterprise. The minimum capital needed for the establishment of Kyŏngbang was 250,000 *yen,* which was about 55.5 percent of Kim's family's total annual income from rents in 1919.[34]

The Formative Period of Kyŏngbang

Until Kyŏngbang had acquired its own headquarters, its office was situated in Kim Sŏngsu's residence. Due to many difficulties and obstacles, the first Kyŏngbang products did not come on line until April 1923.

After the birth of Kyŏngbang, although he was one of the five managing directors, Kim Sŏngsu kept a low profile. As the president, Pak Yŏnghyo was a figurehead, and daily management was done by Pak Yonghŭi, the executive managing director, and Yi Kanghyŏn, technician, engineer, and manager. Pak Yonghŭi was an interesting person because of his adamant anti-Japanese stand. As the son of a big landlord and *kaekchu* (inland market broker) from P'aju, Kyŏnggi province, Pak Yonghŭi graduated from the most prestigious Japanese high school (Daiichi Kōtō Gakkō) and the most prestigious university (Tokyo Imperial University), under the auspices of the government. He earned a reputation for not wearing or using any Japanese products. After his return from Japan, he preferred to wear traditional Korean clothes and rubber shoes (*komusin*).[35] Kim Sŏngsu knew him from his years in Tokyo. Pak helped when Kim took over Chungang School, and worked for Kim at the Kyŏngsŏng Cord Company as manager.[36]

Despite the preparations, Kyŏngbang's beginning was difficult, partly due to inexperience and partly due to natural disaster. It did not help that the Japanese and Korean economies were sluggish in response to the reconstruction boom of the European economy after World War I; Chōbō shortened its working hours, and the poorly financed Kyŏngbang felt the constraints.[37] Kyŏngbang's major financial loss took place even before the company began its first test run, not in Korea but in Japan.

In 1919, shortly after Kyŏngbang was established, Yi Kanghyŏn, the company's chief engineer and manager, went to Nagoya, Japan, to purchase Toyoda looms for the Kyŏngbang factory, and proceeded to Osaka to secure a supply of cotton yarn.[38] Without any previous experience in commodities transactions and without much knowledge of the world economy and changing market conditions, Yi invested large sums of cash in Osaka's market in cotton, cotton yarn, and cotton cloth (called *"Samp'um"* or *"Sampin"* in Japanese), speculating on a windfall. Known as the *Samp'um* incident, it was a great financial loss, totaling 50,000 *yen*.[39] Construction of the Kyŏngbang headquarters building was halted, and the company faced closure before operations began.

Kim Sŏngsu did not know what to do about the financial crisis. At the meeting of the board of directors, Pak Yonghŭi strongly urged declaring bankruptcy, because he believed that there would be no way the company could survive such financial burdens in the midst of an economic recession. Some board members supported Pak's position. One commented, "It was impossible from the beginning to establish a company of this scale solely with Korean capital."[40]

Kim Sŏngsu was determined to continue the company, even if he had to do it alone. Other board members were encouraged by Kim's determination, but insisted on reprimanding Yi Kanghyŏn for his mistake. Pak Yonghŭi, known to be gentle and mild in his temper, commented that, without putting responsibility (on the person who caused such a financial disaster), the company could not be rejuvenated.[41] Kim Sŏngsu replied to Pak Yonghŭi and other board members that he thought about reprimanding Yi, too. Even if Yi left Kyŏngbang, it would not be helpful for the company. If the company was to make Yi go, the company might end up losing an important employee. It would be as if the passengers wanted to get rid of the captain of a sailing boat that wrecked on a reef because of the mistakes made by the captain. If the company disregarded what Yi had done to the company, Yi would do his best for the company. If the company made Yi resign, the company would end up losing both money and a very valuable human resource. Knowing that without Yi's service and dedication reconstruction of Kyŏngbang could not be achieved, Kim asked Pak to leave the solution to Yi and himself.[42] Kim Sŏngsu's response to Pak Yonghŭi about reprimanding Yi Kanghyŏn became widely known, and it was considered an example of Kim Sŏngsu's characteristic style of personnel management; once Kim trusted someone, he would continue to do so, even if that person let him down occasionally. In fact, Yi Kanghyŏn tendered his resignation, but at their meeting on June 21, 1920, the board of directors refused to accept it. Yi kept the same position and title.

As soon as the board of directors' meeting concluded, Kim Sŏngsu went to Chulp'o to seek financial assistance from his parents. When he explained to Kijung what had happened, even his adoptive father, who had been supportive, showed anger and disappointment and did not say anything for a day. Kijung thought that his adopted son lacked the ability to judge people. The next day, after his long silence, Kijung handed over a batch of land deeds to his son, saying that those were all the family assets. Kijung told his son to use the incident as a lesson, not to make any further mistakes in doing business.[43] Even though the Kims were one of the richest families in Korea at the time, they were experiencing fiscal restraints after establishing the *Tonga Ilbo*. In July 1920, using his land deeds as collateral, Kim Sŏngsu was able to get an 80,000 *yen* loan that allowed construction of the factory in Yŏngdŭngp'o to resume.[44]

Kyŏngbang's struggles never seemed to end. As the company had barely recovered from Yi Kanghyŏn's misjudgment, two years after the first products rolled out from the factory, heavy rains in July 1925 caused the Han River to flood. Kyŏngbang's factories and offices in Yŏngdŭngp'o were inundated, and company equipment and raw materials were damaged. The employees spent a month drying wet broadcloth under the sun in order to prevent decay.[45]

More serious than natural and man-made disasters was the problem of capturing a market dominated by the Japanese. As is the case in the present time, Korean consumers then regarded Japanese imports more highly than domestic products. The economic recession that followed World War I was also threatening Kyŏngbang. The new Government-General headed by Saitō was keenly aware of the need for special protection to save industries on the Korean peninsula, especially those that were Japanese-owned. Government subsidies were introduced, with Japanese-owned industries the major beneficiaries. Chōbō was eventually granted a subsidy of 7 percent of its paid-in capital.[46] After a time, the

Government-General's subsidies extended to other Korean industries. Eckert states, "without regular government assistance in its early years of existence Kyŏngbang would probably never have survived."[47] In terms of the Koreans' pride and their notion of the purity of nationalistic Korean capital, it is difficult to understand how such subsidies were justified. As an answer to this question, on June 11, 1922, *Tonga Ilbo* reported Kyŏngbang management's statement to the effect that, if Chōbō were entitled to receive such a subsidy, why should not Kyŏngbang, which is so important to Korea's industry and economy, receive one also?[48]

Kyŏngbang was struggling to maintain itself financially and to carve out a place in a Japanese-dominated market. In the meantime, Kim Sŏngsu, busy running the *Tonga Ilbo,* was looking for a leader with business talent to build Kyŏngbang into a modern business enterprise. Kim Sŏngsu was impressed by his brother, Yŏnsu. While Yŏnsu was managing director of the Kyŏngsŏng Cord Company, he worked so relentlessly that he could be found sleeping and eating in the company plant. Impressed by his zeal and business talent, Kim Sŏngsu appointed his younger brother managing director of Kyŏngbang in April 1922.[49] As Eckert notes,

> Sŏngsu's real interests lay in education and publishing, and when his younger brother Yŏnsu returned to Korea with a degree in economics from Kyoto Imperial University, Sŏngsu gradually turned the actual management of the textile company over to him. Eventually Yŏnsu and his side of the family came to exercise a controlling ownership, and Yŏnsu became a president of the company in 1935. Either personally or through the company, Yŏnsu eventually extended his business interests, directly and indirectly, into a wide variety of areas that encompassed Korea, Manchuria, and China.[50]

Indeed, Kim Yŏnsu was an especially able businessman, and under his leadership, Kyŏngbang made steady growth.[51]

Under Kim Yŏnsu's leadership, for instance, between 1923 and 1935, Kyŏngbang increased the number of its looms and the number of workers increased. After Kim Yŏnsu became president of the company, Kyŏngbang leaped forward toward a *chaebŏl* or business conglomerate (*zaibatsu* in Japanese), by expanding and investing in a variety of fields. By 1938, Kyŏngbang's profits were about 30 percent and the stock was paying a dividend of nearly 12 percent per year.[52] Eventually, Kyŏngbang's direct investment went to building a new factory in Manchuria in 1939.[53]

Kyŏngbang as a Manifestation of Korean Industrial Modernization

Kim Sŏngsu recognized that, along with Korean-language newspapers and good educational opportunities, Korean-owned industry was essential for Korean modernization, yet of all the projects he founded, he was least qualified to run a business. Although he served as principal of Chungang Hakkyo and Posŏng Junior College and president of the *Tonga Ilbo,* he never served as president of Kyŏngbang, ceding that position to his younger brother, Yŏnsu.

As the head of Kyŏngbang, Kim Yŏnsu planned to construct a new plant in Manchuria. Eckert notes that, "Kim Sŏngsu was apprehensive about the project. His younger brother, who was running the company, however, was confident."[54] That the new plant was built in December 1939 is an indication that Kim Sŏngsu's influence on the Kyŏngbang operation was no more than that of an adviser. In 1939 when the South Manchurian Spinning Company (SMSC) was formally inaugurated and Kim Yŏnsu was elected president, Sŏngsu even resigned from his position as an adviser to Kyŏngbang.

Song Ch'an'gyu relates an entertaining episode that illustrates the new direction of Kyŏngbang under Yŏnsu's leadership and Sŏngsu's decision to be aloof from the Kyŏngbang management. Song, who graduated in commerce from Posŏng Junior College in 1941 and knew Kim Sŏngsu personally from his college years, told me this story during an interview with him on June 20, 1991:

> I started to work at Kyŏngbang upon graduation from Posŏng College in 1941. Being an idealistic young man, I thought Kyŏngbang, as a Korean-owned business, should be different from other businesses and would aggressively pursue national independence. Since I had known Inch'on [Kim Sŏngsu] from our college years and understood his spirit of nationalism, in 1943 (I cannot recall the date) I went to Inch'on in his residence in Kedong to complain about the lack of nationalistic interests at Kyŏngbang. He asked me to have supper with him. The supper table was humble, just like that of any ordinary Korean house. As I was complaining, he simply listened. Finally, he asked me, "Your college major was commerce, wasn't it?" I answered that was correct. Then, he asked me,

"What is the ultimate goal of a business enterprise?" And he himself answered the question for me by saying, "Business enterprise pursues its own interests. If you want to carry out Korea's fight for independence, a business firm might not be the ideal place for you. Kyŏngbang is a business enterprise and it will pursue its business interests. When the company is profitable, then it has done its job for the Korean economy. Because I am not a good businessman, I do not bother to say what Kyŏngbang should or should not do. If I were interested in making profits, then I would be running Kyŏngbang. My brother is a good businessman, and he is running a business enterprise, not fighting for independence." [55]

Although the Kyŏngsŏng Cord Company was one of the largest industrial plants before Kyŏngbang in the history of Korean textile industry, it cannot be characterized as a modern factory. Kyŏngbang, because of its size and equipment, was actually the first modern textile factory, and it contributed to Korean *kŭndaehwa* or modernization in the manufacturing sector. Because Kyŏngbang operated under colonial rule, however, its operating procedures could not be completely free from Japanese control, and, at times, subsidies were a necessity for survival. And, because Kyŏngbang grew and prospered during Japanese domination, Kim Yŏnsu has been accused of being a Japanese collaborator. Standard Korean scholarship, however, shares the view of Lee Ki-baik, who, in reference to Kyŏngbang's policy of hiring only Koreans, states, "the Seoul Textile Company [Kyŏngbang] . . . maintained this special characteristic of a native Korean enterprise throughout its history." [56] Certainly, Kyŏngbang was an integrated component of Kim Sŏngsu's modernization projects. The destiny, management, and transnational operations of the post-Kim Sŏngsu era of Kyŏngbang are well-documented in Eckert's previously cited book. [57]

CHAPTER FOUR

Publishing the Tonga Ilbo

Traditionally, the Korean press contributed in a major way to raising the political consciousness of the Korean people against Japanese aggression. The press also served as an important podium to extend education to the masses. Korea's first newspaper, *Hansŏng Sunbo*, founded in 1883 by the Progressive Party led by Kim Okkyun, introduced Western knowledge, but the paper lasted only one year. In 1896, Sŏ Chaep'il founded a modern newspaper, *The Independent* (*Tongnip Sinmun*), that began as a triweekly and eventually became a daily. It's use of the vernacular script, *han'gŭl*, made it accessible to the Korean populace. *The Independent* provided news reports to the general public and fought to preserve the nation's independence. The *Capital Gazette* (*Hwangsŏng Sinmun*), founded by Namgung Ŏk in 1898 and using a mixed Chinese-*han'gŭl* alphabet, was in the forefront of the resistance to Japanese aggression, even though it placed less emphasis on conveying modern values than did *The Independent*.

As Japanese censorship tightened in order to control open criticism against the Japanese, the English journalist Ernest Bethel together with Yang Kit'ak founded the *Korea Daily News* (*Taehan Maeil Sinbo*). It began by using both Chinese and Korean script, and later published purely in *han'gŭl*, while providing an English edition for foreign readers. The *Korean Daily News* published a revealing story by printing "Kojong's personal letter denying that he had approved the Protectorate Treaty and appealing for the protection of the Western powers."¹ Over the door to the newspaper offices, a sign was hung proclaiming, "No Entry to Japanese," and the paper attacked "Japanese acts of aggression with impunity."² In 1906, Ch'ŏndogyo leaders, such as Son Pyŏnghŭi, O Sech'ang, and others, founded the *Independence News* (*Mansebo*); and, in 1909, the Korea Association published the *Korea People's Press* (*Taehan Minbo*), both critical of the pro-Japanese organization of Ilchinhoe. Headed by Song Pyŏngjun and Yi Yonggu, Ilchinhoe was financed by the Japanese and under the direction of Japanese advisers, in order to propagandize that a protectorate over Korea was not a demand on the part of Japan but rather a response to the wishes of the Korean people.

By 1907, stunned by the impact of the Korean press, the Residency-General enacted a law governing newspaper publication. Itō Hirobumi, the first Japanese Resident-General, revealed the strong influence of the Korean press. Consequently, after the annexation in 1910, the *Korean Daily News* changed its name to the *Daily News* (*Maeil Sinbo*), and became a mouthpiece for the Government-General. During the period of the protectorate, Koreans overseas also published newspapers: the *New Korea People's Press* (*Sinhan Minbo*) in the United States; and the *Mainstream* (*Haejo Sinmun*) in Vladivostok. Limited though its circulation, some of these overseas editions were circulated in Korea. Nevertheless, by 1908, all these newspapers were banned. Ultimately, Koreans did not have their own newspapers that could advocate themselves.

Publication of the *Tonga Ilbo*

Considering his background, it would be less strange for Kim Sŏngsu to publish a newspaper than establishing Kyŏngbang, for his natural father published the Honam Hakhoe's monthly magazine. Although it was published only intermittently and its distribution was limited, *Honam Hakhoe Wŏlbo* and Chang Chiyŏn's the *Korean Self-Strengthening Society Monthly* (*Taehan Chaganghoe Wŏlbo*) were good examples of Korea's early journalism.

Even if Kim Sŏngsu had been interested in founding a newspaper before the March First Movement, the Japanese authorities would have forbidden it. After the March First Movement, the so-called enlightened administration, led by Saitō Makoto allowed the publication of Korean owned newspapers in *han'gŭl*. It appeared to be that the Japanese control of the press was related to the publication of Korean newspapers. Nevertheless, there was a hidden reason behind the Japanese policy of relaxation. Even though there was only one newspaper, *Maeil Sinbo,* which was owned, controlled, and published by the Government-

General, there were as many as twenty-nine underground newspapers, and their circulation was wide. The *Chosŏn Tongnip Sinmun,* for instance, printed 10,000 copies in its first issue on March 1, 1919, to publicize the March First Movement.³ Because it was difficult to control such numerous underground newspapers, the authorities decided to allow a few Korean-owned newspapers whose expressions of public opinions it could monitor and thereby control.

Whatever the motivation behind the Japanese policy toward the Korean-owned press, the new policy provided a good opportunity for Korean nationalists to establish newspapers. Although a rumor that the new Governor-General might allow a few Korean-owned newspapers had spread two months before, Saitō announced his new press policy in early October 1919.⁴ A movement to found a nationalistic newspaper had begun in July 1919. Among several nationalists who considered publishing a newspaper, the most prominent candidates were: Yi Sanghyŏp, who was a former editor for *Maeil Sinbo*; and Chang Tŏkchun, who was a former editor-in-chief of the Korean edition of the Japanese-owned *P'yŏngyang Daily Newspaper (Ilmunji)* and older brother of Chang Tŏksu.⁵ Both Yi and Chang sought funding sources for establishing a newspaper, but they could not find anyone who thought that a newspaper would be profitable. They turned to Kim Sŏngsu. Yi first asked Ch'oe Tusŏn, who was the principal of Chungang School, to ascertain Kim Sŏngsu's interest. Ch'oe thought that Kim would not be interested because he was already deeply involved in Kyŏngbang and because he was also planning to establish a junior college under the tentative name of Hanyang Junior College (Hanyang Chŏnmun Hakkyo). When Kim Sŏngsu first heard about Yi Sanghyŏp's plan to publish a newspaper, he was hesitant, claiming that he did not know much about the press. Kim was also worried about whether a nationalist newspaper could live up to its commitment under Japanese control. Economic considerations concerned him as well, since establishing a newspaper along with operating Kyŏngbang might become burdensome.⁶

Ch'oe Tusŏn recalled that it was Yu Kŭn who persuaded Kim Sŏngsu to seriously consider establishing a newspaper. Yu was the former principal of Chungang, a scholar of Chinese, and the founder and chief editor of the *Hwangsŏng Sinmun.* Yu and Kim's other associates realized that, although education was vital for Korean modernization, a newspaper was of paramount importance. Because of their persistent persuasion, Kim finally agreed to found a paper.⁷ Founding a newspaper must be understood as an extension of Kim's educational program for the Korean populace at large, in accordance with the tradition of the Korean press.

With Kim Sŏngsu's backing, the preparations to start up a nationalistic newspaper accelerated. Knowing that the newspaper had to have nationwide support and that, like Kyŏngbang, it would have to be organized as a joint-stock company, Kim Sŏngsu traveled throughout the country to solicit potential shareholders, even before the preparation team had sought permission from the Government-General. At times, his travels served the dual purpose of selling Kyŏngbang shares as well as shares of the newspaper. Kim found out that it was harder to attract people's attention to the paper than to Kyŏngbang, for many believed that the newspaper could not generate any profit.[8]

Despite Kim Sŏngsu's difficulty attracting potential shareholders, on October 9, 1919, only four days after Kyŏngbang's shareholders' meeting, the preparation team applied to the Government-General for permission to start a newspaper. The name of the newly created newspaper was to be, as Yu Kŭn suggested, the *Tonga Ilbo*, meaning *East Asia Daily*. Permission was granted on January 6, 1920.[9] The *Chosŏn Ilbo* (hereafter *Chosŏn*) and *Sidae Ilbo* also obtained permission from the Government-General to publish as daily newspapers.

The first meeting of the *Tonga Ilbo*'s original investors took place on January 14, 1920. On February 1, 1920, the seventy-eight investors from all thirteen provinces, elected Kim Sŏngsu as their representative and sought permission to organize the *Tonga* as a joint-stock company. Permission was granted promptly on February 6, 1920. The authorized capital had been fixed at one million *yen*, divided into 20,000 shares, and the paid-in-capital was 250,000 *yen*. Out of 20,000 shares, 16,500 were held by the original investors, and the remainder were distributed to others.[10]

The process of beginning the *Tonga* resembled that of Kyŏngbang. At the first meeting of the original investors, the key personnel for the *Tonga* were appointed. Pak Yŏnghyo was elected as president for exactly the same reasons that he served as president of Kyŏngbang. Elderly members, such as Yang Kit'ak and Yu Kŭn, who had experience in journalism and had implacable anti-Japanese records, were chosen to be editorial advisers (*p'yŏnjip kamdok*) to ensure an anti-Japanese and nationalistic tone for the newspaper. The remaining key staff were people who had practical experience in the publication of a newspaper. Publication of the first issue was originally set for March 1, 1920, but it actually took place on April 1, 1920, due to financial shortfalls. The economic recession and the drought of 1919 kept many shareholders from making their first payment to the *Tonga*. As was the case with Kyŏngbang, the *Tonga* was only able to print the first issue with the help of a loan secured with Kim Sŏngsu's collateral.[11] Until it built its own building in 1926, the press had to use the former Chungang School building at Hwadong.

In the inaugural issue of the *Tonga (fig.4.1)*, the editors asserted "its belief in human equality and the necessity of recognizing the political rights of all nations in the Far East, a barely veiled reference to the doctrine of self-determination of nations that had incited the idealism of the March First leaders the year before." [12] *Chujirŭl sŏnmyŏng hanora* (the purpose or principle of publishing the paper) that was published in the first issue was known to have been written by Chang Tŏksu, the editor-in-chief. Michael Edson Robinson points out, "Politically, the new press arrogated to itself both the civilizing task of spreading advanced ideas in the colony and the role of spokesman for the nation." [13] The mission of the press was to represent the masses (*minjung*), to advocate the principles of democracy (*minjujuŭi*), and to encourage the spread of culturalism (*munhwajuŭi*). Later, within the first year of publication, the word, "masses" was replaced with "nation" (*minjok*). The decision not to use the word "nation" from the beginning was made to avoid inciting the Japanese, and also because use of the word "masses" (*minjung*) was popular after World War I. [14]

Robinson reports, "The papers attracted many of the best and brightest Korean intellectuals to their editorial boards and reporting staffs. Here was one honorable career within the colony for politically conscious and patriotic Korean youth." [15] Most of all, they were all young in their twenties. In 1919, for instance, when the *Tonga* sought permission from the Government-General, Kim Sŏngsu was only twenty-eight years old; the editor-in-chief, Chang Tŏksu, was twenty-five; the editorial director, Yi Sanghyŏp, was twenty-seven; and a member of the editorial staff and the section chief for politics, Chin Hangmun, was twenty-six. Among the editorial staff, Chang Tŏkchun was twenty-eight; Kim Myŏngsik, twenty-nine; Nam Sangil, twenty-four; Yŏm Sangsŏp, twenty-three; Han Kiak, twenty-three; Yu Kwangyŏl and Yi Sŏgu, both twenty-one; and Kim Hyŏngwŏn, twenty. Only Kim Chŏngjin and Kim Tongsŏng were older, at thirty-two and thirty respectively. [16] Because of this young staff, people called the *Tonga* the "youth newspaper." By the time the first issue was published, there were seventy-four people working for the paper, with twenty-five bureau offices throughout the country.

The Turbulent Beginning
of the *Tonga*

The Japanese' decision to relax permission for establishing newspapers under the so-called enlightened policy opened the floodgate for Korean publications. "In 1920, the Japanese issued 409 permits under the Publication Law (magazines and books); the number of permits tripled to 1,240 by 1925." [17] *Tonga, Chosŏn,* and *Sidae* were born under such a policy.

Relaxation of the permits did not necessarily mean a freedom to print. The Government-General retained a strong control mechanism—censorship. The newly created High Police Office (Kōtō Keisatsu) handled the monitoring and the enforcing of censorship standards. Although the police interpreted the standards liberally in the first years of the cultural policy era, they began to use all sorts of sanction and censorship, such as seizure, suspension, fines, and even jail terms. The most common form of censorship was erasure.[18]

The *Tonga* had been vulnerable to the censorship, because many bright and young Korean intellectuals saw the *Tonga* as a place where they could display their diverse viewpoints. Some of those views offended the Japanese authorities and other views even outraged certain segments of the Korean population. The Government-General's first ban on sales and distribution of the *Tonga* came on April 15, 1920, less than a half-month after publication of the inaugural issue, as the result of reports on an anti-Japanese demonstration in P'yŏngyang. On the anniversary of the March First Movement, demonstrations took place across the country, but the largest was in P'yŏngyang. For the next six months, until the end of September 1920, when the *Tonga* was suspended, there were four times when certain articles were deleted, twelve times when the paper's sales and distribution were banned, two seizures of issues, and one ban against reporting.[19] After analyzing the secret records of the High Police, Chŏng Chinsŏk reports that from 1920 to 1930 the High Police of the Government-General seized 325 editions of the *Tonga*. In those years, according to Chŏng's account, the highest frequencies of seizure took place when Kim Sŏngsu was president of the *Tonga*, especially from October 24, 1924, to October 21, 1927. During those four years, there were 190 seizures.[20]

The *Tonga*'s troubles were not limited to censorship from the Government-General; they came from Korean readers. Because one of the missions of the newspaper was the spreading of advanced ideas—educating the masses—certain editorials offended a conservative segment of the readership. A furious resentment from the conservative readers came a month after the inaugural issue, on May 4, 1920, when the *Tonga* began to publish a six-part editorial series that attacked the vices of the traditional patriarchal Korean family system. The patriarchal family system was Confucian in its origin. Many Confucian readers were offended by the editorial series as an indirect attack on Confucianism.

The conservative Confucian readers were further annoyed by columns written by Kwŏn Tŏkkyu, Chungang School's Korean language teacher, and published in the *Tonga* on May 8 and 9, 1920. Kwŏn directly criticized Korean Confucianists for their *sadae sasang* (a thought pattern serving the great) toward China. In fact, it is a well known fact that, although it is Chinese in origin, Koreans have been outperformers of Confucianism than those of Chinese. Martina Deuchler states such a characteristic in her book, *The Confucian Transformation of Korea*: "The Korean Neo-Confucians came under the spell of this cannonical literature and interpreted it in the most literal sense.... Nowhere in East Asia, therefore, was the re-creation of the institutions of Chinese antiquity more compelling than in Korea."[21] Nonetheless, such editorials and columns outraged Confucianists. The organization of Confucianists (Yurim) denounced the *Tonga*, lobbied the Government-General to suspend the paper, and ultimately boycotted it.

Pak Yŏnghyo, who was then the president of the *Tonga*, did not like such editorials and wanted to publish an official apology, but Pak's plan to publish an apology was rejected at the editorial meeting. On June 1, 1920, Pak tendered his resignation.[22] Pak's values and ideologies were incompatible with those of the editors and reporters on the paper. The boycott threatened to further damage the already financially ailing paper. Finally, by request of the executives of the paper, Kim Sŏngsu became president, on July 1, 1920.

Kim's presidency was not necessarily smooth. The worst of his troubles was the financial state of the paper. Because of the economic recession, the total amount collected from the first installment payments was only 100,000 *yen*, far less than the 250,000 *yen* originally set. In addition, there were 10,000 subscribers, but many either delayed or were delinquent in the monthly payment, which was 60 *chŏn* (0.60 *yen*).[23] Most of all, income from advertisements, the lifeline of newspapers, was almost nil, because there were not many Korean businesses and industries to speak of, and those few were struggling to survive the recession. This was also the time when Kyŏngbang was suffering deep financial losses resulting from Yi Kanghyŏn's *Samp'um* incident. Kim Sŏngsu arranged bank loans using his land deeds as collateral. Despite such hardships, in order to live up to the original purposes for founding the paper, particularly that of spreading culturalism (*munhwajuŭi*), the *Tonga* sponsored Korean students—Kim Chunyŏn, Kim Toyŏn, and sixteen others—to deliver traveling lectures during their summer vacations, until the tours were prohibited by the Japanese authorities who feared their growing audiences and popularity.[24]

The *Tonga*'s first indefinite suspension came on September 25, 1920, by order of Governor-General Saitō, who gave two reasons for his action. One was *Tonga*'s editorial on September 24 and 25, written by Chang Tŏksu, that dealt with the symbols of the Japanese emperor (a mirror, jewel, and sword, representing wisdom, benevolence, and courage) as if they were the same as those objects often used in idol worship. In fact, in accordance with Harumi Befu, "An important characteristic of the Japanese emperor is his semidivine quality.... His semidevine quality was derived from the presumption that he alone was the lineal descendant of the Sun Goddess, the mythological founder of Japan. This genealogical relationship conferred upon the emperor divine legitimacy to rule."[25] The other was the use of an analogy that likened the British colonization of India to that of the Japanese in Korea. The Government-General seized that day's papers and suspended the *Tonga* indefinitely. Saitō anticipated that the *Tonga* would be a moderate newspaper devoted to cultural affairs, and he was afraid of the overtly critical stand the paper was taking against colonial policy.[26] The *Chosŏn* was also suspended, from September 5 to December 24, 1921. The *Tonga*'s suspension was finally lifted on January 10, 1921, after three and a half months.

The suspension of the two nationalist papers was an example of the difference between the so-called Japanese enlightened policy in words and in deed. Yu Chino recalls the analogy of the *Tonga* being referred to as "roadside trees" (*karosu*), which originated when someone asked the director of the political affairs bureau of the Government-General, "It is good to promote the press, but how could you allow an improper person to publish a newspaper?" The director replied, "That's all right. Don't worry about it. Newspapers are like roadside trees. To save the face of 'cultural policy,' it may be necessary to allow one or two papers. However, if those go beyond just decorating the road and cause trouble, then trim some limbs."[27] This story may well illustrate the intention and hidden agenda of the Japanese enlightened policy of the Saitō administration. In fact, Kim Sŏngsu said to the same Japanese official, "If you ban the *Tonga* permanently, there would be no place to show off the enlightened policy (*munhwa chŏngch'i*)."[28]

Even though the suspension was lifted on January 10, 1921, the financial state of the *Tonga* was at its worst, and the paper could not afford to resume publication. Kim Sŏngsu was in the midst of a financial crisis because of Kyŏngbang's troubles. During the suspension, the reporters were unpaid and some company employees left for other jobs. Local bureaus began to dissolve. The director of the business bureau, Yi Un, resigned from his position and left the newspaper because of his inability to pay employees' salaries. Even if the ban on publishing the paper had been lifted earlier, the paper would probably still have faced difficulties. Min Yŏngdal, a bureaucrat of the Chosŏn dynasty, who refused to receive a Japanese peerage after annexation, salvaged the paper by investing 5,000 *yen,* which was actually a donation, although *Tonga Ilbo* policy prohibited it.[29] The paper resumed publishing on February 21, 1921.

While all those difficulties were going on, Kim Sŏngsu's two closest friends, Song Chinu and Hyŏn Sangyun, were released after spending one-and-a-half years in jail for their roles in the March First Movement. Kim Sŏngsu could now share his burdens with these two confidants. Song eventually became president of the *Tonga* in September 1921, and Hyŏn became principal of Chungang School in April 1922.

The *Tonga* as a Joint-Stock Company

The *Tonga* took the form of a joint-stock company by offering shares for public subscription. However, a great majority of the shareholders were original investors whose first installments were not yet paid in full. Even though publication of the paper resumed on February 21, 1921, the financial squeeze never eased. Employees' paychecks were delayed, at times several months. In an effort to turn the chronic financial situation around, Kim Sŏngsu decided to reorganize the company as a joint-stock company.

As he did in 1919 when he established the *Tonga,* Kim Sŏngsu, this time together with Song Chinu, traveled across the country to solicit potential shareholders. Although they fared better than they had in 1919, they did not reach their goal, mainly due to the poor overall economy of Korea. When Kim and Song returned to Seoul from their trip, they called an executive meeting in order to amend the articles of the company. The authorized total capital was reduced from one million to 700,000 *yen,* and paid-in capital to 175,000 *yen.* The first installment would be only 150,000 *yen,* with the remaining 25,000 to be paid by Sin Kubŏm (15,000 *yen*) and Yang Wŏnmo (10,000 *yen*).[30]

Finally, the *Tonga* became a joint-stock company by expanding the shareholders beyond the original investors. Out of a total of 14,000 shares, the original investors held 9,454 and the public, 4,546. The total number of original investors was now 58; only 33 of the first group of 78 original investors remained. The first meeting of the new shareholders took place on September 14, 1921, with the ten elected directors (*ch'wich'eyŏk* in the old system is *isa* [director] in current Korean terms), including Kim Sŏngsu, Song Chinu, and five auditors (*kamsayŏk*). On the next day at Kim Sŏngsu's residence, ten directors elected Song Chinu as the new president, and Kim Sŏngsu remained as one of the ten directors. Chang Tŏksu became vice-president and also editor-in-chief.[31] The great burden of managing the *Tonga* was transferred to Song Chinu, and Kim Sŏngsu was relieved of the daily operations of the paper. As a result, Kim was able to devote his time and effort to other nationalist self-strengthening programs, including a Korean-financed and managed National University (Minnip Taehak) and the Movement for Encouragement of Native Products (Mulsan Changnyŏhoe Undong).

Even though Song Chinu became president of the *Tonga,* he always discussed important matters with Kim. Song made a habit of visiting Kim's residence nearly every day to discuss ways to rejuvenate the newspaper. It sent reporters abroad to report events outside the peninsula and the misery of Koreans in Japan, including the Korean victims of the 1923 earthquake. Beginning in March 1923, the *Tonga* placed permanent foreign correspondents in New York, Tokyo, and Shanghai. The paper sponsored various events, such as a literary contest for creative writing and a women's tennis tournament.[32]

Despite an ambitious program to build the newspaper, the financial state of the paper remained unsound because many of the shareholders had not paid their second installments. On the surface, *Tonga* was a joint-stock company, yet the company's fiscal health depended largely on Kim Sŏngsu's personal finances. Kim Sŏngsu himself commented that keeping the *Tonga* solvent was like pouring water into a bottomless jar.[33] This financial crisis continued until 1924, when the paper picked up new advertisers, especially from Japan. Chŏng Chinsŏk provided useful statistics to show us how helpful the advertisement income from Japan was. The ratio of advertisements from Korea and Japan in 1923 was 63.9 percent from Korea and 36.1 percent from Japan (21.3 percent from Tokyo and 14.8 percent from Osaka). In 1925, 40.3 percent of advertisements were from domestic sources, and 59.7 percent from Japan (39.9 percent from Tokyo, and 19.8 percent from Osaka). Parenthetically, in 1931, for instance, advertisements from Japan overwhelmed those from Korea: 36.2 percent from domestic, and 63.8 percent from Japan (Tokyo 36.2 percent, Osaka 27.6 percent).[34]

The *Tonga* as a Major Vehicle for the Cultural Nationalist Movement

As the *Tonga* barely began to overcome the seemingly everlasting financial crisis, *Tonga*'s mission and Kim Sŏngsu's modernization projects had begun. However, this mission confronted Japanese colonial authorities on the one hand and Koreans who opposed cultural nationalism on the other hand. As Kim Sŏngsu and his cultural nationalists used the *Tonga* as their launching pad, the opposition made the paper a target.

The cultural nationalists advocated a gradual move toward Korean independence through modernization. They advocated self-strengthening by means of raising the level of knowledge and the moral standards of the Korean people;

fostering education; and, achieving economic strength through the development of industry. The self-strengthening program had its intellectual origins in the early nineteenth century, but it was then reinvigorated from time to time, especially in the late nineteenth and early twentieth centuries. The Korean Self-Strengthening Society, for one, was formed in 1906 to carry on social and cultural movements "that sought to establish a foundation for the recovery of Korean sovereignty through promoting the development of native industry and making educational opportunities more widely available to the Korean populace."[35] After it was dissolved by the Residency-General for its opposition to Japan's demand for Kojong's abdication, it soon reappeared in 1906 under the name of the Korea Society.

Kim Sŏngsu made his decision to pursue modern education at Kŭmho Hakkyo in Kunsan after attending a lecture delivered by Han Sŭngi of the Korea Society. A great influence on Kim, Han was instrumental in Kim's having studied in Tokyo. It was Kim Sŏngsu's turn to become an advocate of the cultural nationalism whose basic tenet was similar to that of the Korea Society. He would use the *Tonga* as a vehicle.

The National University
(Minnip Taehak) Movement

The National University (*Kukchagam*) has a long history, going back to its establishment in 992, during the Sŏngjong reign in the period of the Koryŏ dynasty (918–1392). It was established principally for the study of Chinese traditions and classics. The movement to establish a Korean National University (Minnip Taehak), to disseminate modern currents of thought and scholarship among Koreans, had begun in response to the discriminatory policy of the Japanese toward higher education for Koreans. Eckert and his fellow historians relate:

> the National University Movement led by the Society for the Establishment of a National University (Minnip Taehak Kisŏng Chunbihoe), was the natural outcome of the intelligentsia's interest in educational issues. The heavy stress in the colonial schools on Japanese language acquisition, cultural values, and Japanized Korean history had outraged nationalist intellectuals from the beginning. Even more galling was the fact that with few opportunities beyond middle school available in the colony, college-bound Koreans increasingly ended up in

Japan to complete their education. To counter the undesir-
able socializing effect inherent in such a system, nationalists
mounted a drive to establish a truly Korean university.[36]

Korean cultural nationalists, including Kim Sŏngsu, planned a major campaign, to be spearheaded by the *Tonga*. The Society for the Establishment of a National University was officially formed on November 23, 1922, and the first meeting took place March 29 the following year. It was to continue a fund-raising effort begun in 1907 to repay thirteen million *yen* that Korea borrowed from Japan in 1905. Because the government was unable to pay off the debt, some conscientious Korean citizens, knowing that Korea had to be economically independent from Japan in order to be politically independent, launched a fund-raising movement known as the Repay the National Debt Movement (Kukch'ae Posang Undong). The movement started in Taegu and Pusan in January 1907. Yang Kit'ak served as the director (*kansa*), and was supported by two newspapers, *Taehan Maeil Sinmun* and *Hwangsŏng Sinmun*, advocating "no smoking" and "no drinking" in order to save money for the funds.[37]

The fund-raising effort became futile, however, as Japan ultimately annexed Korea. Yun Ch'iho, Yu Wŏnp'yo, Namgung Ŏk, Pak Ŭnsik, No Paekin, and Yang Kit'ak (who was the director of the fund-raising) decided to use the funds to establish a Korean National University. They submitted a proposal for such a university to the office of the Government-General, but Governor-General Terauchi Masatake turned down the proposal. Later, one year after the March First Movement in 1920, the group sought permission again, from Governor-General Saitō Makoto. To create a reason for refusing permission, Saitō countered with a proposal for a National University to be established jointly by Japanese and Koreans. Finally, the Koreans withdrew their proposal.[38]

The other cause for the formation of the Society for the Establishment of a National University was a *Tonga* editorial on February 3, 1922, under the title, "To Advocate the Necessity of a National University."[39] The major reason for the *Tonga*'s insistence on a Korean National University was the passage of a new educational law on January 25, 1922, that called for vocational schools, junior colleges, colleges, and universities to offer education congruent with the educational systems in Japan. Seeing the law as providing a means for the Japanese to further assimilate Koreans, the *Tonga*'s editor advocated creating a Korean National University that would protect Koreans from the Japanese policy of assimilation through public university education.[40] The *Tonga*'s editorial rekindled a National University Movement among cultural nationalists, including Yi Sangjae, Yi Sŭnghun, and Yu Chint'ae.

Carter J. Eckert and his co-authors of *Korea Old and New* state:

> A venerable ex-Chosŏn official, Yi Sang-jae, was chosen as
> leader of the Society for the Establishment of a National Uni-
> versity in November 1922. Song Chin-u, then editor-in-chief
> of the *Tonga Ilbo*,[41] helped to prepare the organizational frame-
> work for a national fund-raising campaign. The goal was to
> raise ten million yen for the university, and the low, one yen
> subscription meant that if every Korean donated the goal
> would be met. . . . Within six months, however, what had be-
> come the largest movement since March First began to falter.[42]

The movement generated a national network of offices that worked closely with
various groups, clubs, and churches. The Society for the Establishment of a
National University (Minnip Taehak Kisŏng Chunbihoe) was formed in November 1922 with 1,170 supporters in presence. Song Chinu and Hyŏn Sangyun
were chosen to join the thirty-member central committee, and Kim Sŏngsu and
Kim Pyŏngno were included as two of the seven members of the committee
for the management of funds,[43] some of which came from collecting activities
in Manchuria and the United States.[44] The projected endowment was set at ten
million *yen,* four million for the first phase, and six million for the subsequent
completion of the university.

The goal to establish a National University was noble. The movement
drew in a large group of moderate nationalists—educators, youth leaders, literary
figures, journalists, ministers, and many others. As Michael Edson Robinson indicates, "Even radical critics of the cultural movement agreed that education
was a key to Korean survival. . . . It [the cultural movement] went on to declare
that although mass education was necessary for overall development, a society was judged, in the end, by the quality of its upper level educational system,
which, in turn, produced national leaders."[45] The Society for the Establishment
of a National University was the largest national effort since the March First
Movement.

The *Tonga,* under the leadership of Song Chinu, publicized the movement and provided it broad and extensive coverage. Editorials appealing directly to Koreans to participate in the movement appeared in the issues of December 16, 1922, and January 14, February 23, March 28, and April 4, 1923. An
editorial on March 29, 1924, expressed regret that the movement was unable to
raise more than half of the projected amount of ten million *yen.*[46]

The movement had become moribund for several reasons. Eckert and
his fellow historians assert that the Society failed due to: "Mismanagement of

donations, infighting between chapters, and vitriolic criticism from more radical nationalists, including the withdrawal of support from the important All Korean Youth League . . ."[47] Leftist critics started to question the efficacy of establishing a university that would serve such a small segment of the population. Insufficient contributions from Koreans were another reason for the failure of this movement. On January 1, 1924, by the end of the first year, barely one million *yen* had been pledged. Therefore, the *Tonga* editorial of March 29 blasted Koreans who did not donate even though they could afford it.[48]

The Japanese helped guide this movement to failure, employing the tactics of "divide and conquer" to cultural nationalists and radical leftists. Ultimately, before the Koreans' self-help drive to establish their own National University, Japanese authorities had announced plans for the building by 1926 of an imperial university in Seoul to be called Keijō Imperial University, which further diminished public interest in a Korean National University.[49] Soon the movement withered away, but *Tonga* stayed with it from the beginning to the end.

The dream of a Korean National University never died in some cultural nationalists. Kim Sŏngsu, for one, made a faithful attempt to build a National University. Kim's drive materialized in 1932, when he took over Posŏng Junior College and eventually expanded it to Koryŏ University, after Korea became independent from Japan after World War II.

The Korean Production Movement and the Role of the *Tonga*

The Korean Production Movement (Chosŏn Mulsan Changnyŏ Undong) was a manifestation of the idea of self-sufficient national economic development. The movement prevailed even before the *Tonga* played an active role in it. The Repay the National Debt Movement during the protectorate was a similar patriotic appeal. Later, during the March First Movement, many Korean merchants and citizens participated spontaneously in a "buy Korean" movement. In the fall of 1919, Ch'oe Chin and several others in Seoul established the Promotion of Korean Production Corporation.[50] In P'yŏngyang, Cho Mansik, often called the "Gandhi of Korea,"[51] Kim Tongwŏn, and fifty other Koreans, mostly Christians, created in July 1920 the Society for the Promotion of Korean Production.

The movement dwindled for a couple of years, however, until the *Tonga* rekindled it in its editorials on November 1, 12, and 13, 1922, and launched a major campaign. Accordingly, in December of the same year, Yŏm T'aejin, who was a student at Yŏnhŭi Junior College, and fifty other Koreans formed the Self Production Association (Chajakhoe) to raise national consciousness by rejecting the use of imported goods in favor of products made by and for Koreans. The organization opened a consumer cooperative in Sŏdaemun to display and sell Korean products. Beginning January 5, for four consecutive days, *Tonga* editorials reiterated the rationale for the Korean Production Movement in an effort to bring it to the attention of Koreans.[52]

On January 9, 1923, a coalition of twenty organizations, including intellectuals, students, businessmen, and journalists, formed an association to prepare for the Korean Production Movement. On January 20 of the same year, the first organizational meeting took place. Cho Mansik, who created the Society for the Promotion of Korean Production in 1920, joined the national organization of the Korean Production Movement. The association adopted several agenda and put them into action: self-production and self-supply, the promotion of Korean products and of frugality in Korean consumption, and no smoking and no drinking. February 16, 1923, the lunar New Year's Day, was designated as the date for the Promotion of Korean Production.[53]

The movement generated tremendous initial enthusiasm, and rallies and parades took place in provincial cities. At its height in the summer of 1923, the movement had become the most successful mass mobilization of Koreans, which was comparable to that of the March First Movement. Also, it somewhat altered Korean consumption habits. The *Tonga* provided its fullest support for the movement, using its editorial pages, columns, and contributions by readers.[54] Although the movement involved the populace, a few businessmen played major roles, including Kim Sŏngsu and Kim Tongwŏn, president of the Kyŏnggi Spinning Company.

Kyŏngbang's policy of hiring only Koreans largely concurred with the principal idea of the movement. More specifically, Kyŏngbang developed a new label, T'aegŭksŏng (Star of the Great Ultimate), with the Korean flag in the center encircled with eight stars that symbolize the eight Korean provinces. The idea of the label originated with Yi Kanghyŏn, and it appeared on clothing in the market beginning in 1924. The label depicted the mood of the Korean Production Movement and symbolized Kyŏngbang's promotion of itself as a nationalist enterprise. Parenthetically, seeing what looked like the Korean flag on the new label, the Japanese police authorities called up Yi Kanghyŏn and requested an explanation. Yi explained to the authorities that the *s* mark, which is similar to that of the Korean flag, is the initial for "spinning" and not a replica of the Korean flag.[55] At any event, the movement continued into the 1930s.

Kyŏngnyun and the Tonga

Throughout the two major national movements, the National University Movement and the Korean Production Movement, some cultural nationalists had experienced two major obstacles. One was, as expected, the persistent Japanese interference; the other was the challenge of Korean leftists. In fact, 1923 was the year when Korean nationalists witnessed the manifest differences between their two factions, the gradual approach of the cultural nationalists versus the radical approach by the leftists for Korean independence. While some cultural nationalists blamed the Japanese authorities for hindering those movements, others, notably Kim Sŏngsu and his close associates, recognized the culpability of Koreans themselves in not having a centralized political organization like the Indian National Congress.

In 1885, during British colonial rule, Indians established the Indian National Congress with British approval. The congress served as a political debating society where Indians could discuss their problems. Members of the organization came from every part of India, and from many religious groups and castes. The congress lost favor with the British when it began striving for self-government. In 1920, Mohandas K. Gandhi became the leader of the Indian National Congress, which had grown to be India's most important political organization. Gandhi persuaded the congress to adopt his program of nonviolent disobedience against the British, which included the nonpayment of taxes and refusal to enter British schools and courts. Many of his followers gave up well-paying jobs that involved cooperating with the British. Via the Indian National Congress, Gandhi expanded India's independent movement from a few educated Indians into a mass movement of millions of Indians.

Wanting to adopt the Indian National Congress as a model and acknowledging the necessity of such a political organ, in late December 1923, several gradual nationalists held an organizational meeting at Kim Sŏngsu's residence. These nationalists included many prominent Koreans from various organizations: Kim Sŏngsu, Song Chinu, and Ch'oe Wŏnsun from the Tonga; Sin Sŏgu and An Chaehong from the Chosŏn; Ch'oe Rin and Yi Chongrin from Ch'ŏndogyo; Yi Sŭnghun from the Christian circle; Pak Sŭngbin, Cho Mansik, Kim Tongwŏn, Sŏ Sangil, et al. With 100,000 yen, including 20,000 yen from Kim Sŏngsu, they named the organization Yŏnjŏnghoe (political study club), and started to organize local chapters. An Ch'angho also introduced the club in Beijing.[56] The major objective of the Yŏnjŏnghoe was to carry on the spirit of the March First Movement, as Gandhi did India's independence movement through the Indian National Congress. As the Indian National Congress had been founded and functioned with British approval, Kim Sŏngsu and his colleagues wanted to establish Yŏnjŏnghoe legitimately, within the limits of colonial rule.

On January 2, 1924, as Yŏnjŏnghoe's organizing effort was gaining a foothold, Yi Kwangsu published a five-part editorial in the *Tonga* entitled *Minjokchŏk Kyŏngnyun* (National Statecraft) as an attempt to clarify and amplify his controversial thesis on national reconstruction.[57] Yi called for a master plan for the future development of the nation and for the creation of a comprehensive organization that could accomplish any objective.[58] The basic tenet of Yi's *Kyŏngnyun* was the same as the one he outlined in his long essay under the title *Minjok Kaejoron* (Treatise on the reconstruction of the nation), published in May 1922 in *Kaebyŏk*.[59] In his essay, Yi described the gradualist and cultural-nationalist vision of political independence. Publication of Yi's *Kyŏngnyun* in the *Tonga* led to a short-lived boycott of the newspaper by the left wing of nationalists. *Kaejoron* and *Kyŏngnyun* both stimulated a fierce reaction in the left wing of the national movement. There was a growing sense of crisis among nationalist intellectuals, and cultural nationalists in particular.

The primary goal of cultural nationalism was not only nation-building, but also the preparation of the groundwork for successful demand for independence. Considering the reality of the Japanese military power and their brutal tactics to suppress the Korean nationalist movement, cultural nationalists decided that it would not be realistic to confront the Japanese directly through social revolution and overt resistance to Japanese imperialism, as younger, more radical nationalists advocated. Yi's *Kyŏngnyun* escalated the leftist attacks against cultural nationalism and thereby threatened the Yŏnjŏnghoe movement.

Kim Sŏngsu and his fellow cultural nationalists might have been overly anxious to adopt the Indian model or too naive to estimate the explosive nature of the issue of accommodation. Robinson points out the differences between the Korean cultural nationalists' independence movement and that of the Indians: "While [the Korean] cultural nationalists searched for ways to operate within the limits of the cultural policy, Gandhi was urging Indian nationalists to ignore British law, constitutional reform, and the lure of appointments in the bureaucracy of the British Raj."[60] In any event, publication of Yi's writing in the *Tonga* placed the newspaper, Kim Sŏngsu, and Song Chinu in an embarrassing position politically. Yi Kwangsu promptly tendered his resignation from the *Tonga*.

Parenthetically, it is ironic that, while Korean radical leftists and their followers charged the organizers of Yŏnjŏnghoe as accommodationists or collaborators, a secret document (*Kōtō Keisatsu Yoshi*) prepared in 1934 by the Japanese High Police Bureau to be used as a textbook for training the High Police Force to oppress Korean independence fighters classified the movement of Yŏnjŏnghoe as a stage that would evolve into a non-compromising national independence movement.[61] To the Japanese authorities, the collaboration charge made by the leftists against the cultural nationalists was a great opportunity to divide Korean nationalists into two factions, and to promote internal struggles and fighting within the Korean nationalists. In the midst of all these, Kim Sŏngsu maintained a low profile. This was a great strategic victory for the radical leftists.

The Pak Ch'un'gŭm Incident and the *Tonga*

The *Tonga* experienced difficulties as it became the target of leftists after Yi's publication. Moreover, Japanese oppression of the newspaper did not slacken. In late January 1924, the director of the bureau of political police, Maruyama Tsurukichi, hired Pak Ch'un'gŭm to threaten the *Tonga*. A native Korean, who never had any formal education and was a hoodlum, Pak extorted money from Korean laborers in Japan. Eventually, the Japanese made Pak a cat-is-paw to oppress and terrorize Korean independence organizations.[62] Pak and his followers came to the *Tonga* armed with knives and clubs, demanding money that had been raised by the paper to assist overseas Koreans.

On March 25, 1924, Maruyama organized the League of Elite Groups (Yujiyŏnmaeng) by mobilizing various pro-Japanese factions to counter the nationalist movement. An editorial in the *Tonga* on March 30, 1924, blasted the league for its potential harm to the nationalist movement. On the same date, Yi P'ungjae paid a social call on Kim Sŏngsu and Song Chinu and invited them to have dinner at Siktowŏn (a restaurant). Yi, using his acquaintanceship with Kim and Song, set the stage for Pak and his fellow mobsters to terrorize Kim and Song for the league. As Kim and Song entered the restaurant, there were several league members present. At dinner, they complained about the *Tonga*'s criticism of the league. Pak and his followers entered and threatened Kim and Song with knives and pistols. Kim's and Song's clothes were torn off by the knives. They demanded a public apology for the *Tonga*'s criticism, and asked for 3,000 *yen* from Kim, to be used in managing the league. Under extreme threat, Song at last wrote a note to the effect that even if it had been his "personal view," he regretted publishing such personal criticism in the newspaper. Kim

Sŏngsu promised to deliver 3,000 *yen*, and the next day, he delivered 3,000 *yen* to Maruyama at the bureau of political police (*kemu kyoku*), instead of handing it over to Pak directly. Maruyama pretended that he was unaware of the incident, but it was everyone's knowledge that he had set it up.[63]

After learning of the incident, Yi Chongrin and forty other Koreans met at the Yuilgwan restaurant and decided to launch a mass demonstration against Japanese policy toward the Korean media. Members of the Korean bar association filed a protest in the offices of the Government-General and the public prosecutor. Pak Ch'un'gŭm was arrested, but, by arrangement with Maruyama, fled to Japan.[64]

Twenty days after the Pak incident, on April 25, 1924, the director of the editorial department, Yi Sanghyŏp, a charter member of *Tonga,* resigned from the paper, demanding Song Chinu's resignation from his presidency, protesting what in the world the president of the *Tonga,* who represents the national press, could be doing apologizing to mobsters.[65] The *Maeil Sinbo* (the official newspaper of the Government-General) stirred up the situation by reporting Song's apology to mobsters without giving a full story. Song resigned promptly, and Kim Sŏngsu also resigned his seat on the board of directors. Worse, when Yi Sanghyŏp left the *Tonga* for the *Chosŏn,* he took several key editorial department members with him. The *Tonga* faced its worst crisis since its founding.

In order to provide leadership for the *Tonga* in this vacuum, Yi Sŭnghun became the new president on May 14, 1924. Yi was thirty years older than Kim Sŏngsu, one of the thirty-three representatives for the Declaration of Independence during the March First Movement, the founder of Osan School in Chŏngju, and one of the most respected Korean nationalists of the time. Yi assumed the presidency as a personal favor to Kim Sŏngsu and led the *Tonga* for four months. On October 21, 1924, Kim Sŏngsu returned to the paper as president. Yi remained as an adviser until his death.[66]

Completion of a

New *Tonga* Building

While *Tonga* was experiencing a crisis internally as well as externally after the Pak Ch'un'gŭm incident, it still moved forward. The most urgent task was to build a new building to replace the old building in Hwadong, which was too small and located in an inconvenient place for transportation and communication. A plan to build a new building was completed in early 1924, and in March 1924, the building site in Kwanghwamun (currently 139 Sejongno) was purchased. The site was located on one of Kwanghwamun's busy streets, and the new *Tonga* building would be within sight of the new Government-General building, which had been under construction since 1916. The Japanese authorities could not avoid seeing the *Tonga* building.[67] Indeed, the physical setting of the two buildings made them look as if they were confrontational in their relationship. Parenthetically, at last in 1996, the former Government-General building, which has remained a symbolic residue of the unpleasant past as a Japanese colony, was dismantled. Nevertheless, the *Tonga* building still stands there.

During his tenure as *Tonga*'s fifth president, Kim Sŏngsu faced two challenges. One was to acquire the necessary funds for the building construction; the other was to overcome Japanese suppression of the paper in the form of an indefinite suspension. *Tonga*'s second indefinite suspension was the result of publishing a message from the headquarters of the International Farmers' Association in Russia to Korean farmers on March 5, 1926. The message, dated March 1, revealed sympathy for Korean farmers in their struggle for independence on the seventh anniversary of the March First Movement.

The indefinite suspension was not the only punishment *Tonga* had to endure. Song Chinu, the editor-in-chief, was indicted for a violation of the Security Law, and Kim Ch'ŏlchung, director of the department of paper distribution, was also indicted, for the violation of laws regulating the newspapers. The suspension, lasting a month-and-a-half, brought financial pressure on the paper, while construction of the new building created an additional financial burden. Kim Sŏngsu received 30,000 *yen* from his younger brother to help the paper, but it was not sufficient. As had happened many times previously, Kim wrote to his adoptive father for an additional 25,000 *yen* and again won his support.[68] Despite these financial difficulties, the new *Tonga* building *(fig.4.2)* was completed in December 1926. In October 1927, Kim Sŏngsu handed over his presidency to Song Chinu and remained as a director *(ch'wich'eyŏk)*. In March 1928, Kim also resigned from his position as a director of Kyŏngbang. He then made plans for a long journey around the world.

Campaign against Illiteracy

and for a

Korean Language Movement

One of the three missions of the *Tonga* was to encourage the spread of culturalism *(munhwajuŭi)*. Thus, the newspaper launched various projects and cultural programs, some halted by the Japanese authorities. Elimination of illiteracy (Munmaeng T'ap'a Undong) was one such project. *Tonga* planned a nationwide campaign to eliminate illiteracy (it was estimated that 90 percent of Koreans were illiterate), to be launched on the newspaper's eighth anniversary. After mobilizing three hundred branch offices of the newspaper, on March 16, 1928, *Tonga* issued posters and solicited a song to promote the elimination of illiteracy, awarding 50 *yen* to the winning songwriter. It would be the first nationwide Korean vernacular (*han'gŭl*) movement. The *Tonga* movement was based on the assumption that the simplicity of *han'gŭl*, with its twenty-four letters, would make it easy to teach to the masses. On March 17, *Tonga* ran an editorial (a portion of which was deleted by Japanese censorship), stressing the urgent need to eliminate illiteracy in Korea, and giving a detailed plan for the campaign. Originally, the Japanese perceived the movement as harmless. As it took on the shape of a nationalistic movement, however, the Japanese authorities forced the cancellation of the project three days before the official campaign was to begin.[69]

Tonga's support of the Korean vernacular movement remained strong, even though its own campaign for eliminating Koreans illiteracy was annulled by the Japanese authorities. The language movement in Korea was considered to be the center of nationalist movement ever since the Independence Club propelled the language issue to the center of the nationalist movement. Indeed, *han'gŭl* was a national identity and core of cultural nationalism. *Tonga* took the movement seriously, and played a major role to promote Unified Orthography (*Match'umbŏp T'ongilan*) in the early 1930s.

Chu Sigyŏng, who scientifically studied the use of vernacular Korean, believed firmly that language was the most fundamental expression of national identity. (I personally learned about Chu and his vernacular movement when I was in Chungang High School because Chu's grandson, Yŏngil, was my intimate friend who sat next to me when we were seniors.)

In 1921, linguists and Korean intellectuals formed the Korean Language Research Society (Chosŏnŏ Yŏn'guhoe), to study, monitor, and support the Korean vernacular movement.[70] Cultural nationalists used the language issue politically. The Japanese authorities kept their eyes on this movement. A report on the language movement was published in *Unified Orthography* in 1933 by twelve scholars, including Kwŏn Tŏkkyu, Kim Yun'gyŏng, Yi Hŭisŭng, Ch'oe Hyŏnbae, and others.

One year before the official report was published in *Unified Orthography*, the officials of the Korean Language Society (Chosŏnŏ Hakhoe), including Kwŏn Tŏkkyu, Kim Yun'gyŏng, Yi Kŭngno, Yi Pyŏnggi, and Yi Hŭisŭng, visited Kim Sŏngsu and asked that the Korean vernacular be used in the *Tonga*, realizing that the success of the movement would depend on wide implementation of the vernacular by Korean publishers and newspapers. Both parties were apprehensive about the receptivity of Korean readership; if readers of the newspaper rejected the vernacular, the expense of changing the type characters would be wasted. On April 1, 1933, the *Tonga* published an editorial in the vernacular before the Korean Language Society published its orthography of the vernacular. *Tonga* also published a supplementary manual to the orthography and distributed it widely. To produce new type fonts in accordance with the changes, the newspaper spent 70,000 *yen,* which was not a small amount.[71] According to Yi Hŭisŭng, who was a member of the task force for the publication of the orthography, Kim Sŏngsu donated funds to the endeavor on various occasions. The exact amounts are unknown. When it was published, the orthography acknowledged Kim Sŏngsu's role, and linguist Ch'oe Hyŏnbae, onetime president of the language society and member of the publication team for the orthography, published a poem of tribute to Kim Sŏngsu for his strong support of the vernacular movement.[72] The language movement was one of the few to draw the support of virtually every Korean.

The Publication of

Monthly Magazines

While Kim Sŏngsu was on his world tour (1929–1931), *Tonga* suffered another suspension, from April 1930 until September 2, 1931, because it published the speech of the editor-in-chief of an American magazine, the *Nation,* in *Tonga*'s tenth anniversary issue. Despite such difficulties, when Kim Sŏngsu returned in November 1931, *Tonga* initiated its monthly magazine, *Sindonga* (*New Tonga; fig.4.3)).* Even before the *Sindonga,* beginning in the early 1920s, Korea experienced a renaissance in the publication of monthly magazines. Hundreds were launched—*Kaebyŏk (Creation), Sinsaenghwal (New Life), Tongmyŏng (Eastern Light), Sinch'ŏnji (New World), Chosŏn Chigwang (Light of Korea)* were just a few. A few magazines, such as *Kaebyŏk,* the brainchild of the Ch'ŏndogyo, lasted a long time, publishing seventy-two issues (1920–1926). Most of the magazines, however, had very short lives.

When the *Tonga* began publishing the *Sindonga* as a sister magazine of the newspaper, some of the leading magazines, such as *Kaebyŏk* and *Chosŏn Chigwang,* had ceased to exist. Publication of the *Sindonga* induced other newspapers to publish their own monthly magazines, such as *Chungang* (1933) by the *Chosŏn Chungang,* and *Sin Chosŏn* (1934) by *Chosŏn.* Similarly, after the

Tonga started to publish a women's magazine, *Singajŏng (New Family; fig.4.4)*, in 1933, the *Chosŏn* followed suit and launched its own women's magazine, *Yŏsŏng (Women)*, in 1936.

Intensified Japanese Control

Tonga's longest suspension began on August 27, 1936, after the 11th Summer Olympics in Berlin, during the rule of Adolf Hitler. During the Olympics, Son Kijŏng, a Korean, won first place, and another Korean, Nam Sŭngyong, won third place, in the marathon. Every Korean was delighted, even shocked. However, the Korean athletes wore the uniforms of their occupiers, marked with the red Japanese flag. To most Koreans, it was an intolerable shame. And, whereas Japanese presses reproduced Son's picture in their newspapers, the ill-equipped Korean national presses, including *Tonga,* lacked the capability to publish the picture of Son's glorious moment. *Tonga* did obtain a picture of Son taken during the awards ceremony by copying it from a Japanese weekly newspaper, *Asahi Sport,* ten days after the event.[73] In the first evening edition of August 25, 1936, the Japanese flag was clearly visible on Son's uniform, but by the second edition, alas, the flag was obliterated.

This expurgation of the Japanese flag was executed by low-echelon reporters. Yi Kiryong, a sports reporter, asked Yi Sangbŏm via intercom whether the Japanese flag on Son's uniform could be erased. Yi Sangbŏm answered, "I understand. I will do what I can."[74] He promptly erased the flag from the picture and handed it to Paek Unsŏn, who in turn produced a copper plate and printed it in the second issue of the paper. The September 1936 issue of the *Sindonga* printed the same picture without the Japanese flag, as did the *Singajŏng,* which printed a close-up photograph of Son's legs alone.[75]

The Japanese retaliated against *Tonga* and its two magazines by confiscating the evening issue of the newspaper along with copies of *Sindonga.* They forced *Singajŏng* to erase some portions of its publication. On August 27, 1936, newly appointed Governor-General Minami Jirō suspended *Tonga* and *Sindonga* indefinitely. *Singajŏng* could not go on when its two major affiliated publications were suspended, because it would not have been reciprocated financially by *Tonga* and *Sindonga* and because it could not afford to distribute its issues outside the network.

There followed a series of arrests. All the reporters who were involved in the incident—Paek Unsŏn, Sŏ Yŏngho, Chang Yongsŏ, Im Pyŏngch'ŏl, Sin Akkyun, Yi Sangbŏm, Yi Kiryong, Hyŏn Chin'gŏn from *Tonga,* and Ch'oe Sŭngman, Song Tŏksu, and Yang Wŏnmo from *Sindonga*—were arrested by the

Kyŏnggido police department. The editor-in-chief of *Tonga*, Kim Chunyŏn, was also taken to the police station for questioning. Kim and the director of the editorial department, Sŏl Ŭisik, tendered their resignations. Those reporters who were arrested and taken into police custody were released forty days later due to the lack of specific criminal laws to prosecute them, because the Japanese criminal code specified punishment for those who disgrace foreign flags, but not the Japanese flag.[76]

The Japanese authorities were never satisfied with the sanctions they imposed on the *Tonga*. They demanded replacement of the entire staff of the *Tonga*, including president Song Chinu. Song was delegated to resolve the situation. Song even asked assistance from some prominent Japanese who served in the Government-General, such as Seikiya Teizaburō and Mizuno Rentarō. They responded to Song's request and lobbied the Japanese government on Song's behalf. At the same time, they advised Song to change the name of the newspaper. Then, the Government-General demanded the replacement of *Tonga* personnel with pro-Japanese staff.[77]

Through a long period of hard negotiation, Paek Kwansu, a close friend of Kim Sŏngsu from boyhood, was recommended for the presidency of *Tonga* and obtained final approval from the Japanese authorities. Others resigned from their positions: Kim Sŏngsu from his post of director (*ch'wich'eyŏk*), Song Chinu the position of president, and Chang Tŏksu from that of vice-president. Song remained as an adviser. As Paek Kwansu became president of *Tonga* effective May 31, 1937, the drawn-out suspension ceased, and, on June 3, *Tonga* was able to publish again. *Sindonga* and *Singajŏng*, though, were not resurrected in Kim Sŏngsu's lifetime. *Sindonga* was revived in 1964 and *Singajŏng* in 1967, under the new title of *Yŏsŏngdonga*.

A Permanent Closure
of the *Tonga*

The plan to force closure of *Tonga* on August 10, 1940 was part of Japan's assimilation policy under the slogan *Naisen ittai*, literally meaning "Japan and Korea are One Entity." This movement aimed to eradicate Korean national identity by eliminating Korean culture and transforming the Korean people into Japanese imperial subjects (*Kōkoku shimminka*). The movement had escalated after Japan launched a full-scale assault on China in 1937 on the occasion of the famous incident at the Marco Polo Bridge outside Beijing. In 1941, Japan attacked the United States.

As the Sino-Japanese War escalated, Japan considered the Korean peninsula an advance military-supply depot and a source of people, both indispensable to the Japanese war machine. To harness the spirits of the Koreans for their imperial goal, the Japanese imposed the *Naisen ittai* policy, which had several purposes: the promotion of Shintōism and the imperial cult; strict enforcement of the use of the Japanese language in public and quasi-public places as well as in homes, including all educational facilities after 1938; and coercing Koreans into adopting Japanese names (*ch'angssi* or identity creation) beginning in 1940. The Japanese authorities pressured Koreans to adopt Japanese customs and habits in daily life as well as clothing, food, and housing; they attempted to eradicate Korean national identity.

The Japanese authorities thought that the major hindrance to their assimilation movement was the Korean national newspapers and other *han'gŭl* publications. Also a Japanese target was the Korean Language Society. In October 1942, the leaders of the Korean Language Society were arrested; some others such as Yi Yunjae died in prison. The *Tonga* was the Japanese's prime target for permanent closure. The *Naisen ittai* movement meant an official ban against the so-called *bunka* policy. Right after the March First Movement, Japanese policies on cultural nationalism were relaxed on the surface at least until 1937. But, after 1937, the activities of cultural nationalism became the target of Japanese control. Control of writing, speech, books, films, and music was thorough, and anything that obstructed or hindered the implementation of *Naisen ittai* was a target for eradication. In February 1938, even the map of the Korean peninsula with the rose of Sharon (Korean national flower) in the background had to be deleted.

Japanese plans to close the Korean vernacular newspapers, particularly *Tonga,* long had been deliberated and were systematically carried out. In December 1939, before the newspaper was forced to close, the Government-General advised the *Tonga* to shut down voluntarily by February 11, 1940. This was the date the Japanese had set to impose on Koreans the adoption of Japanese names (*ch'angssi*). A recently discovered top-secret paper, however, *Onmon Shinbun Touseian: Ōno Rokuichirō Bunshyō (Proposal for controlling Korean vernacular newspapers),* prepared by Vice Governor-General Ōno Rokuichirō in 1939, proposed several alternatives: consolidate all Korean vernacular newspapers into one; relocate the *Tonga* to Taejŏn and the *Chosŏn* to P'yŏngyang to be regional newspapers; or, combine *Tonga* and *Chosŏn.*[78]

None of Ōno Rokuichirō's alternatives was chosen, and the Japanese opted to close the Korean nationalist newspapers, the *Tonga* and *Chosŏn.* On January 15, 1940, the director of the bureau of political police of the Government-General, Mitsubashi Kōichirō, invited Paek Kwansu and Song Chinu from

Tonga and Pang Ŭngmo, president of the *Chosŏn,* to his official residence to persuade them to close the newspapers voluntarily. If they would, the Government-General would pay all the employees' salaries for a year, and would buy all the facilities, including the rotary-press machinery. The newspapermen promptly rejected Mitsubashi's offer. Mitsubashi then paid a visit to Kim Sŏngsu's residence and told Kim that to carry out an all-out war would result in the inevitable closing of *Tonga.* Kim insisted that *Tonga* was not a newspaper for a few individuals but for all Koreans. Kim reminded Mitsubashi that he was no longer an executive of the *Tonga* but simply a stockholder.[79]

Kim Sangman (1910–1994), Kim Sŏngsu's eldest son, went to Japan on January 16, 1940, to deliver Song Chinu's secret letter to influential Japanese leaders to lobby to save the newspaper from forced closure. The effort delayed the closing date, but could not prevent the shut down. The Government-General this time changed its tactics from suggesting voluntary closure to creating a criminal case against *Tonga* by fabricating a charge of illegal bookkeeping.[80] In early June, several Japanese police officials having dinner at the Myŏngwŏlgwan restaurant found printing paper covering the dinner table and inquired about its source. The owner of the restaurant told them that he had purchased it from *Tonga.* Because of shortages resulting from the war, printing paper was rationed. The police charged that the rationed paper had been sold illegally. A clerk in charge of accounting, Kim Chaejung, and the head of the accounting department, Kim Tongsŏp, were arrested. The paper turned out to be waste (*p'aji*) that could not be used for newsprint.[81]

Searching for illegal use of funds, the Japanese police found that sums of cash were deposited in Haedong Bank under Song Chinu's name, and that 20,000 *yen* of the *Tonga*'s funds had been loaned to Posŏng Junior College. Director (*sangmu*) Im Chŏngyŏp and director of business affairs (*yŏngŏp kukchang*) Kuk T'aeil were arrested. Saiga Shichirō of the Kyŏnggi police department, who had a reputation for cruelty, was assigned to handle this matter. (Of interest, Saiga was shot to death in Wŏnnamdong, Seoul, by an unknown Korean rightist after World War II.) As for the 20,000 *yen,* Saiga accused Kim Sŏngsu, who was then the president (*kyojang*) of Posŏng Junior College, but he was unable to make a case against him, even after questioning Kim for twelve hours.[82]

The Japanese had to come up with another case. This time they fabricated a secret organization (*pimilgyŏlsa*) for Korean independence. This fabrication was based on two actual meetings. One was a dinner held by *Tonga* president Paek Kwansu, his executives, and Song Chinu at Paekunjang restaurant in early May 1940. After the dinner, Song Chinu, adviser to the *Tonga,* had a long visit with Kim Sŏngsu in his home in Kedong. The Japanese authorities alleged that these two meetings were of the secret organization, that the funds in Song's account belonged to the organization, and that *Tonga*'s eight hundred branches throughout the country were regional branches of the secret organization. The Japanese authorities accused the organization of planning to launch a campaign to raise funds for the Korean Provisional Government in Shanghai. Song Chinu, who was lobbying for the *Tonga* in Japan, was arrested in Pusan on his way back home, and the director of the business affairs bureau, Kim Sŭngmun, was also arrested, as was Paek Kwansu. The director of the editorial department, Ko Chaeuk, was sick and could not work. Im Chŏngyŏp (*sangmu*), was critically ill while in jail, and was so badly tortured that he nearly died.[83] *Tonga* lost its leadership and direction.

Song Chinu asked Saiga,"What are you really trying to do?" Saiga replied honestly, "We are following orders from our superiors. If you close *Tonga* voluntarily, everything will be resolved."[84] There was no other alternative to save the newspaper. At an informal executive board meeting in the office of the section chief of investigation (*sach'al kwajang sil*) of the Chongno police station, Paek Kwansu refused to submit an application to close the newspaper. The Japanese police elevated Im Chŏngyŏp, who was nearly unconscious from sickness and torture, to the position of publisher and editor-in-chief in order to get the application submitted. On July 26, at the regular board meeting, the directors voted to ratify the decision that had been made in the police station. In early August 1940, Song Chinu, Im Chŏngyŏp, and Kuk T'aeil were released. Chang Tŏksu, then professor at Posŏng Junior College since his return from the United States in 1937, was in charge of *Tonga* because almost all of its executives were in jail. Chang instructed Kim Chuhan to write a statement about the closure of the newspaper to appear in its 6,819th issue, the final issue, on August 10, 1940.[85] *Chosŏn* was also forced to close. Kim Sŭngmun, Kim Tongsŏp, and Kim Chaejung were not released until early September, after *Tonga* had closed permanently.

The Revival of *Tonga* after World War II

As *Tonga* was forced to close permanently, the company changed its name to Tongbonsa (East Asia Company), hoping that someday the newspaper could be revived. Song Chinu was named to head the revised company. Kim Sŏngsu handed over all his shares to Song Chinu, so that Song could have a free hand to run the company. (When *Tonga* was revived, after Korea became free from Japan, Song returned these shares to Kim.)[86] The *Tonga* resumed publication on December 1, 1945, three-and-a-half months after the war ended. The delay was due mainly to the problem of obtaining printing facilities, since most of the existing printing facilities were occupied by left-wing papers. Political strife among many factions of the left and right wings and between the pro-trusteeship and anti-trusteeship groups was furious. In those chaotic political days, Song Chinu became president of *Tonga* while he was involved in politics as the head of a right-wing party. Song's tenure as the president of *Tonga* was short-lived, for he was assassinated by political terrorists on December 30, 1945.[87] Kim Sŏngsu again took over the presidency of *Tonga,* as he had done many times previously, holding the post from January 1, 1946 until February 20, 1947.

After *Tonga* was reborn, following Korea's independence from Japan, the newspaper dedicated itself to building a democratic society, which had been one of its three missions when it was founded in 1920. Although the country was independent from Japan, the newspaper was not always smooth. At times, the Korean government's oppression was not any better than the oppression under Japanese rule, especially during the long years of military rule after the military coup in 1961. During the Korean War, *Tonga* was unable to publish from June 28 to December 4, 1950, and again from January 4 to 10, 1951, because the newspaper was unable to secure facilities in the temporary wartime capital, Pusan, and because its personnel had been dispersed, some killed or captured and taken to the north. But, the *Tonga* survived the difficult times of modern Korean history.[88]

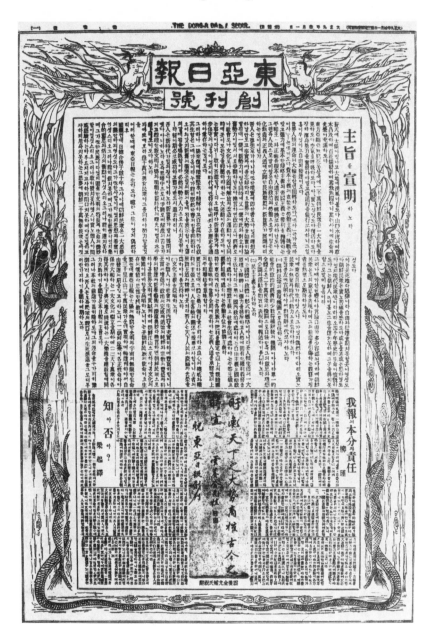

4.1. The first issue of the *Tonga Ilbo*

4.2. The new
Tonga Ilbo building
in Kwanghwamun

4.3. The first issue of
Sindonga

4.4. The first issue of *Singajŏng*

CHAPTER FIVE

The Establishment of Koryŏ (Korea) University for Higher Education

Kim Sŏngsu successfully took over, expanded, and effectively managed a post-elementary school. Notwithstanding, he firmly believed that higher education had to play a major role in Korean modernization, for Korea's future would ultimately be judged by the quality of its upper level educational system and the national leaders it produced. Even critics of Kim agreed that education was key to Korean survival.[1] Kim also faced the reality that in the colony few opportunities were available for college-bound young Koreans, and, increasingly those who could afford it completed their education in Japan. Those who could not afford to pay for their education had no opportunity at all. Kim therefore enthusiastically supported a Korean National University Movement in late 1922 and early 1923. As the movement became moribund, Kim instructed Ch'oe Tusŏn, a teacher at the Chungang School, to develop a plan for establishing a junior college, to be tentatively named Hanyang Junior College (Hanyang Chŏnmun Hakkyo). The plan was halted indefinitely, however, because Kim Sŏngsu was establishing Kyŏngbang and *Tonga Ilbo*.

The establishment of a National University became a reality to Kim when he returned from his prolonged overseas tour. During his travels, Kim was particularly interested in looking at the educational facilities of prominent universities in Europe and the United States. He visited Oxford and Cambridge in England, the Sorbonne in France, Berlin and Heidelberg in Germany, Prague in

Czechoslovakia, and Harvard, Yale, and others in the United States. He not only met and talked with various educators in those universities, but he also took photographs, which were among the major items he brought back with him when he returned.

Taking Over
Posŏng Junior College

Posŏng Junior College, one of the oldest private higher educational institutions in Korea, was founded in 1905 by a statesman, Yi Yongik. Although of humble origins, Yi was appointed to various high government positions. After he assisted Queen Min during the Military Mutiny of 1882 (*imo kullan*), he became a trustee of the royal families assets. He was a strenuous anti-Japanist and a prominent pro-Russian as much as he was a zealous advocate of modern education. He established Posŏng Elementary school, Posŏng Middle school, and Posŏng Junior College. In order to print textbooks for the students, he founded printing facilities, Posŏngsa. Posŏng Junior College taught a two-year program, offering degrees only in law and economics. Because of Yi's personal tie with the royal family, funds to manage the school came from royal family assets. Nevertheless, in 1905, upon the signing of the Protectorate Treaty, Yi took refuge in Russia. Right before his death in Vladivostok in 1907 as an exile, Yi left a note to King Kojong that it was imperative to recover the national independence through educating the talented people by establishing many schools.[2] Nevertheless, in 1907, King Kojong abdicated his throne, and thereafter Posŏng Junior College was unable to sustain itself financially.

Son Pyŏnghŭi of Ch'ŏndogyo took over the management of Posŏng Junior College, but the college soon faced another difficulty: Son and Yun Iksŏn, principal of Posŏng then, were arrested in connection with the March First Movement. The new principal, Ko Wŏnhun, solicited fifty-eight donors and thereby raised sufficient funds to form a foundation, and the school was relocated to the old Ch'ŏndogyo headquarters in Songhyŏndong (*fig. 5.1*). The funds were the minimum needed to qualify as a foundation, and the financial situation of the school never improved. To make matters worse, an internal struggle developed among the big donors of more than 100,000 *yen* each. Looking for someone who could save the school, the board of the foundation delegated member Kim Pyŏngno, a close associate of Kim Sŏngsu, to induce Kim Sŏngsu to take charge of Posŏng.[3]

Not a stranger to Posŏng college, Kim Sŏngsu was one of the contributors who established the school foundation. Although he kept a distance from the actual management of the school, he knew Posŏng's problems, the most chronic and acute of which was financial but which also included a badly structured foundation that was unable to manage the school. Kim's initial response to taking over the school was cautious. Even though he had been unsuccessful in setting up his own Hanyang Junior College, Kim wanted to establish his own college instead of inheriting all the problems surrounding Posŏng.

Kim proposed a compromise: he would take over the school, and his parents would donate land worth 600,000 *yen,* subject to a major structural and organizational change. The changes were to include resignation of all members of the board of trustees and auditors, so that he could replace them with his own team. In addition, Kim wanted to change the regulations governing the school council (*p'yŏngŭiwŏnhoe*), which consisted of the founders of the school and a few alumni representatives, and which had rights to appoint and dismiss board members (*isa*) as well as auditors (*kamsa*). The tenure of some board members was for life. Kim thought that he could not manage the college effectively, if he were to inherit the existing structure and organization.[4]

To Posŏng Junior College, Kim's proposal and conditions meant a total transfer of the school to him. To Kim, it was in essence the same as establishing a new college, without seeking permission from the colonial authorities. If they wanted to salvage the college, the Posŏng board members had no other alternative but to accommodate Kim's proposal. The board requested, however, that Kim guarantee the jobs of current employees, keep the name of college as it is, and construct new school buildings. Kim's original thought was to rename Posŏng to Chungang, in order to match the Chungang School, but he finally concurred with the wish list of the school board. The final deal was made on March 26, 1932. As he planned, Kim named Ch'oe Tusŏn, Kim Yongmu, and himself as the board members (*isa*), and Cho Tongsik and Han Kiak as auditors (*kamsa*). Kim's team took over the college management on June 4, 1932, and, within less than three months, Kim became the principal (*kyojang*) of Posŏng Junior College.[5] Even though the title of the head of Posŏng Junior College was principal, the post was de facto president.

Revival of Posŏng Junior College
under Kim Sŏngsu

Although Kim Sŏngsu founded his various projects when he was in his middle and late twenties, he was forty years old when he took over Posŏng. He admitted to himself that Posŏng might be his last undertaking, and thus he felt a stronger attachment to it than to any of his other projects. For the other projects, he delegated responsibilities to a close friend or an associate, unless it was absolutely necessary for him to be in charge. For Posŏng, Kim remained in charge from the time he took it over in 1932 to 1946, except for a two-year period from May 1935 to May 1937.

In all honesty, Kim Sŏngsu was not an academician who understood the scholarly world or a college professor with an advanced degree. Nevertheless, he had a vision of what an institution of higher education should be. His visits to the world's most prestigious universities in Europe and America had broadened his perspective on colleges and universities beyond those of Japan. In his interview with *Tonga Ilbo* on March 1932, Kim mentioned that an important role for a college should be teaching students, but that it would be equally important for a college to produce a large number of scholars by facilitating research opportunities.[6] He told Yu Kwangyŏl that he was so impressed by the Yale University library that, when he took over Posŏng, his immediate plan was to build a good library like Yale's by acquiring a large site for the college, at least 10,000 *p'yŏng*, near Seoul. Kim envisioned Posŏng as a school for educating people who would rather create jobs for others than work for someone else. Although he knew that many graduates of Posŏng wanted to get jobs upon graduation, Kim realized that, under the Japanese domination, there were not many jobs available for Koreans. He told Yu that Posŏng could fulfill the role of a Korean National University, soliciting the participation of many Koreans as he demonstrated in Posŏng's library construction.[7]

Kim Sŏngsu wanted to make Posŏng an elite educational institution, comparable to Yŏnhŭi Junior College (Yŏnhŭi Chŏnmun Hakkyo, currently Yonsei University), if not to Keijō Imperial University. According to Yu Chino's recollection, when Kim took over, Posŏng was not at all comparable, and was much inferior in its facilities and in its public rating, to Yŏnhŭi.[8] Yu was one of three young scholars Kim recruited, along with Duke-educated O Ch'ŏnsŏk and Japanese-educated Kim Kwangjin.

The poor state of Posŏng's physical facilities, especially the school buildings, was a chronic problem. Even before Kim took over the college, Posŏng had

14,000 *p'yŏng* (about 11.4 acres) of land, but was unable to build on them due to lack of money. In 1933, Kim acquired 62,000 *p'yŏng* (about 50.7 acres) of new land for the school in Koryang county of Kyŏnggi province, then not far from Seoul. By Korean standards, it was a huge school site, considering that Posŏng had a limited enrollment and offered only two degree programs. When Pak Tongjin, the chief architect for Posŏng, asked Kim why he needed such a huge tract of land, Kim replied to Pak that he would not want to be blamed by the next generation for not thinking ahead about future expansion.[9]

Construction of Posŏng's Main Building

In designing school buildings, Kim was heavily influenced by the universities in Europe and the United States. He reviewed slides of many prominent European and American university buildings before working with the architect on plans for the main building. He opted for a long-lasting stone structure in the Gothic style. Kim's residence served as the headquarters for the construction work on the main building of the school, and the chief architect lived with Kim. Considering the expense of Gothic stone buildings, even Song Chinu suggested to Kim that the primary function of the school should be teaching students, not building a fine plant. Nevertheless, Kim insisted on going with granite that could last forever. Despite budget overruns for the construction, the three-story main building was completed in September 1934.[10]

While the construction of the main building in Anamdong *(fig.5.2)* was nearing completion, Kim developed a master plan to expand the campus, including construction of a library, an auditorium, and a gymnasium. He wanted to launch the building project on Posŏng's thirtieth anniversary in 1935. To prepare for the commemorative event, Kim appointed a committee to raise funds nationwide. On November 4, 1933, the commemoration committee for fund-raising (Kinyŏm Saŏp Palgich'onghoe) was formally constituted and elected nine working committee members *(silhaeng wiwŏn)*, including Kim himself. The committee was not limited to raising funds for construction, but also assisted Posŏng in expanding its degree programs to include liberal arts, sciences, medicine, agriculture, and technology. Its plan was to elevate Posŏng from a junior college to a comprehensive university. The funds to be raised were targeted at 300,000 *yen* by the end of 1934. The committee solicited 1,200 prominent potential donors throughout the country, and 464 expressed interest.[11]

Although there are no detailed records of the fund-raising drive, the total funds raised during the campaign were estimated at 170,000 *yen* by the end of 1935, a little over half the goal of 300,000 *yen*. Even if the fund-raising failed to meet its original projection, the campaign revealed that the interest of poor people in higher education was not less but actually greater than the interest of the rich and propertied Koreans. Some well-to-do Koreans donated large sums of money: Kim and his brother donated 20,000 *yen* each; Kim Chongik, 12,000 *yen*; and, Ch'oe Ch'anghak, Ko Kwangp'yo, and Pak Yonghŭi, 10,000 *yen* each. Hundreds of underprivileged and poor Koreans were included among the donors. For example, Kim Sinil, an old woman from Seoul, bequeathed 500 *yen* of her lifetime savings to the Posŏng fund-raising; Cho Tonghŭi, a poor widow from Kimje, and Kim Ilhae from Mujang, north Chŏlla province, donated 1,000 *yen* each; and twelve Korean students in Kobe, Japan, donated 31.50 *yen* from their savings.[12]

The most memorable event of the entire fund-raising was the donation from a widow, An Hamp'yŏng, from Koch'ang of north Chŏlla province. When she visited Kim Sŏngsu, she brought her land deed, which could produce 70 *sŏk* (1 *sŏk* equals 5.1 bushels) of rice annually. That land had been purchased from her lifetime savings earned from running a small tavern (*chumak*) in the remote town of Sach'ŏn, in Hŭngdŏk county, north Chŏlla province. With tears in her eyes, she insisted that Kim take the land to help the expansion of Posŏng. Kim, who was deeply moved by her donation, told her, "In terms of generosity, your 70 *sŏk* will be worth more than my 7,000 *sŏk* of land."[13] On An's death, Kim instructed the office of the Posŏng Foundation to preserve her burial site and to observe annually the traditional rites for a dead person by offering food and paying respect on the date of her death. When the library *(fig. 5.3)* was completed, a section of the library was dedicated to her memory. The An Hamp'yŏng Memorial Room displays information and materials on Korean folklore.

Robinson notes, when Kim Sŏngsu mounted a national endowment drive in 1932 to establish a central library at Posŏng, funds raised for the defunct national university project were funneled to the library campaign.[14] It is an irony that, while the leftists were critical of elite education for the masses, the poor, uneducated, and underprivileged Koreans were zealous in supporting the institution of higher education. However strong support had been, the target proved to be unrealistic. Construction of the library alone would take 220,000 *yen,* and even if they had been able to raise 300,000 *yen,* the sum would not have been sufficient to complete all the projects in the plan. Kim and Posŏng therefore decided to build the library first.[15]

Japanese Interference and
Kim Sŏngsu's Resignation

As Posŏng was shaping up with the construction of its main building at a new site, the recruitment of additional faculty members, and the start of an ambitious new project to build a library, Posŏng faced Japanese interference. The educational bureau of the Government-General chastised Posŏng for not complying with restrictions on school enrollment. The charge was that Posŏng accepted more students than the four hundred maximum allowed. In 1932, the total number of applicants was lower than the number allocated for Posŏng, thus the enrollment ceiling was not an issue. The applicant pool increased in 1933, however, and in both 1933 and 1934, Posŏng accepted a few more students than the maximum allowed, but the bureau tolerated it.

In February 1935, with the expanded facilities at the new campus site, Posŏng sought permission from the bureau to increase its enrollment from 400 to 720, allocating 240 slots for incoming freshmen. The bureau did not notify the school about their decision regarding the request until the entrance examination was over and the school had already notified incoming students of their acceptance. Posŏng assumed that the excess was either approved or tolerated as had been the case in previous years. As it was customary for each school to be permitted to accept two percent over the allowed number for the entering class, Posŏng accepted 264 freshmen. Out of the 264 accepted, 228 registered, and they were scheduled for an entrance ceremony on April 11. On the evening of April 10, however, the bureau of education notified Posŏng that the original request for an enrollment increase had been modified from 400 to 600, not 720. This meant that the freshmen enrollment could be only 200, and that 28 freshmen, who had already registered, had to be denied entrance. Kim ignored the notification. The bureau continuously demanded that the enrollment restriction be enforced. The confrontation escalated to the point that, in May, Kim Sŏngsu resigned from his position as principal, taking full responsibility for defying the bureau's orders. In return, since in effect the bureau had succeeded in forcing Kim out of the post, the bureau made no further issue about the enrollment restriction.[16]

Although Kim resigned as principal, he remained as a member of the board (*isa*), and continued to work on the construction of the library. In commemoration of Posŏng's thirtieth anniversary, construction of the central library began in June 1935. Pak Tongjin worked as the chief architect, modeling the library after that of Duke University. The reading room was designed to contain 250 leather-covered seats, each with a reading lamp. The shelves contained 200,000 books. On the first floor were thirty-two private offices for faculty members for their research. Even at present, the Posŏng library is superior to any other university library building in Korea.

Under the direction of Son Chint'ae, the library solicited donations of rare books. Some Posŏng faculty members donated books that they had kept for generations. Even a Japanese professor at Keijō Imperial University donated sixty books. The reference library stored various works of art, archaeological findings, and materials on folklore, including Kim Sŏngsu's own collections. The reference library's collection of Korean folklore later evolved into a museum.

It appears that Kim Sŏngsu was concerned about the aesthetics of the campus. According to Kim's biography, most of the trees on the campus were transplanted by Kim himself from the nursery near Chungang School. The lawn grass was brought from Chŏngŭp, near Kim's hometown, and flower seeds from Japan and England. An evergreen planted beside the library cost 300 *yen,* which was the equivalent of six months' salary of the average staff member at Posŏng.[17]

A Plan to Offer Degrees in Agriculture and Forestry

Kim Sŏngsu saw that offering degrees in agriculture and forestry, in addition to those in law and commerce, would be urgent for Korean modernization. In the middle of the 1930s, however, there were only two schools of higher education that offered training in agriculture and forestry. As a public school, Suwŏn Higher School for Agriculture and Forestry (Suwŏn Kodŭng Nongnim Hakkyo) accepted sixty-five students; as a private college, Sungsil Junior College (Sungsil Chŏnmun Hakkyo) in P'yŏngyang accepted only thirty students annually. The demand was high, and in the case of Suwŏn Higher School for Agriculture and Forestry, the pool of applicants was five times the available spots in 1934.

In August 1935, Posŏng submitted a proposal to the bureau of education to offer degrees in agriculture and forestry. A three-year degree program would accept 240 students in agriculture and 120 students in forestry, employing seventeen additional faculty and eight adjunct instructors (*ch'okt'ak kangsa*). Posŏng planned to acquire 120 *chŏngbo* (about 290 acres) of land nearby to be used for the new program. All the expenses involved in offering the new degree programs were estimated at 240,000 *yen,* and Kim proposed that they be paid for by selling the crops on land owned by his brother Chaesu and his oldest son, Sang-man. The bureau of education returned the proposal, asking Posŏng to attach further information. Nine months later, the revised proposal was rejected by the bureau on the grounds that the land would not be a stable source of income because the yield of the crop that year had been poor due to bad harvesting. The plan for the new degree programs was halted.[18]

In 1952, in the midst of the Korean War, the degree programs for agriculture and forestry were finally established, and, six years after, Posŏng Junior College became Koryŏ University *(fig. 5.4)*. Paek Nakchun (George Paik), a Yale-educated theologian and educator, who was president of Yonsei University, revealed that Kim had been tenacious in pursuing the goal of offering degrees in agriculture and forestry, even after the proposals had been rejected by the Japanese authorities. Paek recalled, "In Taegu during the Korean War [the government was relocated in Taegu when Seoul was seized by North Koreans], when I was minister of education, I approved the agricultural degree program at Koryŏ University. I became the one who helped Inch'on [Kim Sŏngsu] realize his long-cherished desire to start an agricultural program."[19]

Japanese Mobilization and Its Impact on Posŏng Junior College

After a two-year setback at Posŏng, resulting from the over-enrollment incident, Kim again returned as principal in May 1937. For him, it was rewarding to have the library completed in September of the same year, and to have a plan underway for athletic fields in 1938.

But when Japan started to mobilize Koreans for their war machine, Posŏng was directly affected. The mobilization steadily escalated after July 7, 1937, when Japan launched its full-scale assault on China. Because of the war, Japanese colonial control over Korea entered a different phase, becoming worse than ever before. As president of Posŏng, Kim had to endure humiliation, oppression, and threats at the hands of the Japanese, and his reputation, integrity, and cultural programs for Korean modernization suffered. In the end, Posŏng Junior College became a vocational college. The dream of an elite educational institution ended.

As the war began, Japan carried out a total national mobilization policy and put into effect a variety of extraordinary measures. The measures included the requisition of Korean grain production, various items made of metal, and, most of all, mobilization of Korean manpower. As the fighting grew, in February 1938, the Japanese announced the Special Volunteer Army Act, and some Koreans were mobilized in June of the year in accordance with the act. In 1939, the Japanese proclaimed the National Manpower Mobilization Act, under which Korean laborers and military draftees were involuntarily brought to Japan to compensate for the manpower shortage created by the expansion of the war to Southeast Asia. The mobilized laborers were forced to work in munitions plants and coal mines, and to perform various other forms of physical labor to support the war. Japan also began to recruit volunteer soldiers among Koreans.[20]

As Japan escalated its war effort, the National Mobilization Law in 1942 entrapped increasing numbers of Koreans. Following the Japanese attack on Pearl Harbor, Koreans were subject to the Japanese military draft. The number of Koreans drafted into the Japanese military totaled 364,186 by the end of World War II. These conscripted soldiers were sent to the South Pacific, Southeast Asia, and China. Almost half of them died or were missing in action. The aggregate number of Koreans mobilized throughout the war by the Japanese government in both Korea and Japan reached almost six million.[21]

The Japanese war effort, along with the *Naisen ittai* (Japan and Korea are one entity) policy, brought about many new policies that affected Kim as well as Posŏng. The escalating *Naisen ittai* policy forced cultural nationalists to dismantle their programs to encourage Korean national and cultural identity, and transformed Posŏng into a vocational college. *Tonga Ilbo* was forced to close. The leading figures in the Korean Language Society were arrested in October 1942, and novelists, poets, and other creative writers were forced to produce their works in Japanese. In the end, it was even required that the Japanese language be used exclusively in public and quasi-public places, even in Korean homes.

The mobilization included females ranging from twelve to forty years of age, who served under the designation Women's Volunteer Workers Corps. The mobilized females were forced to engage in harsh manual labor, and a good many of them were sent to the war zone to work in brothels for Japanese soldiers. The Japanese authorities even picked up pregnant women to meet their allocated quotas despite instructions that they draft only single females between the ages of eighteen and twenty-nine.[22]

Naisen Ittai and Its Impact on Posŏng's Curriculum

As a manifestation of the *Naisen ittai* policy, the Japanese authorities required Posŏng to teach "Japan studies" and "military drill" for one hour each week. Every morning, students had to recite the Japanese imperial oath. Instruction was exclusively in Japanese. Beginning in spring 1942, Posŏng was forced to change its term-years from three years to two and to change the first article of the school regulations to specify that the mission of the school was to educate students to become "imperial subjects." At the same time, by changing the educational law to make the Korean school system the same as the Japanese, the common school (*pot'ong hakkyo*) became the small school (*so hakkyo*), and the high common school (*kodŭng pot'ong hakkyo*) was named the middle school (*chung hakkyo*). Posŏng students were recruited for various public-service projects to fill the manpower vacuum created by the wartime mobilization.

Such changes were not limited to Posŏng and other higher educational institution. They were even required for elementary schools. Choong Soon Kim vividly remembers those hard days: "I went to a Japanese-run school for a while. Speaking Japanese was essential for one's survival under Japan's colonial rule. It was the only language Koreans were allowed to speak in public and quasi-public places. Thus I learned Japanese history, culture, and the spirit of their military aggressiveness. As the war neared its end, we school children had to collect various items for war materials every afternoon. These items ranged from hay to brass dishes to chopsticks. I grew weary of school and eventually dropped out of the first grade in the Japanese-run elementary school."[23] Korean school children were forced to indoctrinate in the principles and rites of Japanese Shintōism and the imperial cult. (I still remember how burdensome it was to go to the Shintō shrine every morning during school.)

On February 11, 1940, as part of the *Naisen ittai* campaign, a policy of "identity creation" (*ch'angssi*) was enforced. Under this policy, Koreans were compelled to adopt Japanese-style family and personal names. The Japanese authorities pretended that this policy was voluntary, but in reality it was mandatory. Often police were used to enforce the policy. Those who did not conform to the policy were thought to be anti-imperial subjects and were thereby discriminated against in employment.

As the identity creation movement heightened, the Japanese authorities listed several categories of possible retaliations against those who opposed the policy and for those who retained traditional Korean names: their children would not be able to enter public schools; they could not be employed in the public or private sectors; their documents, if submitted to government agencies, would not be accepted; they would be regarded as anti-imperial or insubordinate Koreans, and thus subjects for investigation and mobilization; they would be excluded from various government rationing programs; and their freight would not be accepted by railroad stations. Many tragic incidents followed. A man from Koksŏng, south Chŏlla province, committed suicide to protest the name-change policy; a person in Koch'ang of north Chŏlla province changed his name to the Japanese style so that his children would be accepted by a school, and committed suicide soon afterward; a writer, Kim Munjip, changed his name to be phonetically the same as "eat dog's waste," and disappeared.[24]

Despite some vehement opposition to the policy, less than four months after the announcement of the policy, 326,105 Korean households (about 87 percent of the total) changed their names.[25] Posŏng students had to change their names in accordance with the new rules, and Yu Chino reveals that, after the name changes, even though he had been a professor for a long time, he became so used to the Japanese names that he could not remember the Korean names.[26] It was doubly difficult for professors to remember the names of their former students, because those who had Japanese-style names changed their names back into Korean after Korea's liberation.

Because of the two-year intensive drive to implement the policy, many Koreans did change their names, but a small minority did not. (I was one of those who adopted a Japanese-style name in order to enroll in a Japanese-run school.) Those who retained their Korean names were considered anti-Japanese, that is, unpatriotic. Kim Sŏngsu and his close associates, including Song Chinu, Hyŏn Sangyun, Chang Tŏksu, Paek Kwansu, and Kim Chunyŏn did not change their names.

The Japanese did not leave Kim Sŏngsu alone, however. They tried to get him to adopt a Japanese-style name. One day in late June 1942, right after the deadline for ch'angssi, the director of the bureau of education (gakumu kyokuchō) called Kim to his office in the Government-General and asked why Kim had not changed his name. Kim used the excuse that his parents were strongly opposed to such a change. The director was not convinced and ordered Kim to reconsider changing his name for his and his children's sake.[27] Yu Chino also reveals that one day after a writers' gathering when the ch'angssi campaign was intensified, Yi Kwangsu asked Yu to have a cup of coffee at a tea room in Sogongdong. Yi, who had already changed his name into Japanese, induced Yu to change his name and asked Yu to persuade Kim Sŏngsu to do the same.[28] There is no evidence as to whether Yi's effort to persuade Kim was on his own initiative or instigated by the Japanese authorities. Most faculty members at Posŏng retained their traditional Korean names. Only five out of thirty faculty members at Posŏng had *ch'angssi,* while all but five faculty members of Yŏnhŭi Junior College had *ch'angssi.*[29] Carter J. Eckert indicated that "the Japanese authorities allowed some 'trustworthy' Koreans to retain their names to preserve the illusion that the name change movement was voluntary (Pak [Hŭngsik][30] had also continued to use his Korean name)."[31] Perhaps some Koreans such as Pak might have been exempted from *ch'angssi.* In Kim's case, his biography indicated that he was in a position not to change his name, not because of rapport with the Japanese authorities but because he did not have to seek employment or depend on government rationing for his livelihood.[32] Nevertheless, without any doubt the Japanese authorities treated Kim cautiously because of his prominent position in Korean society. If this was a privilege, Kim certainly had it.

The Military Draft of Koreans and the Kim Controversy

The major underlying purpose of the *Naisen ittai* policy was to provide justification for using Koreans to supplement Japanese manpower for World War II. The actual recruitment of Koreans began in February 1938 with the acceptance of Korean volunteers, mainly males who were seventeen years old and above. A Korean conscription system was promulgated in May 1942, and, with the initial exception of college and university students, Koreans were drafted beginning in August 1943. As the war intensified, however, the Government-General announced a "special volunteer" system on October 20, 1943, and launched an all-out propaganda campaign to recruit college and university students, calling them "student soldiers" (*haktopyŏng* or *hakpyŏng*). The Japanese authorities at first tried to exclude insubordinate as well as anti-imperial students, but, because so few students were interested in joining, in February 1944, they instituted a full conscription system without exemptions.

Every news medium was used for the campaign, and draft dodgers were arrested and imprisoned. Many prominent Koreans, including businessmen and educators, were mobilized by the Government-General. According to the September 2, 1937, edition of *Tonga Ilbo,* even before the mobilization campaign, Kim Sŏngsu was included in a list of fifty-nine Koreans whom the Japanese authorities wanted to use to promote Governor-General Minami's *Naisen ittai* policy. Kim Sŏngsu would have been valuable to Japan's mobilization campaign. Eckert reports that Kim Sŏngsu participated in a *hakpyŏng* symposium that was sponsored by the *Maeil Sinbo* at Seoul's Citizens Hall (Fuminkan).[33] However, he wonders about the role of Kim Sŏngsu: "There is some question as to the degree of enthusiasm with which the Kims, and especially Kim Sŏngsu, took part in the implementation of the *Naisen Ittai* policy, including the *hakpyŏng* campaign."[34]

There is no doubt that there was intensive coercion imposed upon many prominent Koreans from the Japanese authorities to take active roles for *hakpyŏng* campaign. Even Kim Yŏnsu, a leading businessman, might not have been able to continue his business if he had refused the Japanese request for various donations for the Japanese mobilization effort. The action was reminiscent of the coercion of Korean businessmen to donate to political funds during the postwar military rule. The Korean government controlled Korean business and industry with industrial licensing, price control, rationing, and the allocation of foreign borrowing under government guarantees.

When Japanese efforts to mobilize prominent Koreans for their conscription campaign were at their height, Kim Sŏngsu, on the pretext of illness, secluded himself at his farm in Chŏn'gok, some twenty-five miles north of Seoul. His intention was to avoid participating in the mobilization lecture circuit. According to Kim's biography, on one occasion in 1943, when his pretended sickness failed to convince the Japanese authorities, Kim was forced to participate in a *hakpyŏng* lecture in Ch'unch'ŏn.[35] The biography states that when he was called upon to speak at the Ch'unch'ŏn lecture, Kim simply said, "Because this man does not know how to deliver a speech in front of the public, please listen to the speech of the next speaker, and assume that the contents of his speech will be the same as that of mine."[36] Then he deferred to the next speaker, who was his close friend and associate, Chang Tŏksu. It was a prearranged agreement with Chang, and Kim was able to avoid making a speech.

The most controversial issue concerning Kim's participation in Japan's mobilization campaign focuses on Kim's newspaper article published in the *Maeil Sinbo* (November 6, 1943), urging students to join the war as a part of the *hakpyŏng* campaign.[37] Kim's biography acknowledges the *hakpyŏng* article, and concludes that a reporter fabricated the article after Kim refused to contribute an article himself. Some historians have been questioning whether Kim actually wrote, endorsed, or the newspapers simply attached Kim's name to the article that appeared in the *Maeil Sinbo*.[38]

In fact, Kim's biography and other publications were unable to identify the reporter or explain the circumstances that led up to the fabricated article, but Yu Chino shed light on the incident. Yu worked closely with Kim after Kim took over Posŏng Junior College, and also, as one of its contributors, he was in a position to know about the newspaper campaign.

Yu's version goes something like this.[39] When *hakpyŏng* was a fact and many students were mobilized and sent to the war zones, the Government-General ordered some prominent Koreans to write encouraging articles in the *Maeil Sinbo*. Kim Pyŏnggyu, who was then a reporter for the *Maeil Sinbo,* brought such an order to Yu. Yu knew Kim even when Kim was in high school in Japan, and Kim wrote to Yu occasionally. Kim dropped out of Tokyo Imperial University, where he was majoring in French, when his fellow students in law and liberal arts were drafted as "student soldiers." Upon his return to Seoul, Kim became a reporter for the *Maeil Sinbo.* Yu recalls that the bureau of political police (*keimu kyoku*) of the Government-General prepared the list of potential writers of encouraging articles. The list included Kim Sŏngsu, Song Chinu, Yŏ Unhyŏng, An Chaehong, Yi Kwangsu, Chang Tŏksu, Yu Chino, and one or two additional persons. When Yu told Kim Pyŏnggyu that Kim Sŏngsu was unlikely to write an article, Kim Pyŏnggyu said he would write it for him. Kim Sŏngsu agreed but told Kim Pyŏnggyu that he wanted to see the copy. Yu called Kim Sŏngsu to check and Kim confirmed the story and asked Yu to make sure that Pyŏnggyu's writing was not "shameful." Yu examined the article written by Kim Pyŏnggyu and concluded that, in his judgment, it was not shameful. Yu handed the article to Kim Pyŏnggyu along with his own writing.

Whether Kim Pyŏnggyu ever showed the article directly to Kim Sŏngsu and received his approval is not known. Kim Sŏngsu's biography indicates that Kim Sŏngsu was indignant that the article published in the *Maeil Sinbo* did not accurately reflect the talk he had had with the reporter, but there was nothing he could do about it because the *Maeil Sinbo* was the organ of the Government-General.[40] Most likely, Kim Sŏngsu never saw Kim Pyŏnggyu's article, leaving it to Yu Chino to judge whether it was "shameful" or not. It is also unknown whether the article that Kim Pyŏnggyu wrote for Kim Sŏngsu was changed after Yu reviewed it. Yu explains: "the reason I am revealing the identity of the author of the article published under Kim Sŏngsu's name is that, because of this article, Inch'on [Kim Sŏngsu] was unduly criticized and falsely accused after liberation."[41]

Yu Chino adds that, after the liberation, Kim Pyŏnggyu turned to the left-wing movement. An English version of a pamphlet entitled "The Traitors and the Patriots," prepared by Kim Pyŏnggyu and others in September 1945, included some positive speeches of Yŏ Unhyŏng, who was in charge of an interim administration after World War II and formed a short-lived Korean People's Republic.[42] The pamphlet was initially prepared in response to comments made by Major General Archibald V. Arnold, who replaced Abe as Governor-

General, accusing the leaders of the Korean People's Republic (Chosŏn Inmin Konghwaguk) of being "childish, 'venal' men, 'so foolish as to think they can take to themselves and exercise any of the legitimate functions of the Government of Korea.'"[43] Widely circulated, this pamphlet, according to Yu, was an effort to praise the left wing and discredit the right-wing political movement. Yu firmly believes that, if the left wing intended to reprint all the writings (either pro-Japanese or sympathetic to the Japanese authorities) that were published during the colonial era, the publications would have to include the writings of leftists, like Yŏ Unhyŏng, for fairness. Yu gives the impression that it was propaganda by the left wing.[44]

Regarding the article in the *Maeil Sinbo*, some former Posŏng Junior College students who were "student soldiers" (particularly Yi Ch'ŏlsŭng), do not believe that whatever was written in the newspaper was what Kim Sŏngsu really believed. During my interview with Yi Ch'ŏlsŭng, who represented Posŏng Junior College as one of the instigators of an anti-*hakpyŏng* campaign, he confirmed what Yu had indicated.[45] Yi said that Kim Sŏngsu told him privately: "Why should I be involved in the *hakpyŏng* mobilization? I am devoted to educating young Koreans, not to arranging for their mobilization." Kim added: "The reason why they [the Japanese] are so aggressively mobilizing Korean students is that they have all but lost the war. They want to use mobilization to eliminate educated Koreans. You know what I mean?" Yi interpreted that comment to mean that he should avoid the draft if he could.[46] Some Posŏng professors suggested to students that they dodge the draft. An Hosang, a Posŏng professor, for instance, whispered to Yi during Yi's visit to him while he was hospitalized, "Japanese defeat is certain. Dodge the draft!"[47]

Yi's article in the *Tonga Ilbo* revealed that Kim Sŏngsu instructed him to organize an underground anti-*hakpyŏng* movement.[48] Eckert was skeptical of Yi's credibility.[49] (My lengthy interview with Yi does not allow me to reach any definite conclusion regarding the truthfulness of his article.) Kim thought the war would be over soon and everything would be forgotten, including his article in the *Maeil Sinbo*.

Posŏng's Change to Kyŏngsŏng Ch'ŏksik Kyŏngje Chŏnmun Hakkyo

Whatever the commotion about *hakpyŏng,* on January 20, 1944, Posŏng Junior College students were sent to the war. The Allied war was succeeding on all fronts. In March 1944, the Japanese authorities closed the law and liberal arts programs at all junior colleges. They converted Posŏng Junior College to Seoul Colonial Junior College for Vocation and Economics, beginning with the academic year in spring 1944.

Posŏng Junior College accepted the change without much resistance. The school officials thought that the Japanese could do anything. If the Japanese authorities could change the names of Koreans and mobilize students for the war, it would be a small matter to change the name of a school. The same thing happened to Yŏnhŭi Junior College, whose name was changed to Seoul Junior College for Industries and Management. Because the school was under the auspices of American missionaries, its assets were seized, and a Japanese was appointed president.

Evolution from a Junior College to Koryŏ University

On liberation, the name of Posŏng Junior College was restored. The official restoration of the original name took place on September 25, 1945, and the school resumed the programs that had been closed by the Japanese authorities during the mobilization. Nevertheless, the school did not open until October 5, even though the liberation took place on August 15, 1945 during summer vacation, for many students, who were mobilized during the war as *hakpyŏng* and other conscripted workers, had not yet returned to school.

The Posŏng board elected Kim Sŏngsu executive director of the board (*chumu isa*), and rearranged its curriculum to offer degrees in law, political science, economics, and commerce. Of greatest interest, however, Posŏng Junior College was preparing to become a comprehensive university. Kim Sŏngsu still wanted to dedicate his life to establishing a university, but the sudden liberation created political chaos in the country. The tardy (they arrived a full month later than the Soviet Union did in the north), ill-prepared, and inept United States Occupation Forces worsened the political commotion in South Korea. Hegemonic struggles between left-wing and right-wing forces and fierce fighting between the pro- and anti-trusteeship movements among Korean nationalists led students to fight against each other along factional and ideological lines. On the right, students organized the National League of Students for Anti-Trusteeship (Chŏn'guk Pant'ak Haksaeng Yŏnmaeng or Haknyŏn) and elected Yi Ch'ŏlsŭng, a Posŏng student, as chairman (wiwŏnjang). The left-wing students organized the National League of Students for Unified Actions (Haksaeng Haengdong T'ongil Yŏnmaeng or Hakt'ong). The fighting between the two leagues was bloody and furious. Kim Sŏngsu took a strong anti-communist stand, and because Kim Sŏngsu and Yi Ch'ŏlsŭng came from Posŏng. Posŏng Junior College was a major center for Haknyŏn.

In the midst of the chaos created by the political factions, especially the sharp disagreements between pro- and anti-trusteeship, Song Chinu, who was chief (susŏk ch'ongmu) of the right wing of the Korean Democratic Party (Han'guk Minjudang), was assassinated. Kim Sŏngsu assumed the responsibilities of Song's position and led the party. As a result, Kim resigned from the presidency of Posŏng Junior College on February 19, 1946, before it was elevated to a university. Kim's longtime friend and associate, Hyŏn Sangyun, succeeded Kim in the presidency, but Kim still remained as the executive director of the board, and directed the board to prepare for a comprehensive university proposal.

The ministry of education of the U.S. military government in Korea approved the request for Posŏng to become a comprehensive university on August 15, 1946, the first anniversary of Korea's independence. The name of the school changed to Koryŏ University. Originally, the name Koguryŏ—after the Koguryŏ dynasty (37 B.C.–668 A.D.), which had once extended its territory to Manchuria, was considered; but three syllables would be too hard to pronounce, so it was abbreviated to Koryŏ. (Certainly, it was not named after the middle kingdom of the Koryŏ dynasty, 918–1392 A.D.) Hyŏn Sangyun became the first president of Koryŏ University.

It is indisputable that Koryŏ University, one of the oldest and most prominent of the modern Korean higher educational institutions, was a major player in Korean modernization. Over 150,000 (by the late 1990s) graduates of Koryŏ University were then, as they are now, everywhere in Korean society, playing major roles in leading the nation. Koryŏ University contributed to stopping the autocratic rule of Syngman Rhee during the early 1960s. When the autocratic rule of the Rhee government was at its height, on April 18, 1960, students at Koryŏ University held a demonstration; they were attacked by a gang of thugs mobilized by the government. Triggered by this incident, on the following day, some 300,000 university and high school students marched toward the presidential mansion and were fired upon point blank by police. By the end of the day, about 130 students had been killed and 1,000 wounded. Therefore, it was the demonstration by the Koryŏ University students that sparked the massive student demonstrations that eventually brought about Syngman Rhee's resignation on April 26, 1960, and the end of the first republic. The demonstration is known as the "April 19 Student Revolution."

Despite some revisionist critics among Koryŏ University students in recent years, a great majority of Koryŏ University graduates acknowledge Kim Sŏngsu's contribution to the university and to the nation. As Paek Namŏk recognizes, some graduates of Koryŏ University have taken Kim Sŏngsu as their role model. Kim Sŏnggon, founder of the Ssangyong Group (one of the top-ranking Korean business conglomerates or *chaebŏl*), is an example.[50] A 1937 graduate of Posŏng Junior College who majored in commerce, Kim Sŏnggon established Kŭmsŏng Pangjik (textile), Ssangyong Cement, *Tongyang T'ongsin* (news) and *Yŏnhap Sinmun* (*Yŏnhap Newspaper*). Like Kim Sŏngsu, Kim Sŏnggon established schools, namely Kungmin University and Hyŏnp'ung junior and senior high schools.[51] Kim Sŏnggon was involved in politics in his later years, as was Kim Sŏngsu. Perhaps there will be many more who resemble Kim Sŏngsu.

5.1. Former Posŏng Junior College buildings in Songhyŏndong

5.2. The Posŏng Junior College main building in Anamdong

5.3. The Posŏng Junior College library, modeled on Duke University's

5.4. Campus scene at Koryŏ (Korea) University

CHAPTER SIX

Kim Sŏngsu and His Involvement in Politics

Kim Sŏngsu's biography tended to downplay Kim's interest in politics.[1] We know that his primary interest was in education, and seeing the development of Koryŏ University. When the Korean Democratic Party (Han'guk Minjudang or Hanmindang or KDP) was founded in September 1945, Kim's name was not listed as a member of the party, although he supported the party morally and ideologically. Obviously, no one truly knows whether Kim possessed a deep desire to enter politics or whether he was content to be a man behind the scenes. Judging by his character, however, his avoidance of politics was natural. He left politics up to his alter ego, Song Chinu. In fact, Song even discouraged Kim's involvement in politics because of the uncertainty of the political milieu of the time.

Regardless of his personal feeling about politics, when Song was assassinated, Kim was forced to lead the KDP. As a major leader of the opposition party, Kim became a stout critic of Syngman Rhee when Rhee gradually drifted toward authoritarian rule. Kim was elected vice president under Syngman Rhee. Nevertheless, as Yu Chino asserts, Kim was not as successful in politics as he was in educational endeavors.[2]

Political Chaos
After the Liberation

After the atomic bomb on Hiroshima on August 6, 1945, most Koreans realized the Japanese were defeated. At 4:00A.M. in the early morning of August 10, a middle-echelon Japanese (whose full name is unknown) from the bureau of political police, visited Song Chinu to propose an interim administration to preserve law and order as the Japanese left Korea. Song refused, but he demanded freedom of the press, the release of all political and economic prisoners, and distribution of food to starving Koreans. Song also called for the halt of Japanese surveillance of his residence.[3] The day after the visit of an official from the bureau of political police, a Korean attorney, Kang Pyŏngsun, reassured Song that the Japanese surrender would come within the next few days.[4]

On August 11, four Japanese high officials invited Song to an unidentified Japanese home in Ponjŏng (currently Ch'ungmuro) to induce him to head up an interim administration to preserve the peace.[5] Song refused again, but the Japanese importuned him until the eve of liberation day, saying that he was too ill to accept such responsibilities.[6] Bruce Cumings reports, quoting the accounts of Song's supporters, Song "refused the Japanese offers because (1) he realized that any Korean administration would have to await the sanction of incoming Allied forces; and (2) he believed the Korean Provisional Government (KPG) in Chungking was the legitimate government of Korea. They also say Song did not want to give the Japanese the benefit of cooperation in their time of need."[7]

At the final meeting with the governor of Kyŏnggi province at his office on August 14, Song again refused the Japanese request. Right after the meeting, Song visited Kim Sŏngsu at his residence in Kedong, and explained the meeting and his refusal of the request. Then Song advised Kim to go to Chŏn'gok farm, warning that the next couple of days would be the height of the crisis (*kobi*); he convinced him that it would be safer for him to go to Yŏnch'ŏn (the county where Kim's Chŏn'gok farm was located).[8] Song implied that the Japanese authorities might assassinate some Korean leaders before surrendering to the Allied forces, for there was a rumor that the Japanese police and military police had created a list of Koreans to be assassinated. Song told Kim that thus far it appeared that their major concern was to protect the lives of the Japanese in Korea, but they were so spiteful that no one could know what they would do.[9] Song appeared to be protective of Kim; however, he himself wanted to be active in postwar politics. Kim took Song's advice, and promptly went to his farm in Chŏn'gok, where he celebrated the liberation.

The Japanese were becoming desperate in their need to create an interim administration to be run by an influential Korean. They turned to Yŏ Unhyŏng. According to Bruce Cumings, Yŏ's views were known to be a mixture of socialism, Christianity, and Wilsonian democracy. He always was willing to work with communists, and he embraced Marxism as a "good idea." [10] Cumings further states that ". . . Yŏ had been approached because his 'somewhat radical views' made him popular with students. . . . They hoped that Yŏ's cooperation might help rein in student demonstrations." [11] Eventually, when Yŏ met with Endō Ryūsaku, the Governor-General's secretary for political affairs, in the early morning hours on August 15—the day of the Japanese surrender—he accepted the Japanese offer. Yŏ demanded:

(1) Release all political and economic prisoners immediately throughout the nation; (2) Guarantee food provisions for the next three months; (3) Absolutely no interference with the maintenance of peace or with Korean activities for the sake of independence; (4) Absolutely no interference with the training of students and youths; (5) Absolutely no interference with the training of workers and peasants. [12]

The Japanese authorities had no choice but to accept Yŏ's conditions.

Yŏ did not waste any time. As soon as his meeting with Endō was over, he gathered his people at his home and started organizing activities to create an organizational body for a political movement, above and beyond the interim peacekeeping administration. To form such a broad organization was relatively easy for Yŏ because he already had an underground political organization, the Korean Independence League (Chosŏn Kŏn'guk Tongmaeng or Kŏnmaeng), founded on August 10, 1944. Yŏ and his followers decided to form the Committee for the Preparation of Korean Independence (Chosŏn Kŏn'guk Chunbi Wiwŏnhoe or CPKI). Yŏ approached Song Chinu and Kim Pyŏngno to join him. Yŏ was unsuccessful in gaining their help, but he was successful in inducing An Chaehong, an anti-Japanese activist and the chief civilian administrator of the South Korean Interim Government (SKIG) in 1947, to join the CPKI. When he returned to Seoul on August 17 from his farmhouse in Chŏn'gok, Kim Sŏngsu witnessed the actions of the CPKI. Students were heavily guarding Yŏ Unhyŏng's residence. [13]

Yŏ's CPKI was not smooth sailing, however. It developed an estranged relationship with the Japanese authorities. The Japanese authorities thought that

Yŏ's CPKI went above the original mission, which was limited to peacekeeping. Around August 18, the Japanese demanded to reduce CPKI's functions to the original mission. Furthermore, on August 20, an American B-29 dropped leaflets signed by General Albert Wedemeyer announcing that the U.S. military would arrive soon, and that until then the Japanese authorities should maintain law and order as they did before the end of the war.[14] The Japanese forthwith ordered the dismantling of all law and order political organizations. The leaflets clearly announced that the troops entering Seoul were to be Americans, not Soviets. (The division of Korea along the 38th Parallel was officially announced on September 2, 1945.) Major General Archibald V. Arnold replaced Abe Nobuyuki as Governor-General. Two days later, Endō Ryūsaku and all Japanese bureau chiefs were removed from office. The administration was changed from the Government-General to the Military Government. English became the official language of the occupation. Having lost its vital mission, Yŏ's CPKI gradually shifted toward the organization of communists.

In the meantime, right wingers were encouraged that Seoul and the south would be ruled by American, not Soviet forces, as publicized by communists and leftists. On August 28, Kim Pyŏngno, Paek Kwansu, Cho Pyŏngok, Yi In, Kim Yongmu, Wŏn Sehun, Ham Sanghun, and Pak Ch'anhŭi formed the Korean Nationalist Party (Chosŏn Minjoktang). Other conservatives, including Paek Namhun, Kim Toyŏn, and Chang Tŏksu, wanted to form their own Korean Nationalist Party (Han'guk Kungmindang). On September 4, Kim Sŏngsu, Song Chinu, Sŏ Sangil, Kim Chunyŏn, Sŏl Ŭisik, Chang T'aeksang, Kim Tongwŏn, An Tongwŏn formed a preparatory committee for welcoming the return of the Korean Provisional Government and the Allied Forces (Taehanminguk Imsijŏngbu mit Yŏnhapkun Hwanyŏng Chunbi Wiwŏnhoe). Nevertheless, with the uncertainty of the returning date of the Korean Provisional Government, and with increasing pressure to establish a communist government, they changed to the Preparatory Committee for a National Congress (Kungmin Taehoe Chunbihoe), and scheduled an inaugural meeting at the *Tonga Ilbo* building on September 7. Some 330 members were scheduled to participate, and Song Chinu was delegated to head the committee (*wiwŏnjang*). The birth of the National Congress would provide an opportunity for the conservative right, including Chosŏn Minjoktang and Han'guk Kungmindang, to form a single party.[15]

On September 6, one day prior to the meeting of the Preparatory Committee for a National Congress, Yŏ Unhyŏng and several hundred CPKI activists gathered at Kyŏnggi Girls High School. They declared the formation of the Korean People's Republic (Chosŏn Inmin Konghwaguk or KPR). "The main reason for this hasty action was," according to Bruce Cumings, "the impending arrival of American occupational forces."[16] Yŏ Unhyŏng himself acknowledged in his speech at the assembly of September 6 that the imminent American arrival in South Korea created the exigency of proclaiming the KPR.[17] On September 8, the KPR published a list of its officers and cabinet members and their departments: Syngman Rhee as chairman; Yŏ Unhyŏng, vice chairman; Hŏ Hŏn, prime minister; Kim Sŏngsu, education; Kim Ku, interior; Kim Pyŏngno, justice; Kim Kyusik, foreign affairs; Ha P'ilwŏn, economics; Cho Mansik, finance; Sin Ikhŭi, communication; Kim Wŏnbong, military; Ch'oe Yongdal, security; Yi Kwansul, public relations; Kang Kidŏk, agriculture and forestry; and Yi Wisang, labor. The list indicated two objectives: both left and right wing were included; cabinet members were chosen according to their various specialties. At the same time, out of fifteen cabinet posts, the names of seven key members, including Syngman Rhee, Kim Ku, Kim Kyusik, Kim Wŏnbong, Cho Mansik, Kim Pyŏngno, and Kim Sŏngsu, were listed without their knowledge. Cabinet posts went not only to leftists like Yŏ and Hŏ Hŏn, but also to rightists, such as Kim Sŏngsu and Syngman Rhee.

About the KPA, Carter J. Eckert and his colleagues conclude:

> Scholars disagree about the political character and legitimacy of the KPR. Standard South Korean and American scholarship has tended to view the KPR as a communist front whose popularity was directly proportional to the degree it was able to camouflage its real intentions. . . . Revisionist studies of the period . . . have suggested that the KPR represented a genuine attempt at a leftist coalition government and that it had a strong popular backing.[18]

The communists must have been confident enough to allow the rightists a place in the new government for the sake of national unity. In any event, Kim Sŏngsu's name appeared on the KPR list for the first time, even if it was without his approval.

The Korean Democratic Party (KDP) and the Role of Kim Sŏngsu

An organizational meeting of the united front of the rightists and conservatives to form the KDP was scheduled for September 16 at the Ch'ŏndogyo building in Kyŏngundong. The meeting of the National Congress Committee on September 7 at the *Tonga Ilbo* building was the prelude of the KDP. Most of the attenders at the National Congress Committee meeting were the ones who were preparing for the KDP. It was a party that united four factions (*p'a*): Kiho (Paek Kwansu, Kim Pyŏngno, Hong Sŏngha), Haewoe (Chang Tŏksu, Kim Toyŏn, Hŏ Chŏng, Cho Pyŏngok, Yun Posŏn, Yi Yŏngjun, Yun Ch'iyŏng), Pukp'ung and Hwayohoe (Wŏn Sehun, Kim Yaksu, and Pak Ch'anhŭi), and Hwanghae (Paek Namhun and Ham Sanghun) *p'a*.[19] These factions shared the same values and ideology. All were anti-communist, conservative, and politically right wing.

At the first convention of the KDP, they wanted to elect Song Chinu as party chairman (*tangsu*). Song refused to accept the title, mainly because he wanted to yield to the overseas independence fighters, either Syngman Rhee or Kim Ku. Instead, Song took the post of the executive director of general affairs (*susŏk ch'ongmu*).[20] Regardless of the title, Song was de facto chairman of the party. Although almost all the rightist forces were united under the KDP, some critics indicate that "unlike the KPR (Korean People's Republic), the KDP never tried to reach across Korea's political divisions and include Koreans on the Left."[21] Although Kim Sŏngsu shared the basic philosophy of the KDP and saw the necessity of the formation of the party of rightists against the growing communists, he never held any position in the party until Song was assassinated.

Kim Sŏngsu's Role in the United States Army Military Government in Korea

The dramatic conclusion to the war left Koreans unprepared for their own self-governing body. The Commanding General of the United States Armed Forces in Korea (USAFIK), John Reed Hodge, was also ill-prepared to rule over fifteen million Koreans. Nor had the General any experience in dealing with Asians and their culture. The General appeared to be ignorant about Korea, according to a report on September 4, 1945, because "General Hodge instructed his own officers that Korea 'was an enemy of the United States' and therefore 'subject to the provisions and the terms of the surrender.'"[22] A lack of knowledge about Korea and Hodge's ambiguous policy created further confusion regarding the role of America.[23]

Hodge and his Military Government needed the advice of some influential Korean leaders. On the recommendation of Im Yŏngsin (Louis Yim), who was a KDP supporter and also had close ties with Hodge's Military Government, Kim Sŏngsu became a member of the advisory council for education in the bureau of education in the Military Government, along with Yu Ŏkkyŏm, Hyŏn Sangyun, Paek Nakchun, Ch'oe Hyŏnbae, Cho Tongsik, and Kim Hwaran (Helen Kim).[24]

Paek Nakchun, who had developed his ties with the Military Government from the beginning and who was also a member of the advisory council with Kim Sŏngsu, relates:

> The American military forces wandered from their mission and lacked a clear policy and goal. After they decided to install a Military Government, they contacted some Koreans with whom they could communicate freely [in English without interpreters], developed rapport, and eventually became closer. I was one of those who could talk freely. Some of us with an interest in education talked about the reconstruction of Korean education with the American authorities. Several Koreans who were concerned about Korean education said to the American authorities that, if we are concerned about the future of Korean education, we must invite Kim Sŏngsu and his close associates to form an advisory council for education. With the approval of the American authorities, I visited Kim Sŏngsu, who was then with Hyŏn Sangyun. I asked both of them to serve on such a council.[25]

According to Paek's account, Kim was uncertain about the policies of the Military Government. Kim asked Paek, "In a time like this, as the American forces are occupying Korea, how can [you] ask me to serve [in such a council]?" Paek explained to Kim, "I have made contact with Americans, and am still in close contact with them. [According to my experiences] I do not believe that they are interested in occupying the [Korean] territory, making Korean nationals [their] slaves, or extorting things from Korea. They are willing to cooperate with us."[26] Kim and Hyŏn were convinced by Paek's view of Americans, and finally accepted the Americans' offer via Paek. Paek Nakchun also reports that, when Korea took over Keijō Imperial University (currently Seoul National University), some had recommended Kim Sŏngsu to be president of the university. Kim refused the offer. Instead, he insisted on expanding his Posŏng Junior College.[27]

Because of the ties through the advisory council on education, Kim Sŏngsu was selected on October 5 to be a member of an eleven-member advisory council to Military Governor Archibald V. Arnold. The list of the council members included Kim Sŏngsu, Chŏn Yongsun, Kim Tongwŏn, Yi Yongsŏl, O Yŏngsu, Song Chinu, Kim Yongmu, Kang Pyŏngsun, Yun Kiik, Yŏ Unhyŏng, and Cho Mansik. They elected Kim Sŏngsu as chairman of the council.[28] Yŏ Unhyŏng, the only one representative chosen from the left, never participated in the council, except on one occasion, October 5; it was his first and last attendance. Nevertheless, according to Cumings, Yŏ "promptly quit and walked out, asking Hodge if a nine to one advantage was his idea of working together."[29] Yŏ's action displeased the occupation command, and ultimately led to an official condemnation of the KPR on October 10.

The official condemnation of the KPR enhanced the position of the KDP. The occupation command viewed the KDP as supportive of the American plan. Thus, the KDP began to receive full support from the American Military Government. Subsequently, an official welcoming ceremony for the American forces by the KDP was held at the square of Chungangch'ŏng, formerly the building that housed the Japanese Government-General.[30] This was a manifestation of the "American-KDP camaraderie," in Bruce Cumings's words.[31]

Trusteeship, Song's Assassination, and Kim Sŏngsu's Involvement in Politics

Because of the rapport developed between the Military Government and the KDP, the Military Government supported the KDP's request for the return of Syngman Rhee and the KPG leaders. Subsequently, Rhee returned on October 16, and Kim Ku and twenty other KPG leaders returned on November 23. Their return, however, created further complications in the already existing factional strife in Korean politics.

Although the KDP was instrumental in the return of the KPG leaders, the KPG leaders were critical of the KDP, and Syngman Rhee and his dogmatism. Rhee was openly saying, "Follow me. If we unite together around me, we will accomplish our objectives."[32] The KDP created a supporting association for the KPG returnees (Hwan'guk Chisa Huwŏnhoe), and delivered 9 million *wŏn* for their living expenses. When the KDP leaders delivered the money, some KPG leaders, including Sin Ikhŭi, even refused to accept the money, saying "there would be some dirty money in the funds," and charged the association with collaborating: "How could you survive in Korea without being pro-Japanese?"[33]

An estranged relationships between the KDP and the KPG quickly developed: (1) If the KPG leaders were to exercise political hegemony, they had to put down the KDP leaders; but KPG leaders were inferior to those of the KDP in personal qualifications and talents; (2) the KDP supported Syngman Rhee instead of the KPG leaders.[34] For Hodge and his advisors, Kim Ku and his followers were less trustworthy than Syngman Rhee.

While this was going on, at a conference in Moscow in December 1945, the foreign ministers of the United States, Great Britain, and the Soviet Union adopted a trusteeship plan as a means of solving the Korean problem. The underlying assumption of the trusteeship was that Koreans were not yet prepared to govern themselves at the end of the war. This plan would place Korea under a four-power (the United States, Britain, China, and the Soviet Union) trusteeship for a period of up to five years. The trusteeship announcement reached Korea on December 27, via foreign news sources, and triggered public outrage and violent opposition from Koreans. Resistance against the trusteeship issue was instantaneous and practically unanimous. Almost all Koreans simply could not accept the idea of trusteeship after all the years of fighting and longing for independence. Some stores and businesses in Seoul were closed in protest, and demonstrations were continuous during the last months of 1945. Although at first the communists joined in the anti-trusteeship movement, "Then on January 2, 1946, the Communist groups in Korea, doubtless on Russian instruction, suddenly changed their attitude and came out in favor of trusteeship. Well-rehearsed demonstrations in favor of trusteeship were held in north Korea and leftist groups in the south dutifully fell into line, while the nationalists stubbornly maintain[ed] their opposition."[35]

Song Chinu, along with Kim Chunyŏn, attended the Extraordinary People's Assembly (Pisang Kungmin Hoeŭi) at Kim Ku's residence to discuss the strategies for anti-trusteeship. The meeting took place on the night of December 29. Originally, every Korean vehemently opposed the trusteeship, until January 3, 1946, when the Soviet Union demanded that the communists and leftists change their position. There were, however, differences in choosing methods to launch an anti-trusteeship movement. Kim Ku and his KPG leaders insisted on not only using radical and violent means, if necessary, but also clashing head-on with the Military Government. They urged Koreans to denounce the Military Government, to declare national independence, and to seize power.

On December 28, Song attended a meeting at Kyŏnggyojang (Kim Ku's residence). At the meeting, Song agreed with the KPG leaders on opposing the trusteeship in principle, but insisted on using a legitimate means of expressing national sentiment against the trusteeship. Song urged the avoidance of direct confrontation with the Military Government. If such a confrontation occurred, Song believed, only the communists would reap advantages. The fundamental argument between Song and the KPG continued until 4 o'clock in the early morning of December 29. At the meeting, they agreed to form a Committee for Total National Mobilization Against Trusteeship (Sint'ak T'ongch'i Pandae Kungmin Ch'ongdongwŏn Wiwŏnhoe), selected forty-one central committee members, and scheduled a massive rally to be held at Seoul Stadium on December 30 and a nationwide rally on December 31. Kim Sŏngsu was one of twenty-one standing members of the central committee. Song's position was basically that of the cultural nationalists during the Japanese colonial period—gradual, legitimate, and non-confrontational.[36]

According to Song's biography, because of disagreement about the means of launching the anti-trusteeship movement, the KPR and the communists accused Song of influencing the Military Government to condemn the KPR, claiming that he supported American tutelage. They did everything to strain the relationship between Song and the leaders of the KPG.[37] Some historians painted Song and his KDP leaders as pro-trusteeship.[38] Whatever the charges and allegations against Song, the communists and leftists were the ones who shifted their positions on the trusteeship.

At 6:15 A.M. on December 30, Song, then fifty-six years old, was assassinated at his home.[39] Song's assassination inevitably led to a call for Kim Sŏngsu to undertake the leadership role for the KDP. Until that time, Kim had remained politically behind the scenes, supporting Song and the KDP indirectly. Kim's rocky journey toward Korean politics started bizarrely.

Kim Sŏngsu and the KDP

The KDP desperately needed a leader to fill the vacuum created by the assassination of Song Chinu. On January 7, 1946, the central standing committee (Chungang Chip'aeng Wiwŏnhoe) of the KDP elected Kim Sŏngsu as the executive director of general affairs. Chang Tŏksu informed Kim about the selection, but Kim refused to accept the responsibilities. Sŏ Sangil and Paek Kwansu tried to persuade him, but Kim refused again. Finally, on the third attempt, Kim Pyŏngno told Kim Sŏngsu that the party would be dismantled if he refused to accept the directorship.

According to Kim's biography, after calling a family meeting, Kim Sŏngsu reluctantly accepted the responsibility. Kim's younger brother, Yŏnsu, committed himself to donate funds for the party as needed.[40] Other sources indicate that Kim Yŏnsu promised to donate 200,000 *wŏn* per month.[41] On January 1, 1946, Kim Sŏngsu had assumed the position of president of *Tonga Ilbo,* to take Song's place, although the board did not approve his presidency until February. As he undertook the responsibilities of the KDP, on February 19 Kim Sŏngsu resigned from the presidency of Posŏng Junior College. This would be his last direct involvement in an educational institution.

When Kim Sŏngsu was involved in party politics, the anti-trusteeship movement became the anti-communist movement, because the communists shifted their position from anti-trusteeship to pro-trusteeship on January 3, 1946. As the leader of the KDP, Kim made it clear that the KDP unabashedly opposed the trusteeship. And, Kim sent an anti-trusteeship message to Secretary of War Robert F. Patterson. At the same time, he made it clear that he and the KDP supported the KPG leaders, and persisted in an effort for cooperation between Syngman Rhee and Kim Ku.[42]

In the midst of such political commotion, meetings of the U.S.-Soviet Joint Commission to implement the Moscow Agreement were held in January and March 1946. Despite the opposition of the U.S. delegates, the Soviets intended to exclude the democratic nationalists from the interim government in order to organize it with communists alone. Consequently, the talks broke off in May 1946. The deadlock of the Joint Commission brought further disarray to the Korean political situation.

In the meantime, Syngman Rhee organized a National Headquarters for Unification (Minjok T'ongil Ch'ong Ponbu) to establish an autonomous Korean government. Kim Ku and others from the Korean Independent Party (Han'guk Tongniptang or Handoktang) also formed a National Assembly (Kungmin Hoeŭi) to succeed the Extraordinary People's Assembly in launching an anti-trusteeship movement and in bringing about national unification between the leftists and rightists. On March 27, 1946, Kim Sŏngsu arranged a meeting with Kim Ku and Cho Wan'gu from Handoktang, An Chaehong from Kungmindang, and Kim Yŏsik from Sinhanminjoktang for a possible coalition. In order to persuade Kim Ku and his Korean Independent Party to form a coalition, Kim Sŏngsu proposed a new party with Syngman Rhee and Kim Ku as the leaders. Kim Sŏngsu had in mind the creation of the largest party, with Syngman Rhee as president, Kim Ku as vice pr0esident, and Kim Kyusik as prime minister. The proposal initiated by Kim Sŏngsu, Paek Namhun, and Chang Tŏksu, however, was rejected on April 9 by the central standing committee of Kim Sŏngsu's own KDP.[43]

Concurrently, there was another moderate rightist movement led by Kim Kyusik. With the support of the Military Government, Kim Kyusik worked with the moderate leftist Yŏ Unhyŏng to bring about unity between leftists and rightists. On the basis of Kim Kyusik's moderate group, the Military

Government announced the formation of the South Korean Interim Legislative Assembly (Namchosŏn Kwado Ipŏp Ŭiwŏn) in 1947. The assembly would comprise ninety members, forty-five of them to be appointed by the government and forty-five elected by the public. Syngman Rhee, Kim Ku, and the communists boycotted the election in October 1946.

Kim Sŏngsu ran for election in Seoul at large, and won, along with his KDP leaders, including Chang Tŏksu and Kim Toyŏn. This was the first time Kim had run, and he was elected by the people. Nevertheless, Kim Kyusik declared that, in Kangwŏn province and Seoul, election was manipulated by the National Society for the Rapid Realization of Korean Independence (Taehan Tongnip Ch'oksŏng Kungminhoe or NSRRKI), organized by Syngman Rhee. Hodge decided to nullify the results from Kangwŏn province and from the Seoul election as well. Even without the Kangwŏn and Seoul figures, the results of the election showed that thirty-one out of forty-one of the people elected supported Syngman Rhee. In contrast, of the forty-five appointed members (except one each from the KDP and the NSRRKI), forty-three were moderates or from the KPG. In the Kangwŏn province and Seoul reelections, Kim Sŏngsu did not run. The assembly elected Kim Kyusik as chairman.[44]

In the meantime, the left-wing political parties formed the Democratic National Front (Minjujuŭi Minjokchŏnsŏn) and carried on a unified pro-trusteeship campaign. The left wing hoped that giving positive support to the work of the Joint Commission might create the trusteeship concept. Nevertheless, Lee Ki-baik delineates the fate of the left-wing forces that "when the police found evidence of large-scale currency counterfeiting at a press used by the Korean Communist Party (May 1946), the U.S. authorities put out an order for the arrest of its leaders, whereupon the Communists went underground."[45]

As the U.S.-Soviet Joint Commission reconvened in May 1947, the United States proposed referring the Korean issue for further discussion to a conference of the foreign ministers of the four powers. When the Soviet Union rejected the proposal, the United States submitted the question of Korea's independence to the United Nations. The key U.S.-U.N. decision was that general elections be held in Korea under United Nations supervision. To do this, a U.N. Temporary Commission on Korea was created to oversee and facilitate the carrying out of this endeavor. But, the U.N. Temporary Commission was unable to enter North Korea because of Soviet opposition. On the basis of the Commission's report, in February 1948, the Interim Committee of the U.N. General Assembly authorized elections to be held in those areas of Korea open to the supervision of the Commission, which meant to only the southern half of the country.

The United Nations decision for a general election nullified the trusteeship issue. Syngman Rhee, of course, welcomed the U.N. decision because it concurred with his position, which he had presented in a speech in Chŏngŭp on June 3, 1946.[46] Kim Ku seemed to be supportive of the U.N. plan in his announcement on December 1, 1947: he regretted that the election could not be held in the north because of the Soviet Union's interference; his position was to leave room for North Korea to participate in the election when such an obstacle (created by the Soviet Union) was removed; and, his position was basically no different from that of Syngman Rhee.[47]

At this juncture, it appeared that a coalition among the nationalists, especially between Syngman Rhee and Kim Ku, could be accomplished. The mood of a united movement was shattered, however, after the assassination of Chang Tŏksu, on December 2, 1947. Chang was then preparing the KDP strategies for the forthcoming general election. It was the second time that Kim Sŏngsu would lose a longtime friend and trusted associate. Chang was a trusted confidant who carried out many difficult tasks for various of Kim's projects, ranging from the Chungang School and Posŏng Junior College to *Tonga Ilbo*.[48] Chang's assassination became a political issue. During the trial of Chang's assassin, the Military Government even called Kim Ku as a witness.[49]

An effort to unite the positions of Korean leaders on the issue of elections and unification failed. Syngman Rhee and Kim Sŏngsu insisted that elections be held in the South exclusively, if the Soviet Union refused entry into the North. Kim Ku and Kim Kyusik urged further dialogue between the North and South.[50] Despite a boycott of the election by those who favored direct talks between political leaders of the North and South, the first general election in the history of Korea, if only in the South, was carried out on May 10, 1948. One hundred seats were allocated to the northern provinces, and two hundred representatives were chosen by the South Korean voters.

Kim Sŏngsu did not run for a seat in the newly created National Assembly, although the party officials insisted that the chairman of the party should have a seat in the assembly. Kim's biography explains that his primary reason for not running was so that Yi Yunyŏng, vice chairman of the Korean Democratic Party (Chosŏn Minjudang, not the same as KDP), could be elected from Kim's congressional district of Chongno Kapku. The Chosŏn Minjudang was founded by Cho Mansik, who was under house arrest from January 1, 1946 until he was imprisoned on July 9, 1947 in North Korea for his anti-trusteeship agitation. Kim Sŏngsu allocated his district for Yi out of his respect for Cho and Cho's Chosŏn Minjudang.[51]

During the election, communist disturbances were not minor: 846 people were killed, and 1,040 communist terrorist acts and assaults were reported. Despite those disturbances, out of 8,300,000 eligible voters, 7,840,000 (96.4 percent) registered to vote, and 7,400,000 (95.5 percent) voted.[52]

Kim Sŏngsu as a
Leader of the Opposition Party

The general election resulted in the following distribution of the assembly seats: fifty-five members from Rhee's NSRRKI; twenty-nine from the KDP; twelve from Yi Ch'ŏngch'ŏn's Great National Youth Corps (Taedong Ch'ŏngnyŏndan); six from Yi Pŏmsŏk's Korean National Youth Corps (Chosŏn Minjok Ch'ŏngnyŏndan); thirteen from several small social and political parties; and eighty-five from independents (*musosok*). For the KDP, it appeared to be a disappointing performance, however, counting those KDP members who ran with other affiliations, the KDP actually had eighty-four members in the assembly. According to pro-KDP sources, if the KDP were to count others who were not KDP members but who held the same ideology, the number of members would come to over a hundred.[53] Others estimated that the KDP was able to influence about eighty assembly members.[54] Kim Sŏngsu realized that the KDP was not popular, mainly because of criticism from the leftist forces and mistakes made by the Military Government. Nevertheless, many elected assembly members were tilting toward the KDP, expecting that the cabinet would be selected from leaders of the KDP.[55]

Syngman Rhee's
Betrayal of the KDP

The post-election political mood seemed to indicate that Syngman Rhee would be the first president of the newly created republic, while Kim Sŏngsu would assume the role of prime minister. Rhee had been able to carry out his political objectives, with strong support from the KDP leadership. Kim Sŏngsu even provided "one million *wŏn* ($67,000) from his own pocket" to assist Rhee.[56] In reality, Rhee used the KDP as a means to achieve his political goals, and, as Yu Chino indicates, Rhee politically manipulated Kim Sŏngsu and Sin Ikhŭi.[57]

Rhee's first shrewd political maneuver was adopting the first Korean Constitution. The principal architect of the first constitution, Yu Chino, witnessed Rhee's political manipulation. Yu was asked by the Military Government (in January 1948) and by Kim Sŏngsu (in March) to draft the constitution.[58] According to Yu's account, his original draft of the constitution included a parliamentary system, which was approved by the major political factions, including Kim Sŏngsu, Sin Ikhǔi, and even Syngman Rhee. The Committee of the Constitution and the Organization of the Government of the National Assembly were prepared to approve the constitutional draft without major changes. It was scheduled for a vote on June 21. On June 15, 1948, however, Syngman Rhee suddenly appeared before the committee and urged a change from the parliamentary system to a presidential system, and on June 20 Rhee invited the committee members to his residence and lobbied them to change. Instead of forwarding the draft of the constitution to the General Assembly for vote, Rhee threatened not to accept the presidency if the constitution called for a parliamentary system. Rhee said he would remain a civilian and launch a movement to change the constitution.[59] This was a drastic shift of Rhee's position, because at his press conference of June 7, he had indicated that he would adhere to the vote of the National Assembly.[60]

Rhee sought Kim Sŏngsu's help. Rhee warned Kim that if the KDP would insist on a parliamentary system, the KDP had to find another person to be president.[61] Kim's explanations of the benefits of a parliamentary system never satisfied Rhee. Kim then called up his party leaders and the committee members, to persuade them to go along with Rhee's wishes, and, at that time, summoned Yu Chino to his residence. Yu recalled that several KDP leaders had drafts of the constitution in their hands. Yu still opposed the presidential system. Kim asked Yu whether there would be any logical inconsistencies and conflicts among the remaining articles if the constitution were changed from a parliamentary to a presidential system. Yu responded: "What's the point of worrying about some minor logical incongruities and conflicts when the major change is a fundamental shift of the power structure?"[62] Yu then left the scene. Yu believed that Kim Chunyŏn put the final touch on the change of power structure in the first constitution.[63] Some critics say that the KDP leadership must take responsibility for the autocratic government structure that allowed a single man to wield the power of the government in accordance with his will.[64] The revised version of the constitution passed the General Assembly on July 12 and was formally promulgated on July 17, 1948. In accordance with the constitution's provisions, the National Assembly held a presidential election July 20. As everyone had assumed, Rhee was the winner.

Syngman Rhee's most surprising political move was his choice for prime minister. Under the provisions of the presidential system of the Korean constitution, the president appoints the cabinet ministers, including the prime minister, and seeks approval of the assembly. Considering the influence of the KDP in the assembly, the role of the KDP in Rhee's victory, and cooperation of the KDP in adopting Rhee's wish for a presidential system, almost everyone assumed that the KDP's leader, Kim Sŏngsu, would be appointed as the prime minister. Yu Chino believed that Sin Ikhŭi, who at first advocated a parliamentary system and later bowed to Rhee's presidential system, was also a contender for the prime ministership.[65]

Against all expectations, Rhee surprised everyone, including Hodge. At a banquet given by the U.N. Commission on Korea on July 24, after a toast to Syngman Rhee's election as president, the U.N. Commissioner, K. P. S. Menon, offered a toast to Kim Sŏngsu as the future prime minister of the new republic. At that moment, Syngman Rhee told the audience that he had to delegate Kim Sŏngsu for a position that would be more important than that of the prime minister."[66] It was surprising news to the attenders, and no one understood what Rhee meant by a "position that is more important than the prime minister," since vice president Yi Siyŏng had already been elected by the National Assembly.

To explain and justify his declaration at the banquet, on July 27 Syngman Rhee appeared before the National Assembly and announced Yi Yunyŏng as this nominee for prime minister. This move was a symbolic gesture advocating national unification with North Korea, because Yi was vice chairman of Chosŏn Minjudang (chairman, Cho Mansik, remained in North Korea then), which had its roots in the North. Rhee was committed to avoiding anyone who was strongly identified with a particular political party or organization, because, if that person became prime minister, then the interests of a particular party would be in conflict with the best interests of the people. The National Assembly, however, did not approve Rhee's nomination of Yi Yunyŏng, believing that he was not prime minister material.

Rhee then nominated Yi Pŏmsŏk, who was an extreme rightist, a leader of the Restoration Army (Kwangbokkun), and onetime officer in the Chinese Kuomintang "Blue Shirts." His second choice once again surprised everyone. This time Rhee and the nominee actively sought KDP support. Yi himself visited Kim Sŏngsu, and asked for KDP's support. At this point, Kim told Yi that if he would allocate six out of twelve cabinet posts to KDP members, then he might be able to persuade the KDP leaders. Yi acknowledged that Kim's request was reasonable considering the role of the KDP in the whole process of establishing an independent nation, and promised to do his best. Subsequently, with the backing of the KDP, Yi's nomination was confirmed by the National Assembly, but KDP members were excluded from cabinet appointments, excepting Kim Sŏngsu, who was named minister of finance.

The KDP leaders viewed Rhee's appointment of Kim Sŏngsu as an insult. Kim himself expressed disappointment, and, also, it was so surprising that he did not know what Rhee was talking about for a while.[67] Rhee made persistent efforts to bring Kim Sŏngsu in as a cabinet member, but Kim Sŏngsu turned down

Rhee's offer. Regarding Kim's refusal to serve as minister of finance, some who know Kim well and admire him, such as Yun T'aekchung, believe that Rhee's intention was not an insult. According to Yun, under a presidential system, the prime minister does not have any specific role other than pleasing the president and coordinating the cabinet members. The American-educated Rhee, according to Yun, held that treasury secretary was the most important cabinet post. Yun insists that if Kim had been truly interested in politics, and if the KDP intended to be a ruling party, Kim Sŏngsu should have taken Rhee's offer.[68]

To most Koreans the title of prime minister connotes the same as prime minister under a parliamentary system. Even at the present time, many Koreans consider the prime minister as "below one person (king or president), but above everyone else." Under a presidential system, the role of prime minister is ambiguous, limited, and often debatable.

In any event, Kim Sŏngsu and his KDP leaders were more concerned about Kim's face, dignity, and honor. By refusing Rhee's offer, when the Republic of Korea was proclaimed on August 15, 1948, Kim Sŏngsu sat on stage at the celebratory ceremony as the head of the opposition party.

Emergence of the Democratic National Party

Because the KDP was losing its popularity, some KDP party members who were elected under other affiliations did not return to the KDP. A block of twenty-nine KDP members in the assembly was not strong enough to check Rhee's drift toward autocratic rule. The KDP needed to broaden its horizons and membership. Kim Sŏngsu wanted to mobilize right wing and moderate forces to control younger members in the National Assembly.

After a series of meetings, Kim Sŏngsu established the Democratic National Party (Minju Kungmindang, Minguktang, or DNP) in 1949. It was a coalition of the KDP (represented by Kim Sŏngsu), Korean National Party (Taehan Kungmindang, represented by Sin Ikhŭi), and the Great National Youth Corps (Taedong Ch'ŏngnyŏndan, represented by Yi Ch'ŏngch'ŏn).[69] The newly formed DNP elected Kim Sŏngsu, Paek Namhun, Sin Ikhŭi, and Yi Ch'ŏngch'ŏn as members of the party's supreme committee (*ch'oego wiwŏn*). Formation of the DNP altered the distribution of the assemblymen in terms of their affiliations. With several seats, the DNP had the largest number with seventy seats, and the remaining 130 members were divided among four other factions, including the independents.

The DNP, as the largest opposition party in the history of the Korean republic, challenged the power of the Rhee government. On January 20, 1950, the DNP adopted a resolution to propose constitutional amendments that would change the current presidential system to a parliamentary system, because: (1) under the current presidential system, accountability of the cabinet members was uncertain; (2) realistically, it would be almost impossible for the DNP to remain as the majority party with the necessary two-thirds majority needed to amend the constitution in the next election. Rhee began to manipulate his power to make sure the next election would be in his favor.

On January 27, on behalf of the DNP, Sŏ Sangil submitted the proposal for constitutional amendments to the National Assembly. Syngman Rhee launched a strong anti-amendment campaign. The Korean National Party (Taehan Kungmindang or Kungmindang), formed on November 12, 1949, launched a counter-campaign. The tally of the final vote on March 14, 1950, indicated that out of 179 members present only 79 voted for the amendments. Thirty-three voted against the amendments, 66 abstained, and one vote was invalid. The number fell far short of the 144 votes that the DNP anticipated for the amendment. While the defeat was a severe blow to the DNP, Syngman Rhee basked in victory. Again, Syngman Rhee's keen political skills had been demonstrated.

After the DNP's challenge to the constitution, Syngman Rhee displayed a peculiar relationship toward the National Assembly. Many members complained that Syngman Rhee almost ignored the assembly. He even overlooked the constitution. Before the vote on the constitutional amendments proposed by the DNP, Rhee announced that the national election for the second National Assembly would take place on May 10, 1950. After the vote on the amendments, he became vague about the election. In a memo to the speaker of the assembly, for instance, he said the election was to take place before the end of June, even though the two-year term of the first assembly would expire on May 31. Furthermore, after Rhee's victory over the DNP constitutional amendments, Rhee's Taehan Minguktang confused the assembly by proposing its own constitutional amendments, which included presidential election by popular vote, a bicameral legislature, and extension of the term of the first assembly members from two to four years. To compound the confusion, on March 17, Rhee told the foreign correspondents that the general election would be postponed until November 1950.[70]

Kim Sŏngsu, along with Yi Ch'ŏngch'ŏn and Paek Namhun, visited Rhee and reminded him that postponement would be in violation of the constitution. Rhee told them that, if the assembly passed his proposed budget for the fiscal year, he would hold the election. The U.S. Secretary of the State, Dean Acheson, warned that, if elections did not take place, the United States would halt all aid to Korea. On April 19, Rhee announced May 30 as the date of the general election.[71] Realizing that increased criticism from the DNP was the result of poor management of the government, Rhee dismissed Yi Pŏmsŏk as prime minister. When Rhee's nomination of Yi Yunyŏng for prime minister was, once again, not confirmed in the assembly, he appointed Sin Sŏngmo, who was minister of defense, as acting prime minister. As acting prime minister, Sin's appointment would not be subject to the approval of the assembly.

Despite Rhee's ambivalent attitude toward the general election, it took place on May 30, 1950. Unlike the first general election, almost all factions participated. In the first election, 948 individuals ran for 200 seats, but in this election, 2,209 ran for 210 seats.[72] The election was highly competitive. Again, Kim Sŏngsu did not run for his district's assembly seat; he was planning to retire from politics as soon as the DNP was back on track.[73]

The outcome of the election was disappointing to Kim Sŏngsu and his DNP. The DNP secured only twenty-four seats, the same number as Rhee's ruling party. Several key leaders of the DNP, including Sŏ Sangil, Paek Namhun, Cho Pyŏngok, Kim Chunyŏn, Paek Kwansu, Kim Toyŏn, and Yi Yŏngjun, were not elected. Yun Ch'iyŏng, who was the central figure of the ruling party, was also defeated. On the other hand, 126 independents were elected, and formed a majority. Emergence of the neutral or moderate faction was noticeable, including Cho Soang, An Chaehong, Wŏn Sehun, Yun Kisŏp, and Chang Kŏnsang.[74] Such a motley assembly membership augured an uncertain prospect for the assembly and a turbulent political future. The DNP, however, was able to salvage the position of speaker of the assembly with Sin Ikhŭi. The ruling party was significantly weakened.

Outbreak of the Korean War

At dawn on June 25, 1950, North Korea attacked South Korea along the 38th Parallel. The South Korean army was caught completely off guard.[75] Some revisionists, such as I. F. Stone, hypothesize that the South provoked the war.[76] Recently, however, documents relating to the origins of the Korean War have come to light from Russian sources, following the reorganization of the former Soviet Union. These papers confirm that it was the North that attacked the South, putting the earlier claims, hypotheses, and speculations to rest. Park Myung-Lim's comprehensive and voluminous book on the outbreak and its origins of the Korean War supports the conventional view.[77]

The South Korean armed forces, vastly inferior to their northern counterparts in manpower and equipment, had to give up Ŭijŏngbu on the second day
of the war. The city was the gateway to Seoul. While Syngman Rhee assured the
frightened citizens of Seoul over the radio that he would make every effort to
secure the capital city, North Korean tanks reached Seoul on June 28. The South
Korean army then blew up the Han River Bridge, cutting off the major route leading south. Over one-and-a-half-million Seoulites were thus isolated and trapped,
panic-stricken and unable to flee. Many prominent South Koreans were forced
to work for the North Koreans, and others were taken to the north.

On the second day after the war broke out, Kim Sŏngsu met with DNP leaders at Cho Pyŏngok's house to deal with the emergency situation. At the time,
however, even in the Kyŏngmudae (currently Ch'ŏngwadae, the official residence
of the South Korean president), no one had accurate information about the war
and its strategies. It would have been doubly hard for the opposition party leaders to access classified information. By way of a phone call from Colonel Kim
Chŏngo, an acquaintance of Kim Sŏngsu, Kim learned that Syngman Rhee had
already fled to the south, despite his earlier radio announcement. The colonel insisted that Kim had to escape to Seoul as soon as possible. Kim managed to
head south in the early morning of June 27, before the Han River Bridge was
blown up.[78]

Loss of Close Friends in the War

The tide of the war was not to be reversed right away, even after the in-
tervention of the U.N. Forces, which continued to retreat through July as North
Korean troops advanced farther south. The communists occupied most of the
southern peninsula. They controlled the zone thoroughly and systematically,
using well-organized and fully thought-out war plans, and deploying large numbers of North Korean security guards. The invaders ferreted out reactionary elements, including members of the South Korean armed forces, police, anti-
communist rightists, nationalists, politicians, leaders of various civic and social
organizations, landowners, and public officials, who were subject to arrest, imprisonment, abduction, and prosecution. Open trials, called "people's courts,"
were held to convict the arrested persons at locations that were likely to attract
great public attention throughout the occupied southern part of the peninsula.
There were innumerable massacres by the communist occupation authorities.[79]
On July 1, the standing committee of the North Korean Supreme People's Congress had issued an ordinance on wartime mobilization that forced the residents
of the occupied area to collaborate with the People's Army. Volunteer corps, stu-

dent army corps, youth leagues, and women's leagues were mobilized to recruit volunteers on the street. The number of volunteers recruited and drafted from the entire occupied portion of South Korea was estimated to be approximately 200,000.[80] Many South Korean political leaders, respectable scholars, intellectuals, and prominent writers, who were unable to escape Seoul, were kidnapped. As General MacArthur's forces made their spectacular amphibious landing at Inch'ŏn on September 15, 1950, the tide of war turned abruptly in favor of the United Nations. Seoul was recaptured on September 28, and U.N. troops broke out of the Pusan perimeter. As the North Korean army retreated northward, the U.N. Forces crossed the 38th Parallel and marched north, securing the area of the Yalu River, which serves as a natural boundary between North Korea and Manchuria.

Kim Sŏngsu returned to Seoul on October 12. The buildings of Chungang, Koryŏ University, and *Tonga Ilbo* were not damaged, but the Kyŏngbang factories in Sihŭng, Ŭijŏngbu, and Yŏngdŭngp'o had been destroyed. The greatest losses for Kim Sŏngsu were his close friends and aids: *Tonga Ilbo*'s editorial board member, Ko Yŏnghwan, and business affairs bureau chief, Chŏng Kyunch'ŏl, who were shot to death. Former president, Paek Kwansu, chief of the editorial bureau, Chang In'gap, general affairs bureau chief, Kim Tongsŏp, and director of the photographic section, Paek Unsŏn, had been forcibly taken to the north. Most of all, he lost his closest friend, Hyŏn Sangyun, who was president of Koryŏ University. After Kim lost his two closest associates and friends, Song Chinu and Chang Tŏksu, Hyŏn was the only remaining friend in whom he could confide.

Kim also endured another personal tragedy, the death of Yi Insu, a young English professor of Koryŏ University. Kim knew Yi from his boyhood and cared for him as if he were one of his own sons. Upon completing his studies in England, Yi taught English in Chungang School and after the liberation taught English at Koryŏ University. When Yi was trapped in Seoul during the northern invasion, he was forced by the North Koreans to do propaganda work against the United States. Later, Yi was pressed into the People's Army. He managed to escape the north, and surrendered to the U.S. Army, for which he worked for a time. Then, at the request of Korean army intelligence, Yi was handed over to the Korean authorities.

When he heard a rumor that Yi might be executed, Kim Sŏngsu visited defense minister Sin Sŏngmo to plead for Yi's life. Sin told Kim that he would try, yet Kim was skeptical about Sin's promise. Kim went to Paek Nakchun, the minister of education, to discuss the possibility of appealing to Syngman Rhee for Yi's life. While Kim and Paek discussed the possibility of appeal, Sin entered the room and told them that Yi had just been shot to death. Kim angrily asked

Sin, "Look, Minister Sin! Didn't you tell us that we would win the war? Then, you ran away without informing the citizens. When you return, should you kill a man who was forced by the North Koreans to do some English broadcasting just to survive?"[81] Kim condemned Sin's lack of compassion toward the trapped Seoulites who were forced to work for the North Koreans during their occupation. In fact, Sin's reputation as minister of defense and as a humane person was at an all time low, but Syngman Rhee still regarded him highly. (During my tenure as a senior Fulbright scholar at Yonsei University [1993–1994], I had an opportunity to meet Yi Insu's son, who is an English professor at the university, and to learn the relationship between his family and Kim Sŏngsu.)[82]

Kim Sŏngsu was not the only one to endure personal losses during the war. Human tragedy engulfed the entire peninsula. Even eight members of the National Assembly were killed during the war, and twenty-seven members were missing. Some of these had been kidnapped and taken to the north, and some went to the north by their own will.

The recapture of Seoul did not last long. In fact, the war then moved into a new, more complicated stage as the Chinese People's Volunteer (CPV) appeared at the front in October and then in late November. More volunteer forces crossed over from Manchuria and struck strongly, employing so-called human-wave tactics. During the initial CPV attack in late October and the massive Chinese counteroffensive in late November, great numbers of Chinese troops entered North Korea.[83] "The U.N. command estimated that about 486,000 enemy troops, or twenty-one Chinese and twelve North Korean divisions, were committed to the Korean front, and that reserves totaling over one million men were stationed near the Yalu, in Manchuria, or were on the way to Manchuria."[84] When Chinese troops crossed the 38th Parallel and entered Seoul on January 4, 1951, the South Korean government and the U.N. troops pulled out of Seoul and abandoned the port of Inch'ŏn. Once again they had to face the evacuation of refugees. Kim Sŏngsu and his family left Seoul for Pusan December 20, 1951, and later he acquired a small house in Chinhae to avoid the crowded city of Pusan. By that time, he had delegated most of his party politics to Sin Ikhŭi; he remained a supporter of the party outside the political arena of the National Assembly.

Elected as Vice President

After he became president, Syngman Rhee controlled Korean politics thoroughly. As Carter J. Eckert and his colleagues sum up the political milieu of the time: "South Korean politics of the 1950s tended to revolve around or against one man: Syngman Rhee. . . . The kind of assembly that Rhee and his fellow Club members had advocated, however, was essentially an expanded advisory group to the king that would not have ultimately threatened royal supremacy."[85] Although Rhee's tendency to ignore the National Assembly was revealed as soon as he became president, his autocratic ideas grew stronger during and after the Korean War. His skilled political manipulation, enhanced by a strong anti-communist slogans and aided by sycophantic subordinates, allowed him to wield enormous power during and after the war.

A major governmental political scandal in the temporary wartime capital of Pusan was the Kŏch'ang incident. In February 1951, in the Kŏch'ang area of south Kyŏngsang province, a contingent of South Korean troops was led by Colonel Kim Chongwŏn. Kim was one of Rhee's favorites, who later became head of the national police. He massacred some five hundred innocent villagers for allegedly harboring communist guerrillas.[86] Cho Pyŏngok told Rhee about the incident, and subsequently Rhee ordered Sin Sŏngmo, a typical sycophantic subordinate, to investigate the incident. Sin told Rhee that it was fabricated. Rhee believed Sin's words. Rhee's confidant and the central figure of the incident, Kim Chongwŏn even interfered with the National Assembly's investigation of the incident.

Another scandal surrounded the National Guard (*Pangwigun*), which had been formed in December 1950 to mobilize all male Koreans aged seventeen through forty to serve as a reserve army. While half a million guardsmen were retreating southward during the CPV's offensive in the winter of 1950, some high-ranking officers of the guard embezzled the supplies of food and clothes for their own troops, leaving hundreds of thousands of ill-supplied guardsmen to starve that harsh winter, and several thousand to die from the cold. Again, Sin Sŏngmo, minister of defense, and Kim Yun'gŭn, commander of the National Guard, denied the charges, and countercharge that National Assembly investigators were communist instigators, whom they even tried to bribe. Finally, an investigation by several zealous assemblymen revealed the truth. Sin Sŏngmo, who was involved in both incidents, turned in his resignation without incurring any further criminal charges, although his subordinates were sentenced for their crimes, and some were executed. Outraged by the incidents and Rhee's handling of them, Yi Siyŏng, vice president, resigned. It was up to the National Assembly to elect his successor.[87]

On the one hand, Rhee's ruling party was working to elect Yi Kapsŏng as vice president. Yi was one of the thirty-three signers of the Declaration of Independence during the March First Movement. The DNP worked to elect Kim Sŏngsu. At the election on May 16, from the 151 members present, Kim Sŏngsu had sixty-five votes, Yi Kapsŏng fifty-three, Ham T'aeyŏng seventeen, Chang T'aeksang eleven, Yi Ch'ŏngch'ŏn two, and Kim Ch'angsuk one. No one received the two-thirds majority required for confirmation. In the second ballot, again no one secured the needed votes. At the final run-off between Kim Sŏngsu and Yi Kapsŏng, Kim won by a narrow margin; seventy-eight to seventy-three. Kim did not accept his election, saying, "Yi Siyŏng took the position without knowing what it would be like. I know the position. I don't want to be a scapegoat for the Rhee government's misrule." [88] Under the presidential system, the vice president was insignificant other than that he inherited the presidency in case of death or imprisonment of the president. Because of his associates' persistent pleas, however, Kim reluctantly accepted the position, and made his acceptance speech at the National Assembly on May 18, 1951.

The Estranged Relationship between Rhee and Kim

The day after Kim was elected vice president, Syngman Rhee suddenly announced that he would propose constitutional amendments that would call for election of the president, the vice president, and a bicameral legislature by popular vote. Soon after, by merging several factions, Rhee's ruling group, Konghwa Minjŏnghoe, was able to acquire 108 seats, while the DNP was left with only 39.[89] Although Rhee's faction could not muster the two-thirds majority that was necessary to pass the constitutional amendments, it had twenty-one seats above a simple majority.

Despite their differences, Rhee's attitude toward his vice president was not distant, at least at the outset. During Kim's first visit with Rhee after his election, Rhee insisted that Kim attend the cabinet meetings, and Kim agreed to do so. The vice president, as an ex officio member, could attend and speak at the cabinet meetings, but could not cast a vote. Although Kim was critical of Rhee's policies, there had been mutual admiration between them. It appeared that Rhee was willing to take Kim's advice. Nevertheless, some cabinet ministers resented Kim's participation in the cabinet meetings, and spoke disparagingly of Kim to Rhee. As their calumniations continued, Rhee's attitude toward Kim began to change, and eventually their relationship became estranged.

Rhee's arbitrariness and self-righteousness were again in evidence on June 26, 1951, at the cabinet meetings regarding the appointment of a Korean Representative to Japan.[90] To everyone's surprise, Rhee suddenly said, "Raise your hands, those who are in favor of appointing Sin Sŏngmo as Korean Representative to Japan."[91] (It became known later that Rhee had already received Japan's approval on June 23 for Sin's appointment.) Kim Sŏngsu opposed Sin's appointment because Sin was responsible for the Kŏch'ang massacre and the National Guard incident, although both cases were still pending. Kim argued that the person who was ultimately responsible for both incidents could not be appointed de facto ambassador to Japan and allowed to escape the country. Rhee ignored Kim's arguments, and repeated his earlier command. No one at the meeting raised his hand. When the cabinet meeting reconvened in the afternoon, Rhee asked the council to reconsider the decision.

Not feeling well, Kim Sŏngsu did not attend the afternoon session, when Sin's appointment was defeated by a 4–6 vote. Ignoring the vote of the cabinet meeting, Rhee appointed Sin to the post anyway. Kim's indignation about Rhee's highhandedness caused his illness to worsen, and his face became partially paralyzed. Ignoring this early warning of what was to be a fatal illness, in an attempt to soothe his anger and frustration, Kim even drank in the company of Paek Namhun, Cho Pyŏngok, and Yi Yŏngjun on the evening of June 28. The next morning, Kim found that his right arm was numb and immobile, and he experienced some difficulties in speaking.[92]

Pae Sŏp, who was a secretary to Kim during his vice presidency, told me that he believed that Kim Sŏngsu's illness was aggravated by his anger at Rhee's arbitrary action. Clearly, Kim suffered a minor stroke, although his physician, Ko Yŏngsun, did not diagnose it; he advised Kim to drink a few glasses of liquor and to rest and forget about everything. Kim's illness was cerebral thrombosis. Drinking alcohol after having a minor stroke worsened his illness.[93]

Kim's disability made Syngman Rhee's job much simpler by providing him an opportunity to wield his absolute power without any interference from a major political rival. Assassination and illness had eliminated several, potential political competitors: Song Chinu in 1945; Yŏ Unhyŏng in 1947; Kim Ku in 1949; and finally Kim Sŏngsu in 1955.

Resignation from the
Vice Presidency

While Kim Sŏngsu was suffering from his illness, Rhee was building up his power base. He employed a new and more subtle tool for controlling the National Assembly. In late 1951, Rhee formed the Liberal Party (Chayudang), which was composed of a motley assortment of opportunists, who employed police surveillance, armed thugs, and gangs. In 1952, when Rhee was up for reelection, he again proposed the constitutional amendments that the National Assembly failed to approve in 1951. Election of the president, the vice president, and a bicameral legislature by popular vote. Rhee declared martial law and arrested several dozen assemblymen. Rhee herded the assemblymen, who were unwilling to go along with Rhee's constitutional amendments, into the assembly building and locked them up until the amendments were passed.

While Rhee's political thugs and gangs dominated the political arena, Kim Sŏngsu had no power in his position as vice president; he resigned his position on May 29, 1952. His lengthy letter of resignation, condemning Rhee's autocratic rule, was read in the National Assembly. He specifically indicated that he had become ill as a result of Rhee's appointment of Sin Sŏngmo as Korean representative to Japan. Kim's resignation was accepted officially on June 28, 1952. The DNP relinquished hope that Kim Sŏngsu would run for president against Rhee in the forthcoming election. Kim was unable to stop Rhee's increasing authoritarianism.

On August 20, 1953, after a cease-fire was declared, Kim Sŏngsu returned to Seoul via Taegu for a few months of treatment. Kim left the leadership role of the DNP to Sin Ikhŭi, and remained as an advisor. The DNP was no match for Rhee's Liberal Party, which not only employed various immoral, unethical, and illegal tactics, but also mobilized thugs and gangs in addition to the police forces. By 1954, Rhee's Liberal Party had achieved a clear majority in the assembly. In order to amend the constitution to make him president for life, Rhee and his party employed every available means to bribe, banish, or threaten independents in the assembly. The vote for the constitutional amendments on November 27, 1954, resulted in 135 in favor, 60 against, 1 invalid, and 6 abstentions. The vote fell one short of the 136 required for passage. The next day, Rhee's Liberal Party came up with a mathematic principle, which said that two-thirds of 203 was 135.33, but 0.33 should be rounded down, so that the required votes should be 135, not 136. As a result the amendments passed.[94] Clearly, Rhee's dictatorship, self-righteousness, and arbitrariness could not be contained or stopped by Kim and his minority party.

As a strategy to fight against Rhee's dogmatic rule, Kim Sŏngsu induced the DNP leaders to dismantle the old party and organize a new party that, by broadening its membership, would mobilize all the opposing forces. Kim's effort to unite anti-Rhee factions continued as late as January 1955. Without seeing the results of his effort to form a new party, Kim died on February 18, 1955. The new Democratic Party (Minjudang) was finally formed on September 19, seven months after Kim's death. Many current political leaders, notably Kim Young Sam (Kim Yŏngsam), former president of South Korea, and Kim Dae Jung (Kim Taejung), the current president, were descendants of the

Democratic Party that was prompted by Kim. Kim Sŏngsu made his contributions to postwar Korean politics as the leader of opposition parties, not as vice president.

6.1. Kim Sŏngsu with President Syngman Rhee *(r.)* when he was vice president of the Republic of Korea

6.2. Kim Sŏngsu when he was vice president of the Republic of Korea

6.3. Syngman Rhee offers condolences on Kim Sŏngsu's death

6.4. Kim Sŏngsu's residence in Kedong *(below)*, designated for his memorial

CHAPTER SEVEN

The Legacy of Kim Sŏngsu

K im Sŏngsu's accomplishments for Korean modernization through his various projects are remarkable. All the institutions he founded survived Japanese colonial rule, struggled through postwar political chaos, and are successfully functioning at the present. Kim's life history is almost a narrative of modern Korean history.

Like anyone else, Kim Sŏngsu had strengths and weaknesses. He made mistakes in judgment at times. He was not infallible. And, like most Koreans who lived as colonial subjects, Kim had to work within the colonial rules. Nevertheless, he successfully accomplished several monumental projects that propelled Korean modernization.

While the standard Korean scholarship and Kim's supporters and advocates praise Kim highly for his remarkable accomplishments, some others criticize Kim for not directly confronting the colonial authorities. Some critiques of Kim call him a "collaborator" with the Japanese.[1] A wave of criticism of Kim welled up amid campus unrest, labor disputes in protest against the military-led government, and social and economic injustice in the late 1980s. Even tenant farmers from Kim's home county, Koch'ang, were among the demonstrators. Recently, Nancy Abelmann, an anthropologist, documented a detailed ethnography of the Koch'ang tenant farmers movement.[2] Ironically, most demonstrators have been Koryŏ University students and farmers from Kim's hometown. Also, in the late 1980s, students' threats to desecrate Kim's resting place were so frequent that his family exhumed Kim's grave near Koryŏ University and reburied him in another location. Debates on the pros and cons of Kim's projects appeared in student publications at Koryŏ University as late as May 1995.[3]

Some scholars, Chin Tŏkkyu for one, believe that the polarization of views on Kim and his work stems from the ideologies of the critics. The radicals and leftists have been critical of Kim for his conservative, bourgeois background and strong anti-communist stand; conservatives, moderates, and rightwingers have praised him as virtuous and legendary.[4] Nevertheless, Korean scholars and intellectuals, regardless of their ideological stands, agree that such contradictory views of Kim were in part the result of skillful Japanese manipulation that divided Korean nationalists in order to conquer them effectively. The polarized views of Kim might have colonial origins. Even a half century after Korea's independence from Japanese occupation, many Koreans have not thrown off the influence of the Japanese colonialists.

In evaluating Kim and his work, either praising his accomplishments or criticizing his failures, one must consider who Kim actually was, rather than who one wishes he had been, and what Kim did, rather than what Kim should have done differently. Kim's background, his upbringing, and his idiosyncrasies combined to make Kim who and what he was. In summarizing Kim and his work, I would characterize him as a realist, a cultural nationalist, and an educator, but not a statesman.

Kim Sŏngsu as a Realist

According to his family and close friends, Kim possessed a rather short temper, although he was perceived by others as calm and warm-natured.[5] Even though Kim received a modern education in Japan, he was deeply imbued with Confucianism from his early education in Confucian tutorial school. His adoptive father indoctrinated him with the family precepts, stressing that if one could not be kind to and tolerant of himself, he could not be kind to and tolerant of others.[6] Confucian ethics, coupled with his family precepts, inclined him to be unusually frugal in his personal life relative to his wealth. Everyone acquainted with Kim would testify to his humbleness and modest lifestyle. Yet, he was generous with his money and willing to help people, including Song Chinu and many others.

Kim's socialization process made him a patient realist. His dream was attainable. His approach was cautious at best; not taking any risks, he was able, quietly and methodically, to accomplish his goals. Docile and meek in appearance, he was strong internally and thus able to survive personal humiliation. Yu Chino reports that once Yu had become angry when an official of the Government-General addressed him as *kimi,* a non-honorific expression meaning something like "hey, you," used to address a junior or subordinate. When Yu told Kim about it, Kim said that he had been addressed the same way by that same official (although he was older and more prominent than Yu). Furthermore, Kim added, once the same official had addressed him as *Kin kun,* meaning literally "boy Kim." [7] This is an insult to a person of Kim's stature, but Kim did not appear to be ruffled by it.

Kim's humble attitude, however, did not allow him to be a dynamic or charismatic leader, as was his political opponent Syngman Rhee, or even his friend Song Chinu. At the same time, Kim's patience and realism served him well in his political life. Yi Sangdon, who worked for Kim at *Tonga Ilbo,* related the following incident to me:

> It was one afternoon in early August 1940, after the Japanese authorities ordered the *Tonga Ilbo* to cease publication. Having lost my job at the *Tonga Ilbo,* I was talking to Inch'on [Kim Sŏngsu] about my temporary job at the Ch'ŏnil Pharmaceutical Company. Song Chinu came in, completely soaked from a summer shower. Inch'on looked at Song and remarked, "You should stay away from rain showers. You could wait under the overhang of any house until the shower passes. You know, a summer shower is always brief. You don't have to brave it. Waiting it out won't hurt anything." [8]

According to Yi, Song Chinu easily understood the analogy between the rain showers and Kim's view of the Japanese occupation of Korea, including the closing of *Tonga Ilbo.* Everything is transitory.

Koreans, who understood Kim's genuine motives and his method of dealing with the Japanese authorities, accept Kim as a person of strength and wisdom. These are the Koreans who were close to Kim, and who experienced his qualities of endurance and modesty. Others who did not understand him well or who have come to him only through written records tend to think Kim was conciliatory toward the Japanese. They interpret his gradual and cautious approach to mean that he was a collaborator. They take his behind-the-scenes work in behalf of cultural nationalism as not confrontational enough. They see his avoidance of mass demonstrations during the March First Movement as evasive rather than pragmatic.

In addition to socialization and Confucian ethics, the socioeconomic and political conditions of Korea contributed to Kim's patient realism. When he established the Chungang School under Japanese colonial rule, Korea was unable to match Japan's might militarily, economically, and otherwise. Any direct confrontation with Japan was analogous to "hitting rocks with eggs" (*kyeranŭro pawich'igi*), as a Korean proverb has it. Kim learned the reality of the Japanese brutality and the determination to control Korea through retaliation against Koreans during and after the March First Movement. Their methods of retaliation, from imprisonment to mass killings, were inhumane, as evidenced by the Cheamni massacre. Changsoo Lee and George De Vos report a cruel massacre following after the March First Movement in a rural Korean village:

> A nearby Japanese garrison had come to the village [Cheamni]. Some of the soldiers had roughed up several male inhabitants believed to have joined in the general active protest. The protesters had been part of the Christian community of this village. Two days after this unpleasant episode, some troops returned. They told all the villagers present to assemble in the Church. The villagers did so, thinking they were to hear some word of apology for the brutal behavior of the Japanese soldiers. Once they were all inside, the troops barred the doors, nailed them shut, and poured gasoline about the wooden structure, setting it afire. Everyone inside was incinerated.[9]

Kim's view was that direct confrontation with the Japanese would only increase the casualties. Koreans, Kim believed, had to abide with patience but at the same time strengthen the nation by laying the foundations for the future.

In determining the destiny of Korea during the postwar period, Kim remained a realist as he worked toward establishing a legitimate and democratic nation, even if it had to be south of the 38th Parallel. No Korean wished the country to be divided into two parts, yet Kim saw that it would be unrealistic to expect the communists to yield to those who wanted to create a single nation. He had the foresight to see that any delay in establishing a republic in the south could easily allow communization of the entire peninsula. And, he urged a general election in the south in order to create an anti-communist regime at a time when not many young Koreans could understand the threat of communism, and could know how horrifying an experience it would be. (I vividly remember my father, older brothers, and uncles hiding every night to avoid the communist terrorism that could strike them if they were suspected of being rightists. I had to be a messenger going from shelter to shelter.) Communist brutality against right-wing Koreans was as bad as Japanese brutality against Koreans during the colonial rule. Very little written history reveals the details of the horrifying tactics that communists used to threaten and terrorize; many people who never experienced the cruelties firsthand cannot imagine them.

Kim Sŏngsu as a Cultural Nationalist

A realistic assessment of the Korean socioeconomic and political conditions during the period of the Japanese domination and eventual annexation led Kim to embrace cultural nationalism, a movement to raise the general level of national consciousness, literacy, and economic development in Korean society. At that time, for instance, the level of educational attainment of Koreans was very low: "Only five percent of Korean students passed beyond the primary level, and although there was a tremendous expansion of student numbers over time, in 1945 only about twenty percent of the population had received some schooling, while the general rate of literacy was still below fifty percent." [10] With this situation in mind, Kim decided that cultural nationalism offered Korea the best possibility of laying the foundation for future independence via education, newspapers, and industry.

Kim's approach to building for the future was painstakingly gradual, non-violent, and non-confrontational against the colonial authorities. This approach differed from that of radical nationalism, which pressed for social revolution and overt resistance to Japanese colonial rule. As a realist, Kim's view was that, because political independence was then unobtainable, social, cultural, and economic self-strengthening was an acceptable secondary goal.

Most of the time, Kim was successful in avoiding collaboration with the Japanese. During the *Naisen ittai* period, for instance, he was able to retain his original name, despite pressure from the Japanese that he cooperate with the policy. In the middle of February 1945, Endō Ryūsaku, Vice Governor-General (1944–1945), invited Kim to his office and informed him that the Governor-General was going to recommend that Kim be awarded a barony (*Nanshaku*). He would become a member of the House of Peers (*Kizokuin*). Kim declined the offer.[11] Instead, Kim told Endō that he would like to be a person like Fukuzawa Yukichi.[12] Fukuzawa devoted his entire life to education without carrying any peerage or title.[13] Kim was avoiding a difficult situation. The following day, Endō called Kim and told him to forget about the conversation they had had earlier regarding the peerage, for Endō wanted to "save face" as well as the credibility of the Governor-General. When the Government-General announced seven Koreans for the House of Peers on April 3, Kim's name was not included on the list.[14]

As indicated elsewhere, however, Kim made a major mistake when he could not stop publication in the *Maeil Sinbo* of an article under his name that was actually written by Kim Pyŏnggyu. If he had derailed publication of that article (which was intended to induce Korean youths to join the Japanese mobilization) the way he had derailed the peerage, his record as a cultural nationalist would have been untainted. Nevertheless, this one unusual incident should not label Kim a Japanese collaborator.

Because he had been born into a wealthy family, the authenticity of Kim's devotion to cultural nationalism has been questioned by radical left-wing forces that classify Kim's position as brazen hypocrisy—bourgeoisie class interest masquerading as nationalism. But, "even orthodox North Korean historians—no great admirers of the Korean bourgeoisie—have subscribed to the view that businessmen like the Kims were, at least initially, 'national reformists' rather than outright comprador or 'subordinate' capitalists."[15] Despite his status as a landlord, Kim was not an advocate of landlords. For example, when Yu Chino was drafting the Korean constitution, he included an article on land reform. Yu thought that Kim, being a landowner, might not like the idea of land reform. To Yu's surprise, Kim willingly supported the principle.[16] In fact, Kim supported the June 1949 Land Reform Act that called for the Korean government to remain as the mediator in the transfer of land from landlords to tenants. "While land reform may temporarily have reduced productivity per acre, this was far outweighed by the political and social consequences."[17] Further, as Chin Tŏkkyu indicates, Kim did not use his land to accumulate further wealth.[18] When Kim died, in fact, he left a modest house in Kedong, which was later designated his memorial, some forest land that was not subject to land reform by law, and some stocks.[19] He had spent his wealth on cultural-nationalist projects.[20]

Without question, Kim was conservative, rightist, and anti-communist. Conservatism is not a hindrance to progress, however. The Korean economic "miracle," as it is called, that began in the late 1960s, was accomplished under conservative ideology. Furthermore, Kim as a conservative was, as Eckert describes him, a national reformist.[21] As far as Kim's strong anti-communist stand is concerned, the majority of South Koreans welcomed it. Without the effort organized by Kim and his KDP to check the expansion of communism during the Cold War era, the south could readily have come under control of the communists. Judging what communism has done to the North Koreans, not many would argue that communizing Korea was the answer to unification.

Kim Sŏngsu as an Educator, Not a Statesman

As his biography delineates, Kim Sŏngsu's heart was not in politics. He did not have the stomach to ruthlessly eliminate political rivals, as Syngman Rhee had done. Nor had he the aptitude to be a statesman, unlike his colleagues Song Chinu and Chang Tŏksu. If Song had not been assassinated, he would have continued to lead the KDP, and Kim would have remained the power behind the throne. In many ways, Kim was more an organizer and supporter than a statesman. As Yu Chino depicts Kim, he was neither a politician nor a statesman, but rather a cultural nationalist.[22]

If he had had political ambitions, Kim could have realized them by using Syngman Rhee (who had no political roots in Korea), or Kim Ku and his KPG leaders, or even the organization and influence of the KDP. Instead, Kim was a vigorous supporter of all these leaders and political organizations, to the point that he willingly relinquished the National Assembly seat in his district to Yi Yunyŏng in the general election. Although Kim was better known and more influential than many other Koreans, including Song Chinu, the Japanese authorities, recognizing that Kim was more an educator than a political leader, asked Song Chinu to head the interim peacekeeping administration. Even the U.S. military government viewed Kim as an educator, and thus invited him to serve as chair of the advisory council for education. After the liberation, some people even recommended Kim to head Keijō Imperial University, knowing that his skills and interests lay in education; and, when the leftists and moderates formed the Korean People's Republic under the leadership of Yŏ Unhyŏng, they listed Kim as minister of education. Whereas Kim's role as a statesman was confined primarily to checking Rhee's autocratic rule by mobilizing opposition leaders, as an educator, Kim's record of accomplishments and contributions is distinguished.

The Legacy of Kim Sŏngsu

Chin Tŏkkyu points out that Kim dedicated his life energy to advocating three principles; nationalism, liberal democracy, and the practice of rational gradualism.[23] To put these principles into practice, Kim used his personal wealth to establish schools and a newspaper. The *Tonga Ilbo* did much more than provide news and information; it raised the national consciousness and promoted literacy. Kyŏngbang was more than a regional manufacturing plant; it was the prototype of modern Korean industry's harnessing of national capital. Although critics may carp about the composition of the KDP, without the unified right-wing forces, the south would have fallen to the communists, and the Western model of liberal democracy may never have breathed life on the peninsula.

To succeed, Kim's advocacy of cultural nationalism, his pragmatism, and his belief in gradualism required conciliatory gestures toward Japan. Thus, he has been vulnerable to charges of collaboration. From a radical, revolutionary, and revisionist standpoint, Kim Sŏngsu and his approach to cultural nationalism must be puzzling. The Korean struggle for independence, however, cannot be viewed monolithically. Armed resistance, such as Righteous armies and inde-pendence fighting abroad, as well as the diplomatic solutions sought by Syng-man Rhee, were critically necessary. Nonetheless, just as critically important was Kim's cultural nationalism. For example, the institutions that Kim created served as the strongholds and centers for many Korean nationalists. The places were few and far between where Korean nationalists could gather, discuss, and plan na-tionalistic movements, as evidenced in the Chungang School for the March First Movement. In a lecture at Koryŏ University in 1947, two-years after the liberation of Korea from Japan, Sŏ Chaep'il, founder of the Independence Club, said:

> Those Koreans who fought for Korea's independence overseas, and those independence fighters who were arrested and im-prisoned during the Japanese occupation are certainly patri-ots. Nevertheless, those like Inch'on [Kim Sŏngsu] who re-mained in Korea and devoted their lives to laying the foundations for Korea's future independence are also patriots.[24]

We must not overshadow Kim's remarkable cultural nationalist projects with criticism of Kyŏngbang's close ties with the colonial authorities under the leadership of his younger brother, Yŏnsu, who was Honorary Consul-General of Manchuria and even brought to trial in 1949 by the South Korean National Assembly for "anti-nationalist acts." The two, although extremely close as brothers, were different as men. One was a cultural nationalist and an educator, and the other was a keen businessman.

Kim Sŏngsu's two major projects, the schools and a newspaper, had no close ties with colonial authorities. Even Kyŏngbang's ties with the colonial government during the late stages of the war were inevitable, if the operation were to remain in business. In spite of Kyŏngbang's Japanese ties, Kyŏngbang's ef-forts to remain a major nationalistic industry must be acknowledged.[25] One who was close to both brothers, Pae Sŏp, states:

Some think that his younger brother's close ties with the colonial authorities put Kim Sŏngsu at a disadvantage. But, actually, Kim Yŏnsu cultivated the ties to protect his older brother. In addition, Kim Yŏnsu provided financial support for his older brother's various projects. When Sŏngsu reluctantly took over the KDP, for instance, his younger brother donated to the party. In a sense, perhaps Kim Sŏngsu took advantage of his younger brother.[26]

Kim Sŏngsu was not a kind of nationalist who led armed resistance against the Japanese during the Japanese colonial era. Instead, he advocated and successfully practiced self-strengthening programs to lay the foundation for Korea's future independence. His cultural nationalist projects served the nation well during the Japanese domination in the early twentieth century, and will continue in the future.

Finally, I want to try to place the writing this book in the perspective of the rapidly expanding literature in Korean studies. Until the past decade or so, Korean scholars have viewed Kim Sŏngsu in a positive way. They have voiced appreciation both for his role in modernizing Korea and for his participation in the resistance against Japanese domination. His economic, political, and cultural projects were all seen as contributions in both areas. However, in recent years this view has been challenged. Newer and younger scholars have offered evidence that Kim Sŏngsu acquiesced to Japanese colonial policies. They accuse Kim of collaborating with Japanese officials—suggesting that he made the occupation less burdensome by his moderate stance. More importantly, these newer views have been written and translated into English and made available to the huge throng of English-language readers. As of this date, there has been no answer to this iconoclastic view because no scholarly work affirming the patriotism and faithfulness of Kim Sŏngsu has appeared in English. That is why I believe this book had to be written.

It seems entirely possible that many Koreans, even those who have had wartime and colonial experiences similar to mine, will not agree with my descriptions of the colonial period and the Japanese. So be it. I remain convinced that it would be shameful to allow a one-sided view to go unchallenged.

Anthropologists and other social scientists have long argued that observations should be free of ideological biases. History shows that this is not achieved, that none of us really above his or her political and cultural preoccupations. That being the case, it behooves each of us to offer a sober, logical, and at least potentially refutable account of the situations we have investigated. I hope that objective has been achieved here.

APPENDICES

A. LIST OF ABBREVIATIONS

Chōbō: Chōsen Bōshoku

CPKI: Committee for the Preparation of Korean Independence

CPV: Chinese People's Volunteer

DNP: Democratic National Party

DPRK: Democratic People's Republic of Korea

Hakpyŏng: Haktopyŏng

Hakt'ong: Chŏn'guk Haksaeng Haengdong T'ongil Yŏnmaeng

Hakyŏn: Chŏn'guk Pant'ak Haksaeng Yŏnmaeng

Hanmindang: Han'guk Minjudang

KDP: Korean Democratic Party

Kŏnmaeng: Chosŏn Kŏn'guk Tongmaeng

KPG: Korean Provisional Government

KPR: Korean People's Republic

Kyŏngbang: Kyŏngsŏng Pangjik

Minguktang: Minju Kungmindang

NSL: National Security Law

NSRRKI: National Society for the Rapid Realization of Korean Independence

ROK: Republic of Korea

SKIG: South Korean Interim Government

SMSC: South Manchurian Spinning Company

USAFIK: United States Armed Forces in Korea

B. CHRONOLOGY

1891   Kim Sŏngsu (hereafter Kim) was born on October 11 (September 9 in lunar calendar).

1893   Kim was adopted by his heirless uncle, Kim Kijung.

1902   Kim married Ko Kwangsŏk.

1906   Kim attended Ch'angp'yŏng School.

1907   In the spring, the Kims relocated to Chulp'o from Inch'on-ri; during the summer Kim, along with Song Chinu and Paek Kwansu, went to Naesosa (a Buddhist temple) to study.

1908   In March, Kim's adoptive father founded Yŏngsin School in Chulp'o; in May, Kim attended Kŭmho School in Kunsan; together with Song Chinu, Kim went to Japan in October to study, enrolling in the Sesoku English School.

1909   Kim transferred to Kinjo Middle School in April.

1910   A year later, Kim enrolled in Waseda University's preparatory program in April; Korea was formally annexed to Japan on August 29.

1911   In January, Kim's younger brother, Yŏnsu, joined him in Japan.

1914   Kim graduated from Waseda University in July; he returned immediately to Chulp'o from Japan.

1915   In the spring, Kim wrote a proposal to establish a private school (Paeksan School); Kim officially took over Chungang School on April 27.

1917   Kim became principal of Chungang School on March 30; Chungang School relocated to Kedong with new school buildings on December 1; Kim took over the Kyŏngsŏng Cord Company.

1918   Kim resigned as principal of Chungang School on March 30.

1919   The March First Movement was launched on March 1; permission was granted to establish the Kyŏngsŏng Spinning and Weaving Company on October 5; on October 9, Kim applied to the Government-General for permission to start a newspaper, the *Tonga Ilbo* ; Kim's wife, Ko Kwangsŏk, died on October 27.

1920   On January 6, the Government-General granted permission to start the *Tonga Ilbo*; the first issue of the newspaper was published on April 1; the first ban on sales and distribution of the *Tonga Ilbo* was imposed on April 15; the *Tonga Ilbo*'s first indefinite suspension came from Governor-General Saitō on September 25.

1921   Kim married Yi Aju on January 30; Kim resigned from presidency of the *Tonga Ilbo* on September 15.

1922   On November 1, Kim participated in the Korean Production Movement via the *Tonga Ilbo*.

1923   Kim participated in the National University Movement via the *Tonga Ilbo* in January; in December, Kim participated in Yŏnjŏnghoe movement.

1924   Kim became president of the *Tonga Ilbo* on October 21.

1925   On September 27, groud was broken for a new *Tonga Ilbo* building in Sejongno; Kim changed the name of the Kyŏngsŏng Cord Company to the Chungang Commercial and Industrial Company (Chungang Sanggong Chusik Hoesa).

1926   On June 10, about 40 Chungang students participated in a demonstration by the June Tenth Anti-Japanese Movement; Kim faced police inquiry on June 11 regarding the Chungang students' participation in the demonstration; the new *Tonga Ilbo* building in Sejongno was completed on December 10.

1927   Kim resigned from the *Tonga Ilbo* presidency on October 22.

1928   Kim resigned as director of Kyŏngbang on March 28.

1929–31 Kim was on a world tour, including Europe and the United States, from December 3, 1929 to August 12, 1931.

1931   Kim became principal of Chungang School in September; on November 11, the *Tonga Ilbo* published its monthly magazine, *Sindonga*.

1932   Kim took over Posŏng Junior College on March 26; he resigned as Chungang's principal on May 9; Kim took over the management of Posŏng Junior College, becoming its principal on June 4.

1933   The *Tonga Ilbo* published its monthly magazine, *Singajŏng,* in January; the *Tonga Ilbo* published a manual to the orthography of *han'gŭl* on April 1; ground-breaking for Posŏng Junior College's new location in Anamdong took place on August 1.

1934   The three-story main building of Posŏng Junior College was completed on September 28.

1935   Kim resigned as principal of Posŏng Junior College; construction of the central library of Posŏng Junior College began in June.

1936   The *Tonga Ilbo* erased the Japanese flag in a photograph of Son Kijŏng's uniform on August 25; on August 27, the *Tonga Ilbo* and *Sindonga* were suspended indefinitely by Governor-General Minami Jirō; Kim resigned as director of the *Tonga Ilbo* on November 19.

1937   Kim returned as principal of Posŏng Junior College on May 26; Japan launched its full-scale assault on China on July 7; the central library of Posŏng Junior College was completed on September 2; Kim was elected as a board member of Ehwa Women's University, serving until 1952.

1938   The Japanese announced the Special Volunteer Army Act on February 22.

1939   On September 27, the Japanese proclaimed the National Manpower Mobilization Act; Kim resigned from the adviser's position at Kyŏngbang in September.

1940   A Japanese policy of "identity creation (*ch'angssi*)" was imposed on February 11; on August 10, the *Tonga Ilbo* was forced to close.

1941   Chungang School's auditorium was completed on November 11.

1942   In the spring, Posŏng Junior College was forced to change its term from three to two years; the Japanese announced the National Mobilization Law on May 9; the leaders of the Korean Language Society were arrested in October.

1943   On October 20, the Japanese authorities launched an all-out propaganda campaign to recruit "student soldiers" (*haktopyŏng*); Kim's controversial article, "Dying for a Righteous Cause," was printed in *Maeil Sinbo* on November 6.

1944   In the spring, Posŏng Junior College was converted to Kyŏngsŏng Ch'ŏksik Kyŏngjae Chŏnmun Hakkyo; a full conscription system to mobilize Koreans without exemptions was installed in February; in March, the Japanese authorities closed the law and liberal arts programs at all junior colleges; Chungang Sanggong Chusik Hoesa merged with Kyŏngbang.

1945   The liberation of Korea came on August 15; the name of Posŏng Junior College was restored on September 25; Kim was selected as a member of an 11-member advisory council to Military Governor Archibald V. Arnold on October 5; the *Tonga Ilbo* resumed publication on December 1; Song Chinu was assassinated on December 30.

1946   Kim became president of the *Tonga Ilbo* on January 1; Kim resigned as principal of Posŏng Junior College on February 19; the KDP elected Kim as Executive Director of General Affairs on July 7; Posŏng Junior College became a comprehensive university, and changed its name to Koryŏ (Korea) University, on August 15.

1947   Kim resigned from the presidency of the *Tonga Ilbo* on February 20; Chang Tŏksu was assassinated on December 2.

1948   A general election took place in the South on May 10; on July 20, Syngman Rhee was elected as ROK president; the first republic, Republic of Korea, was born on August 15.

1949   Kim was instrumental in establishing the Democratic National Party (Minju Kungmindang, or DNP), and was elected as a member of party's supreme committee (*ch'oego wiwŏn*) on February 10; Kim became adviser to the *Tonga Ilbo* on July 28.

1950   The Korean War began on June 25 as North Korea attacked South Korea along the 38th parallel; Kim left Seoul for the South as a refugee on June 27; the *Tonga Ilbo* was unable to publish due to the Korean War from June 28 to December 4; Kim returned to Seoul as the city was recaptured by U.N. troops on October 12.

1951   As the South Korean government and the U.N. troops pulled out of Seoul, Kim and his family left Seoul for Pusan on January 4; Kim was elected as ROK vice president by the National Assembly on May 16; Kim accepted the position of vice president and delivered his acceptance speech at the National Assembly on May 18.

1952 Kim resigned as vice president on May 29; Kim's resignation was officially accepted on June 28; Koryŏ University was authorized to offer programs in agriculture and forestry in December.

1953 Kim returned to Seoul from the war-time capital, Pusan, on August 20.

1955 Kim died on February 18; his funeral on February 24 was observed as a National Funeral (Kungminjang).

c. GUIDE TO ROMANIZATION

Abe Nobuyuki   阿附信行
an   안
Anamdong   安岩洞
An Chaehong   安在鴻
An Ch'angho   安昌浩
An Chunggŭn   安重根
An Hamp'yŏng   安咸平
An Hosang   安浩相
An Tongwŏn   安東源
budan seiji   武斷政治
bunka seiji   文化政治
bunshyō   文書
chaebŏl/zaibatsu   財閥
Chaeryŏng   載寧
Chajakhoe   自作會
Ch'ambong   參奉
Chang Chien   張謇
Chang Chiyŏn   張志淵
Chang Ch'unjae   張春梓
Chang In'gap   張仁甲
Chang Kŏnsang   張健相
Chang T'aeksang   張澤相
Chang Tŏkchun   張德俊
Chang Tŏksu   張德秀
Chang Tuhyŏn   張斗鉉
Chang Yongsŏ   張龍瑞
Changhŭng Ko   長興高
Ch'anghŭng Ŭisuk   昌興義塾
Ch'angp'yŏng (country)   昌平
Changsŏng (country)   長城
ch'angssi   創氏
Chayudang   自由黨

Chin Hangmun   秦學文
Chin Tŏkkyu   陳德奎
chingnyu   織紐
chinsa   進士
Chinsan   珍山
Chisan (Kim Kyŏngjung)   芝山
ch'wich'eyŏk   取締役
Cho Chihun   趙芝薰
Cho Ch'ŏlho   趙喆鎬
Cho Kehyŏn   曹契鉉
Cho Mansik   曹晚植
Cho Pyŏngok   趙炳玉
Cho Soang   趙素昂
Cho Tonghŭi   趙東熙
Cho Tongsik   趙東植
Cho Wan'gu   趙琬九
Chōbō   朝紡
Ch'oe Ch'anghak   崔昌學
Ch'oe Cheu   崔濟愚
Ch'oe Chun   崔浚
Ch'oe Hyŏnbae   崔鉉培
Ch'oe Hyŏngyŏn   崔炯鍊
Ch'oe Kyudong   崔奎東
Ch'oe Namsŏn   崔南善
Ch'oe Rin   崔麟
Ch'oe Sŭngman   崔承萬
Ch'oe Tusŏn   崔斗善
Ch'oe Wŏnsun   崔元淳
Ch'oe Yongdal   崔容達
ch'oego wiwŏn   最高委員
chokcha   簇子(족자)

ch'okt'ak kangsa 囑託講師
Chŏlla (province) 全羅
Chŏn Pongjun 全琫準
Chŏn Yongsun 全用淳
Ch'ŏndogyo 天道敎
Chŏng Chinsŏk 鄭晋錫
Chŏng Keryang 鄭季良
Chŏng Kyunch'ŏl 鄭均轍
Chŏng Nosik 鄭魯湜
chŏngbo 町步
Chŏnju 定州
Chongnogu 鐘路區
Chŏn'gok 全谷
Chŏn'guk Haksaeng
    Haengdong T'ongil
    Yŏnmaeng
    全國學生行動統一聯盟
Chŏn'guk Pant'ak Haksaeng
    Yŏnmaeng
    全國反託學生聯盟
Chŏngsin 貞信
Chŏngŭp 井邑
Ch'ŏngwadae 青瓦臺
Chōsen Bōshoku 朝鮮紡織
Chosŏn (dynasty) 朝鮮
Chosŏn Chigwang 朝鮮之光
Chosŏn Ch'ŏngnyŏn
    Tongniptan
    朝鮮青年獨立團
Chosŏn Chungang Ilbo
    朝鮮中央日報
Chosŏn Ilbo 朝鮮日報

Chosŏn Inmin Konghwakuk
    朝鮮人民共和國
Chosŏn Kŏn'guk Chunbi
    Wiwŏnhoe
    朝鮮建國準備委員會
Chosŏn Kŏn'guk Tongmaeng
    朝鮮建國同盟
Chosŏn Minjoktang
    朝鮮民族黨
Chosŏn Minjok Ch'ŏngnyŏndan
    朝鮮民族青年團
Chosŏn Minjudang 朝鮮民主黨
Chosŏn Mulsan Changnyŏ
    朝鮮物産獎勵
Chosŏn Tongnip Shinmun
    朝鮮獨立新聞
Chosŏnŏ Hakhoe 朝鮮語學會
Chosŏnŏ Yŏn'guhoe
    朝鮮語研究會
Chosŏnsa 朝鮮史
Chu Sigyŏng 周時經
Chulp'o 茁浦
chumak 酒幕
chumu isa 主務理事
Ch'unch'ŏn 春川
Chungang Chip'aeng
    Wiwŏnhoe
    中央執行委員會
Chungang Hakkyo 中央學校
Chungang Sanggong Chusik
    Hoesa
    中央商工株式會社

Chungangch'ŏng　中央廳
Ch'ungch'ŏng (province)　忠清
Chungch'uwŏn　中樞源
Ch'ungmuro　忠武路
chusik hoesa　株式會社
Endō Ryūsaku　遠藤柳作
Fuji(Mt)　富士
Fuminkan　府民館
Fukuzawa Yukichi　福澤諭吉
gakumu kyokuchō　學務局長
Ha P'ilwŏn　河弼源
Haejo Shinmun　海潮新聞
Haejŏ-ri　海底里
haknyŏn　學聯
hakpyŏng　學兵
Hakt'ong　學統
haktopyŏng　學徒兵
Ham Sanghun　咸尙勳
Ham T'aeyŏng　咸台永
hammyŏng hoesa　合名會社
Han Kiak　韓基岳
Han Man Nyun [Manyŏn]
　韓萬年
Han Sŭngi　韓承履
Han Woo-keun [Ugŭn]
　韓㳓劤
Han Yongun　韓龍雲
Handoktang　韓獨黨
Han'guk Kungmindang
　韓國國民黨
Han'guk Minjudang
　韓國民主黨

Han'guk Tongniptang
　韓國獨立黨
han'gŭl　한글
Hansŏng Kyowŏn Yangsŏngso
　漢城敎員養成所
Hansŏng Sunbo　漢城旬報
Hanyang Chŏnmun Hakkyo
　漢陽專門學校
Hideyoshi Toyotomi　豊臣秀吉
Hŏ Chŏng　許政
Hŏ Hŏn　許憲
Honam　湖南
Honam Hakhoe　湖南學會
Honam Hakhoe Wŏlbo
　湖南學會月報
Honam Hakpo　湖南學報
Hong Myŏnghŭi　洪命憙
Hong Sŏngha　洪性夏
Hŭngdŏk　興德
Hŭngsadan　興士團
Hwadong　花洞
hwajŏk　火賊
Hwanghae (province)　黃海
Hwangsŏng Shinmun
　皇城新聞
Hwan'guk Chisa Huwŏnhoe
　還國志士後援會
Hwimun Ŭisuk　徽文義淑
Hyŏn Chin'gŏn　玄鎭健
Hyŏn Chunho　玄俊鎬
Hyŏn Sangyun　玄相允
Hyŏnp'ung　玄風

Ilchinhoe 一進會
Ilmunji 日文紙
Im Chŏngyŏp 林正燁
Im Pyŏngch'ŏl 林炳哲
Im Yŏngshin [Louis Yim]
　任永信
Imo Kullan 壬午軍亂
Inch'on (Kim Sŏngsu) 仁村
Inch'ŏn 仁川
Inch'on-ri 仁村里
injŏlmi 인절미
isa 理事
Itō Hirobumi 伊藤博文
Kabo Kyŏngjang 甲午更張
Kaebyŏk 開闢
Kaehwadang 開化黨
kaehwasasang 開化思想
kaekchu 客主
kama 가마(니)
kamsa 監事
kamsayŏk 監事役
Kang Kidŏk 康基德
Kang Pyŏngsun 姜柄順
Kang Tongjin 姜東鎮
Kanghwa (Treat of) 江華
Kangwŏn (province) 江原
Kapsin Chŏngbyŏn 甲申政變
karosu 街路樹
kat(hat) 갓
Kedong 桂洞
Kejō Daiichi Kōtō Futue
　Gakkō

京城第一高等普通學校
Keijō Imperial University
　京城帝國大學
Keio (university) 慶應
kemu kyoku 警務局
Kesan (school) 桂山
Kiho Hakkyo 畿湖學校
Kiho Hŭnghakhoe 畿湖興學會
Kim Chaejung 金載重
Kim Chaesu 金在洙
Kim Ch'angsuk 金昌淑
Kim Ch'ŏlchung 金鐵中
Kim Chongik 金鍾翊
Kim Chŏngjin 金井鎮
Kim Chongo 金鐘五
Kim Chongwŏn 金宗元
Kim Chunyŏn 金俊淵
Kim Dae Jung [Taejung]
　金大中
Kim Hakjoon [Hakchun]
　金學俊
Kim Hwaran [Helen Kim]
　金活蘭
Kim Hyŏngwŏn 金炯元
Kim Ilhae 金一海
Kim Inhu 金麟厚
Kim Kijung 金祺中
Kim Ku 金九
Kim Kwangjin 金洸鎮
Kim Kyŏngjung 金暻中
Kim Kyusik 金圭植
Kim Myŏnghwan 金命煥

Kim Okkyun　金玉均

Kim Pyŏnggyu　金秉逵

Kim Pyŏngno　金炳魯

Kim Sanggi　金相琪

Kim Sangman　金相万

Kim Sinil　金信一

Kim Sŏnggon　金成坤

Kim Sŏn'gi　金善琪

Kim Sŏngsu　金性洙

Kim Sŭngmun　金勝文

Kim Tongsŏng　金東成

Kim Tongsŏp　金東燮

Kim Tongwŏn　金東元

Kim Toyŏn　金度演

Kim Uyŏng　金雨英

Kim Wŏnbong　金元鳳

Kim Yohyŏp　金堯莢

Kim Yŏngin　金永寅

Kim Yongmu　金用茂

Kim Yongsŏp　金用燮

Kim Yŏnsu　金秊洙

Kim Yŏsik　金麗植

Kim Young Sam [Yŏngsam]　金泳三

Kim Yun'gŭn　金潤根

Kim Yun'gyŏng　金允經

Kim Yunsik　金允植

Kimje (county) 金堤

Kinyŏm Saŏp Palgich'onghoe　記念事業發起總會

Kizokuin　貴族院

Ko Chaeuk　高在旭

Ko Chŏngju　高鼎柱

Ko Hŭidong　高義東

Ko Kwangjun　高光駿

Ko Kwangp'yo　高光表

Ko Kwangsŏk　高光錫

Ko Sŏkkyu　高錫珪

Ko Wŏnhun　高元勳

Ko Yŏnghwan　高永煥

Ko Yŏngsun　高永珣

Kobu　古阜

Kŏch'ang　巨昌

Koch'ang　高敞

kodŭng pot'ong hakkyo　高等普通學校

Koguryŏ (dynasty)　高句麗

Koh Byong-ik [Pyŏngik]　高炳翊

Kojong (king)　高宗

kōkoku shimminka　皇國臣民化

Koksŏng　谷城

komusin　고무신

Konghwa Minjŏnghoe　共和民政會

Kŏnmaeng　建盟

Koryang (county)　高陽郡

Koryŏ (dynasty)　高麗

Koryŏ (Korea) University　高麗大學校

Kōtō Keisatsu Yoshi　高等警察要史

Kukchagam　國子監

Kuk T'aeil 鞠泰一
Kŭmho Hakkyo 錦湖學校
Kŭmsan 金山
Kŭmsŏng Pangjik 金星紡織
kŭndaehwa 近代化
Kungmin Hoeŭi 國民會議
Kungmin Taehoe Chunbihoe
　國民大會準備會
Kungmindang 國民黨
Kunsan 群山
kunsu 郡守
Kwandong Hakhoe 關東學會
Kwangbokkun 光復軍
Kwangbokkun Ch'ongyŏng
　光復軍總營
Kwanghwamun 光化門
Kwŏn Tŏkkyu 權悳奎
Kwŏn Tongjin 權東鎭
kyeranŭro pawich'igi
　계란으로 바위치기
kyojang 校長
kyoji 校旨
Kyŏngbang 京紡
Kyŏnggi (province) 京畿
Kyŏnggyojang 京橋莊
Kyŏngmudae 景武臺
kyŏngmun 檄文
Kyŏngsang (province) 慶尙
Kyŏngsŏng Chingnyu
　京城織紐
Kyŏngsŏng Ch'ŏksik Kyŏngje
　Chŏnmun Hakkyo

京城拓植經濟專門學校
Kyŏngsŏng Pangjik 京城紡織
Kyŏngundong 慶雲洞
Kyujanggak 奎章閣
Lee Ki-baik [Yi Kibaek]
　李基白
Maeil Sinbo 每日申報
Mansebo 萬歲報
mansŏkkun 萬石君
Maruyama Tsurukichi
　丸山鶴吉
Match'umbŏp T'ongilan
　맞춤법 統一案
Meiji 明治
Min Yŏngdal 閔泳達
Minami Jirō 南次郎
Minguktang 民國黨
minjok 民族
"Minjokchŏk Kyŏngnyun"
　民族的經綸
"Minjok Kaejoron"
　民族改造論
Minjok T'ongil Ch'ong
　Ponbu
　民族統一總本部
Minju Kungmindang
　民主國民黨
Minjudang 民主黨
minjujuŭi 民主主義
Minjujuŭi Minjokchŏnsŏn
　民主主義 民族戰線
minjung 民衆

Minnip Taehak 民立大學
Minnip Taehak Kisŏng
  Chunbihoe
  民立大學期成準備會
Mitubashi Koichirō
  三橋孝一郎
Minzuno Rentarō 水野鍊太郎
Mokp'o 木浦
Mu Wang 武王
Mngunghwa 무궁화
Mujang 茂長
Mulsan Changyŏhoe
  物産奬勵會
munhwa chŏngch'i 文化政治
munhwajuŭi 文化主義
munkwa 文科
Munmaeng T'ap'a Undong
  文盲打破運動
musosok 無所屬
Myŏngwŏlgwan 明月館
Na Wŏnjŏng 羅原鼎
Naesosa 來蘇寺
Nagai Ryutarō 永井柳太郎
Naisen Ittai 內鮮一體
Nam Sangil 南相一
Nam Sŭngyong 南昇龍
Namchosŏn Kwado Ipŏp
  Ŭiwŏn
  南朝鮮過度立法議院
Namgung Hun 南宮薰
Namgung Ŏk 南宮檍
Namsan 南山

Nanshaku 男爵
Nissen Yūwa 日鮮融化
No Paekin 盧伯麟
O Ch'ŏnsŏk 吳天錫
O Sech'ang 吳世昌
O Yŏngsu 吳泳秀
Odoimmun 吳道入門
Ōkuma Shigenobu 大隈重信
Onmon Shinbun Touseian
  彦文新聞統制案
Ōno Rokuchirō 大野綠一郎
Osan (School) 吾山
Pae Sŏp 裵涉
Paek Kwansu 白寬洙
Paek Nakchun [George Paik]
  白樂濬
Paek Namhun 白南薰
Paek Namŏk 白南檍
Paek Unsŏn 白雲善
Paek Yongsŏng 白龍城
Paekche 百濟
Paeksan Hakkyo 白山學校
Paektusan 白頭山
Paekunjang 白雲壯
paji 바지
p'aji 破紙
p'aju 坡州
Pak Ch'anhŭi 朴瓚熙
Pak Ch'angha 朴昌夏
Pak Ch'un'gŭm 朴春琴
Pak Haedon 朴海敦
Pak Hŭido 朴熙道

Pak Hŭngsik　朴興植

Pak Ilbyŏng　朴逸秉

Pak Sŏkhyŏn　朴奭鉉

Pak Sŭngbin　朴勝彬

Pak Sŭngbong　朴勝鳳

Pak Ŭnsik　朴殷植

Pak Tongjin　朴東鎭

Pak Yonghyŭi　朴容喜

Pak Yŏnghyo　朴泳孝

Pang Ŭngmo　方應謨

Pangwigun　防衛軍

Pak Myong-Lim
　(Park Myŏngnim)
　박명림

Pibyŏnnanggong　備邊郞公

pimilgyŏlsa　秘密結社

Pisang Kungmin Hoeŭi
　非常國民會議

Pisŏwŏn　秘書院

Posŏng Chŏnmun Hakkyo
　普成專門學校

pot'ong hakkyo　普通學校

Pusan　釜山

Pyŏn Kwangho　邊光鎬

Pyŏn Yŏngt'ae　卞榮泰

p'yŏng　坪

P'yŏngan (province)　平安

P'yŏngyang　平壤

p'yŏnjip kamdok　編輯監督

P'yŏngŭiwŏnhoe　平議員會

sach'al kwanjang sil
　査察課長室

Sach'ŏn　沙川

sadae sasang　事大思想

Saiga Shichirō　齊賀七郞

Saitō Makoto　齊藤實

Samil Undong　三一運動

Samjŏnnon　三戰論

Samp'um (sampin)　三品

sangmu　常務

sangt'u　상투

sarang　사랑

Sejongno　世宗路

Sekiya Teizaburō　關屋貞三郞

Sidae Ilbo　時代日報

Sihŭng　始興

Siktowŏn　食道園

silhaeng wiwŏn　實行委員

Sim Hyŏngp'il　沈亨弼

Shin Akkyun　申樂均

Sin Chosŏn　新朝鮮

Sin Ikhŭi　申翼熙

Sin Kubŏm　愼九範

Sin Sŏgu　申錫雨

Sin Sŏngmo　申性模

Sinch'ŏnji　新天地

Sindonga　新東亞

Singajŏng　新家庭

Sinhan Ch'ŏngnyŏndang
　新韓青年黨

Sinhan Minbo　新韓民報

Shinhanminjoktang
　新韓民族黨

Sinminhoe　新民會

Sinsaenghwal 新生活
Sint'ak T'ongch'i Pandae
　　Kungmin Ch'ongdongwǒn
　　Wiwǒnhoe
　　信託統治反對
　　國民總動員委員會
sinǔi ilgwan　信義一貫
Sirhak　實學
Sǒ Chaep'il [Philip Jaison]
　　徐載弼
Sǒ Sangil　徐相日
Sǒ Yǒngho　徐永鎬
Sǒbuk Hakhoe　西北學會
Sǒdaemun　西大門
sǒdang　書堂
Sogongdong　小公洞
Sǒhak　西學
sǒk　石
Sǒl Ǔisik　薛義植
Son Chint'ae　孫晉泰
Son Kijǒng　孫基禎
Son Pyǒnghǔi　孫秉熙
sǒnbae　先輩
Song Ch'an'gyu　宋瓚圭
Song Chinu　宋鎭禹
Song Kebaek　宋繼白
Song Pyǒngjun　宋秉畯
Song Tǒksu　宋德洙
Songhyǒndong　松峴洞
sǒngsin　誠信
Sǒnu Hyǒk　鮮于爀
Ssangyong (group)　雙龍

sukchiksil　宿直室
Sungsil Chǒnmun Hakkyo
　　崇實專門學校
Sunjong (king)　純宗
susǒk ch'ongmu　首席總務
Suwǒn Kodǔng Nongrim
　　Hakkyo
　　水原高等農林學校
Taedong Ch'ǒngnyǒndan
　　大同青年團
Taedong Hakhoe　大同學會
Taegu　大邱
Taegǔksǒng　太極星
Taehan Chaganghoe Wǒlbo
　　大韓自强會月報
Taehan Cheguk　大韓帝國
Taehan Hyǒphoe　大韓協會
Taehan Kungmindang
　　大韓國民黨
Taehan Maeil Sinbo
　　大韓每日申報
Taehan Minbo　大韓民報
Taehan Min'guk　大韓民國
Taehan Min'guk Imsi Chǒngbu
　　大韓民國 臨時政府
Taehan Minguktang
　　大韓民國黨
Taehan Tongnip Ch'oksǒng
　　Kungminhoe
　　大韓獨立促成國民會
Taehan tongnip manse!
　　大韓獨立萬歲

T'aehwagwan　泰和館

Taejŏn　大田

Taewŏn'gun (Yi Haung)
　大院君

Taesŏng Hakkyo　大成學校

Tanaka Hozumi　田中穗積

tangsu　黨首

Terauchi Masatake　寺內正毅

T'oegye　退溪

tohangjŭng　渡航證

tojobu　賭租簿

Tonga Ilbo　東亞日報

Tongbok (Kijung)　同福

Tongdaemun　東大門

Tonghak (peasant rebellion)
　東學

Tongmyŏng　東明

Tongnip Hyŏphoe　獨立協會

Tongnip Sinmun　獨立新聞

Tongyang T'ongsin　東洋通信

Tumen (river)　頭滿江

turak　斗落

turumagi　두루마기

Ŭibyŏng　義兵

Ŭigŭmbu　義禁府

Ŭijŏngbu　議政府

ŭiri　義理

Ŭlsa Nŭngyak　乙巳凌約

Ulsan Kim　蔚山金

ungwŏn　雄遠

Wasaeda (university)　早稻田

wiwŏnjang　委員長

woeyu naegang　外柔內剛

Wŏn Sehun　元世勳

Wŏnnamdong　苑南洞

Wŏnp'a (Kim Kijung)　圓坡

Yalu (river)　鴨綠江

Yang Kit'ak　梁起鐸

Yang Wŏnmo　梁源模

yangban　兩班

yen　圓

Yi Aju　李娥珠

Yi Ch'ŏlsŭng　李哲承

Yi Ch'ŏngch'ŏn　李青天

Yi Chongil　李鍾一

Yi Chongrin　李鍾麟

Yi Chunghwa　李重華

Yi Hŭijik　李熙直

Yi Hŭisŭng　李熙昇

Yi Hwang　李滉

Yi Hyŏnhŭi　李炫熙

Yi In　李仁

Yi Insu　李仁秀

Yi Iru　李一雨

Yi Kanghyŏn　李康賢

Yi Kap　李甲

Yi Kapsŏng　李甲成

Yi Kiryong　李吉用

Yi Kŭngno　李克魯

Yi Kwangjong　李光鍾

Yi Kwangsu　李光洙

Yi Kwansul　李觀述

Yi Kyuyŏng　李奎榮

Yi Pŏmsŏk　李範奭

Yi P'ungjae 李豊載

Yi Pyŏnggi 李秉岐

Yi Pyŏnghŏn 李炳憲

Yi Sangbŏm 李象範

Yi Sangdon 李相敦

Yi Sanghyŏp 李相協

Yi Sangjae 李商在

Yi Siyŏng 李始榮

Yi Sŏgu 李瑞求

Yi Sŏngjun 李成俊

Yi Sŏnho 李先鎬

Yi Sŭnghun 李昇薰

Yi Sŭngman [Syngman Rhee] 李承晚

Yi Ukkyu 李禹珪

Yi Un 李雲

Yi Wisang 李胃相

Yi Yonggu 李容九

Yi Yongik 李容翊

Yi Yŏngjun 李榮俊

Yi Yongsŏl 李容卨

Yi Yunjae 李允宰

Yi Yunyŏng 李允榮

Yŏ Unhyŏng 呂運亨

yogang 요강

Yŏm Sangsŏp 廉想涉

Yŏm T'aejin 廉台振

Yŏnch'ŏn (county) 連川

Yŏngdŭngp'o 永登浦

yonggyŏn 勇堅

Yŏngnam Hakhoe 嶺南學會

yŏngŏp kukchang 營業局長

Yŏngsin Hakkyo 永信學校

Yŏnhap Shinmun 聯合新聞

Yŏnhapkun Hwanyŏng Chunbi Wiwŏnhoe 聯合軍歡迎準備委員會

Yonhŭi Chŏnmun Hakkyo 延禧專門學校

Yŏnjŏnghoe 硏政會

Yŏsŏng 女性

Yŏsŏngdonga 女性東亞

Yu Chino 兪鎭午

Yu Chint'ae 兪鎭泰

Yu Kilchun 兪吉濬

Yu Kŭn 柳瑾

Yu Kwangyŏl 柳光烈

Yu Kyŏngsang 劉敬相

Yu Myŏnhŭi 柳冕熙

Yu Ŏkkyŏm 兪億兼

Yu Sŏngjun 兪星濬

Yu T'aero 劉泰魯

Yu Wŏnp'yo 劉元杓

Yuilgwan 唯一館

Yujiyŏnmaeng 有志聯盟

Yuksip Manse 六十萬歲

Yun Ch'iho 尹致昊

Yun Ch'iso 尹致昭

Yun Ch'iyŏng 尹致暎

Yun Iksŏn 尹益善

Yun Kiik 尹基益

Yun Kisŏ 尹基瑞

Yun Kisŏp 尹琦燮

Yun Posŏn 尹潽善

Yun Sangŭn 尹相殷   Yurim　儒林

Yun T'aekchung　尹宅重

NOTES

Acknowledgments

1. Most prominent Koreans have pen names (*ho* in Korean). Traditionally, young people in Korea may not address older people by their actual names. Thus, pen names are widely used, for anyone, regardless of seniority; everyone may be addressed by a pen name. Kim Sŏngsu's pen name, Inch'on, is the name of his home village and means "benevolent" or "virtuous."

2. Ch'oe Sijung, *Inch'on Kim Sŏngsu: Inch'on Kim Sŏngsu sasang kwa ilhwa* [Kim Sŏngsu's thoughts and anecdotes] (Seoul: Tonga Ilbosa, 1985); Kohasŏnsaeng Chŏn'gi P'yŏnch'an Wiwŏnhoe, *Tongnip ŭl hyanghan chimnyŏm: Koha Song Chinu chŏn'gi* [The will to national liberation: A portrait of Song Chinu] (Seoul: Tonga Il-bosa, 1990); Kim Hakjoon [Hakchun], *Koha Song Chinu p'yŏngjŏn: Minjokchuŭi ŏllonin. Chŏngch'iga ŭi saengae* [A critical biography of Song Chinu: A journalist and a states-man: The life and times of a Korean nationalist democrat] (Seoul: Tonga Ilbosa, 1990); Ko Chaeuk, ed., *Inch'on Kim Sŏngsujŏn* [The biography of Kim Sŏngsu] (Seoul: Inch'on Kinyŏmhoe, 1976); Kwŏn Ogi, ed., *Inch'on Kim Sŏngsu ŭi aejok sasang kwa kŭ silch'ŏn* [The patriotism of Kim Sŏngsu in thought and deed] (Seoul: Tonga Ilbosa, 1982); Sin Ilch'ŏl, ed., *P'yŏngjŏn Inch'on Kim Sŏngsu* [A critical biography of Kim Sŏngsu] (Seoul: Tonga Ilbosa, 1991); Yu Chino, *Yanghogi* [Teaching at Korea University] (Seoul: Korea University Press, 1977).

3. See Yun Chaegŭn, *Kŭnch'on Paek Kwansu* [Paek Kwansu] (Seoul: Tonga Il-bosa, 1996).

4. Han Kiak (1897–1941), a pioneer Korean journalist, worked for three major newspapers, *Tonga Ilbo, Sidae Ilbo,* and *Chosŏn Ilbo.* Before his journalism career, however, he worked in behalf of the anti-Japanese independence movement, specifically during the March First Movement in 1919 in Siberia, Tokyo, and Shanghai. See Han Man Nyun, *Irŏp ilsaeng* (Only one job for a lifetime), expanded 2nd edition (Seoul: Il-chokak, 1994), pp. 9–16.

5. Ibid., 382–83.

Introduction

1. Michael Edson Robinson, *Cultural Nationalism in Colonial Korea, 1920–1925* (Seattle: University of Washington Press, 1988), p. 57.

2. Carter J. Eckert, *Offspring of Empire: The Koch'ang Kims and the Colonial Origins of Korean Capitalism, 1876–1945* (Seattle: University of Washington Press, 1991), p. 17.

3. The validity of the "life history," a major method in anthropology has been demonstrated in many anthropological studies. See L. L. Langness, *The Life History in Anthropological Science* (New York: Holt, Rinehart and Winston, 1965).

4. Pertti J. Pelto, *Anthropological Research: The Structure of Inquiry* (New York: Harper & Row, 1970), p. 99.

5. Ibid. Also, this point is well illustrated in John Stands-IN-Timber and Margot Liverty, *Cheyenne Memories* (New Haven: Yale University Press, 1967).

6. Cho Chihun, *Han'guk munhwa sa taege* (A great heritage of Korean cultural history) (Seoul: Minjokmunhwa Yŏn'guso, Korea University, 1970), p. 737; Kang Chujin, "Inch'on ŭi tongnipsasang kwa nosŏn" [Kim Sŏngsu's thought and direction for Korean independence], in *Inch'on Kim Sŏngsu ŭi aejok sasang kwa kŭ sil'ch'ŏn* [The patriotism of Kim Sŏngsu in thought and deed], ed. Kwŏn Ogi, 15–84 (Seoul: Tonga Ilbosa, 1982).

7. Kang, "Inch'on ŭi tongnipsasang kwa nosŏn," pp. 41–42.

8. See the details on An Ch'angho in Chu Yohan, *Andosan chŏnsŏ* [The complete book on An Ch'angho] (Seoul: Samjungdang, 1963).

9. John K. Fairbank, Edwin O. Reischauer, and Albert M. Craig, *East Asia: The Modern Transformation: A History of East Asian Civilization* (Boston: Houghton Mifflin, 1965), 2: 628.

10. Ibid.

11. See Ko, *Inch'on Kim Sŏngsujŏn,* p. 300.

12. Eckert, *Offspring of Empire,* pp. 36–37.

13. Kim Sŏngsu, "Ōkuma Shigenobu wa Chosŏn yuhaksaeng" (Ōkuma Shigenobu and Korean students in Japan), *Samch'ŏlli* 6 (May 1934): 96–99.

14. Shannon McCune, *Korea: The Land of Broken Calm* (New York: D. Van Nostrand, 1966).

15. Choong Soon Kim, *Faithful Endurance: An Ethnography of Korean Family Dispersal* (Tucson: University of Arizona Press, 1988).

16. Sui forces attacked Korea in A.D. 598 and A.D. 612. During the military invasions by the T'ang dynasty of China in the seventh century, many Korean captives from Paekche and Koguryŏ were taken to and relocated throughout China as slaves (Hyŏn Kyuwhan, *Han'guk yuiminsa* [A history of Korean wanderers and emigrants], 2 vols. [Seoul: Ōmungak, 1967], 1: 50–51).

17. During the medieval period of the Koryŏ dynasty (918–1392), scores of people were captured by the Khitans and were taken to Khitan territory. One Khitan province, for instance, included nearly five thousand people from Koryŏ, composing their own province (Hyŏn, *Han'guk yuiminsa,* vol. 1: 55). The most devastating family dispersals occurred during the Mongol invasions of the Koryŏ reign in 1253, 1257, and 1273. During the rule of King Kojong (1213–59) of Koryŏ, 206,000 Koryŏ civilians were captured by the Mongols (ibid., 57–60). After the invasion, the Mongols not only engaged in royal marriages, but also took unmarried females of Koryŏ, most of whom became concubines or slaves of the Yüan emperor and Mongol aristocrats in Beijing (ibid., 68).

18. Japanese pirates during the thirteenth and fourteenth centuries captured some four thousand Koreans and took them to Japan as prisoners (ibid., 2: 273–91). See also, Yoshi S. Kuno, *Japanese Expression on the Asiatic Continent,* 2 vols. (Berkeley: University of California Press, 1937), 1: 176; Edward W. Wagner, *The Korean Minority in Japan: 1904–1950* (New York: Institute of Pacific Relations, 1951), p. 6. Although the Japanese pirates were troublesome, the Japanese attacks on Korea from 1590 to 1597, under the leadership of Hideyoshi Toyotomi, were devastating. Hideyoshi's forces invaded Korea, resulting in a massive number of casualties and captives. The occupational list of those taken captive included highly skilled workmen and artisans such as weavers and porcelain manufacturers. They even captured priests and Confucian scholars. See Mary Elizabeth Berry, *Hideyoshi* (Cambridge, Mass.: Harvard University Press, 1982); Chang-soo Lee and George De Vos, *Koreans in Japan: Ethnic Conflict and Accommodation* (Berkeley: University of California Press, 1981), p. 14.

19. Gregory Henderson, *Korea: The Politics of the Vortex* (Cambridge, Mass.: Harvard University Press, 1968), p. 13.

20. Lee Ki-baik, *Tonga Ilbo,* January 1, 1994.

21. The ideas of the School of Practical Learning took shape in the seventeenth and eighteenth centuries and displayed a broad and varied approach to the reform of Chosŏn dynasty institutions. As a pragmatic scholarship, this school of thought required a pragmatic methodology, and sought always for explicit verification. The major goal of the Practical Learning scholars was to illuminate the history and contemporary workings of political, economic, and social institutions.

22. See the origins of enlightenment thought in Ki-baik Lee (Yi Kibaek), *A New History of Korea*, trans. Edward W. Wagner with Edward J. Schultz (Seoul: Ilchokak, 1984), p. 255. See also Lee Kwangrin (Yi Kwangrin), *Han'guk kaehwasa yŏn'gu* (A study in the history of enlightenment in Korea) (Seoul: Ilchokak, 1993).

23. On *yangban,* see Vincent S. R. Brandt, *A Korean Village: Between Farm and Sea* (Cambridge, Mass.: Harvard University Press, 1971), pp. 11–12; Martina Deuchler, *The Confucian Transformation of Korea: A Study of Society and Ideology* (Cambridge, Mass.: Council on East Asian Studies, Harvard University, 1992), pp. 12–13, 309n22; Takashi Hatada, *A History of Korea,* ed. and trans. W. W. Smith, Jr., and B. H. Hazard (Santa Barbara, Calif.: American Bibliographic Center, 1969), p. 103; Choong Soon Kim, *The Culture of Korean Industry: An Ethnography of Poongsan Corporation* (Tucson: University of Arizona Press, 1992), pp. 14, 32–33; Cornelius Osgood, *The Koreans and Their Culture* (New York: Ronald Press, 1951), p. 44.

24. Martina Deuchler, *Confucian Gentlemen and Barbarian Envoys: The Opening of Korea, 1875–1885* (Seattle: University of Washington Press, 1977), p. xii. A comprehensive study on *Kabo* reform may be found in Lew Young Ick (Yu Yŏngik), *Kabo kyŏngjang yŏn'gu* (Studies on the *Kabo* reform movement) (Seoul: Ilchokak, 1990).

25. Yi Hyŏnhŭi, ed., *Tonghak sasang kwa Tonghak hyŏngmyŏng* (The thought of Tonghak and Tonghak revolution) (Seoul: Ch'ŏnga Ch'ulp'ansa, 1984).

26. Lee, *A New History of Korea,* p. 304.

27. The creation of *han'gŭl,* an indigenous alphabet for Korean people, was initiated by King Sejong (1418–1450) of the early Chosŏn dynasty, and was promulgated in 1446.

28. Fairbank et al., *East Asia,* p. 5.

29. Émile Durkheim, *The Division of Labor in Society* (Glencoe, Ill.: Free Press, 1947); Henry Sumner Maine, *Ancient Law* (New York: Dutton, 1965); Robert Redfield, "The Folk Society," *American Journal of Sociology* 52 (1947): 293–308; Ferdinand Tünnies, *Community and Society,* ed. and trans. Charles P. Loomis (New York: Harper Torchbooks, 1963); Max Weber, *The Theory of Social and Economic Organization,* trans. A. H. Henderson and Talcott Parsons (New York: Free Press of Glencoe, 1957).

30. Kim, *The Culture of Korean Industry,* p. 199.

31. Marion J. Levy, Jr., *Modernization and Structure of Society* (Princeton, N.J.: Princeton University Press, 1966), p. 11.

32. Robert E. Cole, *Japanese Blue Collar: The Changing Tradition* (Berkeley: University of California Press, 1971), p. 7.

33. Fairbank et al., *East Asia,* p. 10.

34. Richard M. Steers, Shin Yoo Keun, and Gerardo R. Ungson, *The Chaebol: Korea's New Industrial Might* (New York: Harper & Row, 1989), p. 129.

35. Fairbank et al., *East Asia,* p. 9.

36. Deuchler, *Confucian Gentlemen and Barbarian Envoys,* p. 223.

37. S. N. Eisenstadt, *Modernization: Protest and Change* (Englewood Cliffs, N.J.: Prentice-Hall, 1966), p. 1.

38. Deuchler, *Confucian Gentlemen and Barbarian Envoys*, xii; LewYoung Ick, *Kabo Kyŏngjang yŏn'gu* (Studies on the *Kabo* reform movement) (Seoul: Ilchokak, 1990), p. 2.

39. Norman Jacobs, *The Korean Road to Modernization and Development* (Urbana: University of Illinois Press, 1985), p. 6.

40. Ko, *Inch'on Kim Sŏngsujŏn*, p. 469. See also Sin Ilch'ŏl, "Han'guk kŭndaehwa ŭi sŏn'gakcha Inch'on Kim Sŏngsu ŭi saengae" (Kim Sŏngsu's career as a leader of Korean modernization), in *P'ŏngjŏn Inch'on Kim Sŏngsu* (A critical biography of Kim Sŏngsu), ed. Sin Ilch'ŏl, 15–73 (Seoul: Tonga Ilbosa, 1991).

41. The concept of nationalism is broad and inclusive. See Karl Deutsch, *Nationalism and Social Communication* (Cambridge, Mass.: MIT Press, 1953); Carlton Hayes, *The Historical Evolution of Modern Nationalism* (New York: Macmillan, 1967); Elie Kedourie, *Nationalism* (London: Hutchison, 1960); Hans Kohn, *The Idea of Nationalism* (New York: Macmillan, 1967); Chong-sik Lee, *Politics of Korean Nationalism* (Berkeley: University of California Press, 1964); Robinson, *Cultural Nationalism in Korea, 8–9*; Anthony Smith, *Theories of Nationalism* (New York: Holmes and Meier, 1983); Arthur N. Waldron, "Theories of Nationalism," *World Politics* 37 (1985): 416–31.

42. Robinson, *Cultural Nationalism in Korea*, p. 15.

43. Ibid., 48; See also Dae-sook Suh, *The Korean Communist Movement, 1918–1948* (Princeton, N.J.: Princeton University Press, 1967), pp. 8–9.

44. Kosaku Yoshino, *Cultural Nationalism in Contemporary Japan: A Sociological Inquiry* (London: Routledge, 1992), p.1.

45. Ibid.

46. Robinson, *Cultural Nationalism in Korea*, p. 74.

47. Ibid.

48. Yoshino, *Cultural Nationalism in Contemporary Japan*, p. 1.

49. Robinson, *Cultural Nationalism in Korea*, p. 100.

50. Eckert, *Offspring of Empire*, p. 47.

51. Kang Tongjin, *Ilcheŭi Han'guk ch'imnyak chŏngch'aeksa* (History of the Japanese imperial policy of aggression in Korea) (Seoul: Han'gilsa, 1980), pp. 170, 397n48.

52. Kim, *Koha Song Chinu p'yŏngjŏn*, p. 173.

53. Yu, *Yanghogi*, p. 87.

54. Robinson, *Cultural Nationalism in Colonial Korea*, passim.

1. A Long Journey from Premodern to Modern

1. According to Cornelius Osgood, before Japanese annexation in 1910, Korean females did not receive proper names other than surnames and nicknames such as "Small baby," "Flat face," "Pretty," etc. See Osgood, *The Koreans and Their Culture*, p. 50. Apparently, Sŏngsu's mother, Lady Ko, did not receive her proper name. It is unknown whether she had a nickname.

2. Yi Hwang explicated neo-Confucianism in Korea and exerted great influence on Confucian scholarship in Japan, which eventually became one of the mainstreams in Japanese Confucian thought.

3. Kim Hwangjung, ed. *Ulsan Kimssi chokpo* (The Ulsan Kim genealogy), 3 vols. (Changsŏng, Korea: Kim Hwangjung, 1977). See also Kim Yongsŏp, *Han'guk kŭnhyŏndae nongŏpsa yŏn'gu: Hanmal-ilcheha ŭi chijuje wa nongŏp munje* (Studies in the agrarian history of twentieth-century Korea: Landlordism and agrarian conflicts in modern Korea) (Seoul: Ilchokak, 1992), pp. 174–75.

4. Kim, *Han'guk kŭnhyŏndae nongŏpsa yŏn'gu*, pp. 175–76.

5. Unlike the practice of Americans, in Korea women retain their maiden names even after their marriages.

6. Ko, *Inch'on Kim Sŏngsujŏn*, p. 44.

7. Ibid., p. 58.

8. Eckert, *Offspring of Empire*, pp. 21–22; Kim Sangha, ed., *Sudang Kim Yŏnsu* (Kim Yŏnsu) (Seoul: Samyangsa, 1985), pp. 34–41; Kim, *Han'guk kŭnhyŏndae nongŏpsa yŏn'gu*, pp. 177–78.

9. Kim, *Han'guk kŭnhyŏndae nongŏpsa yŏn'gu*, p. 177n8.

10. Eckert, *Offspring of Empire*, p. 21.

11. Kim, *Han'guk kŭnhyŏndae nongŏpsa yŏn'gu*, pp. 178, 191–227.

12. Eckert, *Offspring of Empire*, p. 26.

13. Kim, *Han'guk kŭnhyŏndae nongŏpsa yŏn'gu*, p. 185.

14. Eckert, *Offspring of Empire*, p. 32.

15. On the enlightenment movement see Deuchler, *Confucian Gentlemen and Barbarian Envoys*, pp. 151–52; Vipan Chandra, *Imperialism, Resistance, and Reform in Late Nineteenth-Century Korea: Enlightenment and the Independence Club* (Berkeley: Institute of East Asian Studies, University of California at Berkeley, 1988).

16. Lee, *A New History of Korea*, p. 336.

17. Kim, *Han'guk kŭnhyŏndae nongŏpsa yŏn'gu*, pp. 185–233.

18. Kang, "Inch'on ŭi tongnip sasang kwa nosŏn," pp. 25–26.

19. Ko, *Inch'on Kim Sŏngsujŏn*, pp. 56–58.

20. Ibid., p. 57.

21. Kang, "Inch'on ŭi tongnip sasang kwa nosŏn," pp. 29–30; Sin Yongha, "Iljeha Inch'on ŭi minjok kyoyuk hwaldong (Activities of Kim Sŏngsu for national education under Japanese colonization), in *P'yŏngjŏn Inch'on Kim Sŏngsu* (A critical biography of Kim Sŏngsu), ed. Sin Ilch'ŏl, pp. 237–66 (Seoul: Tonga Ilbosa, 1991), pp. 240–41.

22. Japanese writing had a long dependency on Chinese ideograms, *kanji*, but these were now supplemented by *kana*, a phonetic Japanese script based on simplified Chinese ideograms; *katakana*, a mnemonic device using parts of Chinese ideograms; and *hirakana*, a cursive form from *katakana* writing and an art form in itself.

23. Ko, *Inch'on Kim Sŏngsujŏn*, pp. 56–57.

24. Yoshino, *Cultural Nationalism in Contemporary Japan*, p. 1.

25. Kim, *Sudang Kim Yŏnsu*, pp. 47–58.

26. Ko, *Inch'on Kim Sŏngsujŏn*, pp. 68–70.

27. Ibid., pp. 86–87.

28. Ibid., pp. 77–78.

29. Kang, "Inch'on ŭi tongnip sasang kwa nosŏn," p. 35.

30. Ko, *Inch'on Kim Sŏngsujŏn*, pp. 81–82.

31. Ibid., pp. 82–83.

32. Ibid.

33. Ibid., p. 83.

34. Ibid.

35. Ibid., p. 84.

36. Ibid.

2. Education as a Means for Korean Modernization

1. Lee, *A New History of Korea*, p. 332.

2. In 1886, the Paejae School and several other private institutions were founded by American missionary organizations. Also in 1886, U.S. missionaries opened Korea's first educational institution for women.

3. Ko, *Inch'on Kim Sŏngsujŏn*, p. 91.

4. Ibid., p. 97; Sin, "Iljeha Inch'on ŭi minjok kyoyuk hwaldong," p. 244.

5. Lee, *A New History of Korea*, p. 336.

6. Chungang Kyouhoe, *Chungang yuksimnyŏnsa* (Sixty-year history of Chungang School) (Seoul: Chungang Kyouhoe, 1969), pp. 17–86.

7. Ibid.

8. Ko, *Inch'on Kim Sŏngsujŏn*, p. 100.

9. Ibid., p. 102.

10. Ibid, pp. 102–3.

11. Ibid., p. 103.

12. Ibid.

13. Ibid., p. 104.

14. Ibid., p. 105; Sin, "Iljeha Inch'on ŭi minjok kyoyuk hwaldong," pp. 247–48; Kuksa P'yŏnch'an Wiwŏnhoe, ed., *Han'guk tongnip undong saryo* (Historical documents on Korean independence movement) (Seoul: Kuksa P'yŏnch'an Wiwŏnhoe, 1968), 4: 175–76.

15. Ko, *Inch'on Kim Sŏngsujŏn*, p. 104.

16. Pak Kyŏngsik, *Ilbon chegukchuŭi Chosŏn chibae* (Japanese imperial control over Korea) (Seoul: Ch'ŏnga Ch'ulp'ansa, 1986), pp. 151–52.

17. While Kim's biography indicates the land Kim bought for Chungang School was 4,300 *p'yŏng* (Ko, *Inch'on Kim Sŏngsujŏn*, p. 109), *The Sixty-Year History of Chungang* indicates 4,311 *p'yŏng* (Chungang Kyouhoe, *Chungang yuksimnyŏnsa*, p. 83).

18. Ko, *Inch'on Kim Sŏngsujŏn*, p. 109.

19. Chungang Kyouhoe, *Chungang yuksimnyŏnsa*, pp. 82–83.

20. Chin Tŏkkyu, "Inch'on Kim Sŏngsu ŭi chŏngch'i inyŏme taehan sasangjŏk ihae" (An understanding of the conception of the political ideology of Kim Sŏngsu), in *P'yŏngjŏn Inch'on Kim Sŏngsu* (A critical biography of Kim Sŏngsu), ed. Sin Ilch'ŏl (Seoul: Tonga Ilbosa, 1991), pp. 89–91.

21. Ibid., pp. 85–86.

22. Ko, *Inch'on Kim Sŏngsujŏn*, p. 118.

23. Personal interview with Yun T'aekchung, June 14, 1991.

24. Chungang Kyouhoe, *Chungang yuksimnyŏnsa*, pp. 202–3.

25. Ibid., pp. 199–201.

26. Yi Hyŏnhŭi, "Samil undong kwa Inch'on Kim Sŏngsu" (The March First Movement and Kim Sŏngsu), in *P'yŏngjŏn Inch'on Kim Sŏngsu* (A critical biography of Kim Sŏngsu), ed. Sin Ilch'ŏl, pp. 197–236 (Seoul: Tonga Ilbosa, 1991), p. 215.

27. Chin, "Inch'on Kim Sŏngsu ŭi chŏngch'i inyŏme taehan sasangjŏk ihae," p. 44.

28. Ch'oe Hyŏngyŏn, "Samil undong kwa Chungang Hakkyo" (The March First Movement and Chungang School), in *Samil undong osipchunyŏn kinyŏm nonjip* (Collected essays for the 50th commemoration of the March First Movement), ed. Ko Chaeuk

(Seoul: Tonga Ilbosa, 1969), pp. 313–24; Chungang Kyouhoe, *Chungang yuksimnyŏnsa,* pp. 92–101.

29. Frank Baldwin calls Ch'oe Rin the driving force behind the March First Movement. See Frank Prentiss Baldwin, "The March First Movement: Korean Challenge and Japanese Response" (Ph.D. diss., Columbia University, 1969), pp. 54, 247n22, 249–50n33.

30. "In Korea, relationships between *sŏnbae* (senior) and *hubae* (junior) in school are analogous to the relationships between older and younger brothers, and they even address each other using kinship terms of older and younger brother. The *senpai-kohai* (senior-junior) relationships of the Japanese are similar, and both use the same Chinese characters" (Kim, *The Culture of Korean Industry,* p. 50).

31. Ch'oe, "Samil undong kwa Chungang Hakkyo," p. 319; Chungang Kyouhoe, *Chungang yuksimnyŏnsa,* pp. 96–97.

32. Baldwin, "The March First Movement," pp. 54, 247n22, 249–50n33.

33. Yi Pyŏnghŏn, "Naegabon samil undong ŭi ildanmyŏn" (A slice of the March First Movement that I saw), in *Samil undong osipchunyŏn kinyŏm nonjip* (Collected essays for the 50th commemoration of the March First Movement), ed. Ko Chaeuk, pp. 407–11 (Seoul: Tonga Ilbosa, 1969), p. 411.

34. Ch'oe, "Samil undong kwa Chungang Hakkyo," p. 320.

35. Hyoŏn Sangyun, "Samil undong palbal ŭi kaeyo" (A brief summary of the outbreak of the March First Movement), *Sasangge* (March 1963): 44–49. The original article was published under the title "Samil undong ŭi hwoesang" (Recollection of the March First Movement) in *Sinch'ŏnji* (1946).

36. An Kehyŏn, "Samil undong kwa pulgyoge" (The March First Movement and the Buddhist circles), in *Samil undong osipchunyŏn kinyŏm nonjip* (Collected essays for the 50th commemoration of the March First Movement), ed. Ko Chaeuk (Seoul: Tonga Ilbosa, 1969), pp. 271–80.

37. Hŏ Sŏndo, "Samil undong kwa yugyoge" (The March First Movement and the Confucianist circles), in *Samil undong osipchunyŏn kinyŏm nonjip* (Collected essays for the 50th commemoration of the March First Movement), ed. Ko Chaeuk (Seoul: Tonga Ilbosa, 1969), pp. 281–300.

38. Kim Taesang, "Samil undong kwa haksaengch'ŭng" (The March First Movement and student circles), in *Samil undong osipchunyŏn kinyŏm nonjip* (Collected essays for the 50th commemoration of the March First Movement), ed. Ko Chaeuk (Seoul: Tonga Ilbosa, 1969), pp. 301–11.

39. Chŏng Yosŏp, "Samil undong kwa yŏsŏng" (The March First Movement and women), in *Samil undong osipchunyŏn kinyŏm nonjip* (Collected essays for the 50th commemoration of the March First Movement), ed. Ko Chaeuk (Seoul: Tonga Ilbosa, 1969), pp. 335–44.

40. Yi, "Samil undong kwa Inch'on Kim Sŏngsu," p. 219.

41. Hyoŏn, "Samil undong palbal ŭi kaeyo," pp. 44–49.

42. Yi, "Samil undong kwa Inch'on Kim Sŏngsu," pp., 226, 235n121.

43. Ko, *Inch'on Kim Sŏngsujŏn*, p. 134.

44. Ch'oe, "Samil undong kwa Chungang Hakkyo," pp. 321–22.

45. Japanese authorities were responsible for the "incident of 105 persons." When Resident-General (*Tokan*) Terauchi Masatake was to conduct an inspection visit of P'yŏngan province in December 1910, it had been rumored that there would be an assassination attempt. As a result, from September 1911 to March 1912, the Japanese authorities arrested 600 Koreans, and convicted and finally sentenced 105 Korean nationalists. As it turned out, the rumor was unfounded, but it gave the Japanese authorities a pretext to foment a repressive antinationalist campaign. See Kang Chaeŏn, *Sinp'yŏn Han'guk kŭndaesa yŏn'gu* (A newly edited studies of modern Korean history) (Seoul: Hanul, 1986), pp. 402–3).

46. Ch'oe, "Samil undong kwa Chungang Hakkyo," p. 322; Yi, "Samil undong kwa Inch'on Kim Sŏngsu," p. 227.

47. Chin, "Inch'on Kim Sŏngsu ŭi chŏngch'i inyŏme taehan sasangjŏk ihae," pp. 91–92.

48. Chŏng Sehyŏn, "6.10 manse undong" (The June Tenth independence movement), in *Han'guk kŭndaesaron* (Discussion of modern Korean history), ed. Yun Pyŏngsok, Sin Yŏngha, and An Pyŏngjik (Seoul: Chisik Sanopsa, 1977), 2: 401–38.

49. Ibid., p. 425; Chungang Kyouhoe, *Chungang yuksimnyŏnsa*, pp. 126–27.

3. Establishment of an Enterprise for Korean Modernization

1. Woo-keun Han, *The History of Korea* (Seoul: Eul-Yoo, 1981), p. 476.

2. Ibid.

3. Ko, *Inch'on Kim Sŏngsujŏn*, p. 135.

4. See Han, *The History of Korea*, p. 479; see also Lee, *A New History of Korea*, pp. 346–47.

5. Lee, *A New History of Korea*, pp. 347–50.

6. Ibid., p. 355.

7. While Kim's biography and Hwang Myŏngsu date the founding of the Kyŏngsŏng Cord Company as 1911, Carter J. Eckert and Pak state that it was founded in 1910. See Pak Inhwan, ed., *Kyŏngbang yuksimnyŏn* (Sixty years of Kyŏngbang) (Seoul: Kyŏngbang, 1980), p. 50; Eckert, *Offspring of Empire*, p. 28; Hwang Myŏngsu, "Inch'on Kim Sŏngsu ŭi kiŏp hwaldong kwa kyŏngyŏnginyŏm" (Business activity and

management ideology of Kim Sŏngsu), in *P'yŏngjŏn Inch'on Kim Sŏngsu* (A critical biography of Kim Sŏngsu), ed. Sin Ilch'ŏl, pp. 267–308 (Seoul: Tonga Ilbosa, 1991), p. 279; Ko, *Inch'on Kim Sŏngsujŏn*, p. 155.

8. Hwang Myŏngsu is incorrect to state that the first president was Yun Ch'iho (Hwang, "Inch'on Kim Sŏngsu ŭi kiŏp hwaldong kwa kyŏngyŏnginyŏm," p. 279). The president was Yun Ch'iso, the first cousin of Yun Ch'iho.

9. Pak, *Kyŏngbang yuksimnyŏn*, pp. 50–51; Hwang, "Inch'on Kim Sŏngsu ŭi kiŏp hwaldong kwa kyŏngyŏnginyŏm," pp. 279–80; Kwŏn T'aeŏk, *Han'guk kŭndae myŏnŏpsa yŏn'gu* (A study of the history of the modern Korean cotton industry) (Seoul: Ilchokak, 1989), p. 68.

10. Ko, *Inch'on Kim Sŏngsujŏn*, p. 157.

11. Pak, *Kyŏngbang yuksimnyŏn*, p. 51; Hwang, "Inch'on Kim Sŏngsu ŭi kiŏp hwaldong kwa kyŏngyŏnginyŏm," p. 282.

12. Hwang, "Inch'on Kim Sŏngsu ŭi kiŏp hwaldong kwa kyŏngyŏnginyŏm," p. 283; see also Cho Kijun, "Han'guk minjok kiŏp kŏnsŏl ŭi sasangjŏk paegyŏng: Inch'on Kim Sŏngsu ŭi minjok kiŏp hwaldong" (The intellectual background behind the establishment of Korean nationalist businesses: The nationalist business activities of Kim Sŏngsu), in *Inch'on Kim Sŏngsu ŭi aejok sasang kwa kŭ silch'ŏn* (The patriotism of Kim Sŏngsu in thought and deed), ed. Kwŏn Ogi, pp. 85–155 (Seoul: Tonga Ilbosa, 1982).

13. Eckert, *Offspring of Empire*, p. xiii.

14. Ibid., p. 281n66; see also Hochin Choi, "The Process of Industrial Modernization in Korea," *Journal of Social Sciences and Humanities* 26 (1967): 1–33; Sang-Chul Suh, *Growth and Structural Changes in the Korean Economy, 1910–1940* (Cambridge, Mass.: Council on East Asian Studies, Harvard University, 1978), pp. 7–10.

15. Cho, "Han'guk minjok kiŏp kŏnsŏl ŭi sasangjŏk paegyŏng," p. 114.

16. Ko, *Inch'on Kim Sŏngsujŏn*, pp. 159–60.

17. See Cho Kijun, *Han'guk chabonjuŭi sŏngnipsaron* (Discourses on the formative history of Korean capitalism) (Seoul: Taewangsa, 1977), p. 496.

18. Hwang, "Inch'on Kim Sŏngsu ŭi kiŏp hwaldong kwa kyŏngyŏnginyŏm," pp. 280–81.

19. Cho, *Han'guk chabonjuŭi sŏngnipsaron*, p. 497.

20. Hwang, "Inch'on Kim Sŏngsu ŭi kiŏp hwaldong kwa kyŏngyŏnginyŏm," p. 291.

21. Ibid., 299; Ch'ilsimnyŏn P'yŏnjipsil, *Koryŏ Taehakkyo ch'ilsimnyŏnji* (Seventy-year history of Korea University) (Seoul: Korea University Press, 1978), p. 117.

22. Eckert, *Offspring of Empire*; idem., "The Colonial Origins of Korean Capitalism." Also see Dennis L. McNamara, *The Colonial Origins of Korean Enterprise, 1910–1945* (New York: Cambridge University Press, 1990); idem., "The Keishō and

the Korean Business Elite," *Journal of Asian Studies* 48 (1989): 310–23; idem.,"Enterpreneurship in Colonial Korea: Kim Youn-su," *Modern Asian Studies* 22 (1988): 165–77.

23. Ko, *Inch'on Kim Sŏngsujŏn*, p. 161.

24. Cho Kijun indicates, however, that the first stockholders' meeting took place in May 1919 instead of October 5, 1919. See Cho Kijun, *Han'guk kiŏpkasa* (A history of Korean entrepreneurs) (Seoul: Pagyŏngsa, 1983), p. 255.

25. Ko, *Inchon Kim Sŏngsujŏn*, p. 162–64; Hwang, "Inch'on Kim Sŏngsu ŭi kiŏp hwaldong kwa kyŏngyŏnginyŏm," p. 286.

26. Hwang, "Inch'on Kim Sŏngsu ŭi kiŏp hwaldong kwa kyŏngyŏnginyŏm," p. 286.

27. Ibid.

28. Eckert, *Offspring of Empire*, pp. 74–75.

29. Hwang, "Inch'on Kim Sŏngsu ŭi kiŏp hwaldong kwa kyŏngyŏnginyŏm," p. 286.

30. Harold F. Cook, "Pak Yong-hyo: Background and Early Years," *Journal of Social Sciences and Humanities* 31 (1969): 11–24; Lee, *A New History of Korea*, pp. 275–78, 293–94.

31. See Eckert, *Offspring of Empire*, pp. 97–99.

32. Cho, *Han'guk chabonjuŭi sŏngipsaron*, p. 496; Cho, "Han'guk minjok kiŏp kŏnsŏl ŭi sasangjŏk paegyŏng," pp. 145–46; Daniel S. Juhn, "Nationalism and Korean Businessmen," in *Korea's Response to Japan: The Colonial Period, 1910–1945*, Korean Studies Series no. 5., ed. C. I. Eugene Kim and Doretha E. Mortimore (Kalamazoo: Center for Korean Studies, Western Michigan University, 1977), pp. 42–52.

33. Eckert, *Offspring of Empire*, p. 78.

34. Ko, *Inch'on Kim Sŏngsujŏn*, pp. 162–63.

35. Hwang, "Inch'on Kim Sŏngsu ŭi kiŏp hwaldong kwa kyŏngyŏnginyŏm," p. 287.

36. Pak, *Kyŏngbang yuksimnyŏn*, p. 52.

37. Ko, *Inch'on Kim Sŏngsujŏn*, p. 168.

38. Pak, *Kyŏngbang yuksimnyŏn*, p. 60–62.

39. Ibid.

40. Ibid., p. 169.

41. Ibid.

42. Ibid., p. 170.

43. Ibid., p. 171.

44. Pak, *Kyŏngbang yuksimnyŏn*, p. 62.

45. Ibid., pp. 67–69.

46. Eckert, *Offspring of Empire*, p.81.

47. Ibid., p. 84.

48. *Tonga Ilbo*, June 11, 1922.

49. Pak, *Kyŏngbang yuksimnyŏn*, p. 65.

50. Eckert, *Offspring of Empire*, p. 58.

51. Hwang, "Inch'on Kim Sŏngsu ŭi kiŏp hwaldong kwa kyŏngyŏnginyŏm," p. 291.

52. Eckert, *Offspring of Empire*, p. 77.

53. Ibid., p. 177.

54. Ibid.

55. Personal interview with Song Ch'an'gyu, June 20, 1991.

56. Lee, *A New History of Korea*, p. 355.

57. Eckert, *Offspring of Empire*, idem., "The Colonial Origins of Korean Capitalism"; see also McNamara, *The Colonial Origins of Korean Enterprise*.

4. Publishing the *Tonga Ilbo*

1. Lee, *A New History of Korea*, p. 330.

2. Ibid.

3. Chŏng Chinsŏk, "Ŏllonin Inch'on Kim Sŏngsu" (Journalist Kim Sŏngsu), in *P'yŏngjŏn Inch'on Kim Sŏngsu* (A critical biography of Kim Sŏngsu), ed. Sin Ilch'ŏl, pp. 309–38 (Seoul: Tonga Ilbosa, 1991), p. 313.

4. Ko, *Inch'on Kim Sŏngsujŏn*, p. 174.

5. Chŏng, "Ŏllonin Inch'on Kim Sŏngsu," p. 317; Yu Kwangyŏl, *Kija pansegi* (As a reporter for half a century) (Seoul: Sŏmundang, 1970), pp. 272–76.

6. Kim Sŏngsu, "Nan'gwan ŭn tugaji" (Two obstacles); *Pyŏlgŏngon* (February 1927), p. 12; see also Chŏng, "Ŏllonin Inch'on Kim Sŏngsu," pp. 318–19.

7. Ko, *Inch'on Kim Sŏngsujŏn*, pp. 175–76.

8. Kim Sangman, ed., *Tonga Ilbo sasa* (History of the *Tonga Ilbo*), vol. 1 (Seoul: Tonga Ilbosa, 1975), p. 87.

9. Ibid., p. 74.

10. Ibid., pp. 90–96.

11. Ibid., p. 95.

12. The original "Chujirŭl sŏnmyŏng hanora" (The purpose or principle of publishing the paper), *Tonga Ilbo*, April 1, 1920.

13. Robinson, *Cultural Nationalism in Colonial Korea*, p. 53.

14. Ch'oe Chun, "Ilchŏngha ŭi minjok ŏllon: *Tonga Ilbo* wa Inch'on" (National press under Japanese rule: The *Tonga Ilbo* and Kim Sŏngsu), in *Inch'on Kim Sŏngsu ŭi aejok sasang kwa kŭ shilch'ŏn* (The patriotism of Kim Sŏngsu in thought and action). ed. Kwŏn Ogi, pp. 156–203 (Seoul: Tonga Ilbosa, 1982), pp. 169–70.

15. Robinson, *Cultural Nationalism in Colonial Korea*, p. 52.

16. Chŏng, "Ŏllonin Inch'on Kim Sŏngsu," p. 321.

17. Robinson, *Cultural Nationalism in Colonial Korea*, p. 51.

18. Ibid., p. 52.

19. Kim, *Tonga Ilbo sasa*, 1: 125–31.

20. Chŏng, "Ŏllonin Inch'on Kim Sŏngsu," pp. 324–25; see also Chŏng Chinsŏk, *Han'guk hyŏndae ŏllonsa* (History of the modern Korean press) (Seoul: Chŏnyewŏn, 1985).

21. Deuchler, *The Confucian Transformation of Korea*, p. 26.

22. Kim, *Tonga Ilbo sasa*, 1: 138.

23. Ko, *Inch'on Kim Sŏngsujŏn*, pp. 193–94.

24. Ibid., pp. 194–95.

25. Harumi Befu, *Japan: An Anthropological Introduction* (New York: Thomas Y. Crowell, 1971), pp. 29-30.

26. Kim, *Tonga Ilbo sasa*, 1: 149–52.

27. Yu, *Yanghogi*, p. 64.

28. Ko, *Inch'on Kim Sŏngsujŏn*, p. 200.

29. Kim, *Tonga Ilbo sasa*, 1: 161.

30. Ibid., p. 163.

31. Ibid., p. 163–66.

32. Ibid., 1: 182–85.

33. Ko, *Inch'on Kim Sŏngsujŏn*, p. 240.

34. Chŏng, "Ŏllonin Inch'on Kim Sŏngsu," pp. 327-28.

35. Lee, *A New History of Korea*, p. 328.

36. Carter J. Eckert, Ki-baik Lee, Young Ick Lew, Michael Robinson, and Edward W. Wagner, *Korea Old and New: A History* (Seoul: Ilchokak, 1990), p. 290.

37. Robinson, *Cultural Nationalism in Colonial Korea*, p. 95.

38. Kim, *Tonga Ilbo sasa*, 1: 215–20.

39. *Tonga Ilbo*, February 3, 1922.

40. Kim, *Tonga Ilbo sasa*, 1: 215–16; Kohasŏnsaeng Chŏn'gi P'yŏnch'an Wiwŏnhoe, *Tongnip ŭl hyanghan chimnyŏm*, pp. 221–22.

41. Song Chinu was then the president of the *Tonga Ilbo*, not the editor-in-chief.

42. Eckert et al., *Korea Old and New*, p. 291.

43. Kohasŏnsaeng Chŏn'gi P'yŏnch'an Wiwŏnhoe, *Tongnip ŭl hyanghan chimnyŏm*, p. 223.

44. Eckert et al., *Korea Old and New*, p. 291.

45. Robinson, *Cultural Nationalism in Colonial Korea*, p. 86.

46. Kim, *Tonga Ilbo sasa*, 1: 217–20.

47. Eckert et al., *Korea Old and New*, p. 291.

48. Kim, *Tonga Ilbo sasa*, 1: 220.

49. Ibid.

50. Ko, *Inch'on Kim Sŏngsujŏn*, p. 245.

51. "Cho had come in contact with the Gandhian ideas of non-violence and self-sufficiency while attending college in Japan" (Eckert et al., *Korea Old and New*, p. 292).

52. Kim, *Tonga Ilbo sasa*, 1: 211.

53. Ko, *Inch'on Kim Sŏngsujŏn*, p. 246.

54. Kim, *Tonga Ilbo sasa*, 1: 215.

55. Ko, *Inch'on Kim Sŏngsujŏn*, pp. 247–50.

56. Ibid., pp. 260–64.

57. *Tonga Ilbo*, January 1–5, 1924.

58. Yi's *Kyŏngnyun* is well summarized by Robinson. See Robinson, *Cultural Nationalism in Colonial Korea*, p. 140.

59. Yi Kwangsu, "Minjok kaejoron" (Treatise on the reconstruction of the nation), *Kaebyŏk* 3 (May 1922): 18–72.

60. Robinson points out the similarities and differences between the Korean cultural nationalists' independence movement and that of the Indians. See Robinson, *Cultural Nationalism in Colonial Korea*, p. 105.

61. One original copy of *Kōtō Keisatsu Yoshi*, missing a few back pages, was kept by Cho Chihun, and another copy, missing a few front pages, was kept by Chang Kihong. Chang finally combined the two copies and reproduced them in photocopied form in 1970. See Keishōhokudō Keisatsubu, *Kōtō keisatsu yoshi: Bōtoshi henshū shiryo* (A major history of High Police: The editorial materials for the history of rioters) (Keijō: Keishōhokudō Keisatsubu, 1934).

62. Kim, *Tonga Ilbo sasa*, 1: 221–25.

63. Ibid., pp. 223–25.

64. Ko, *Inch'on Kim Sŏngsujŏn*, pp. 275–76.

65. Ibid., pp. 276–77.

66. Kim, *Tonga Ilbo sasa*, 1: 235–38.

67. Ko, *Inch'on Kim Sŏngsujŏn*, p. 287.

68. Ibid., p. 293.

69. Kim, *Tonga Ilbo sasa*, 1: 292–94.

70. Han'gŭl Hakhoe, *Han'gŭl hakhoe osimnyŏnsa* (Fifty-year history of the Korean Language Society) (Seoul: Han'gŭl Hakhoe, 1971).

71. Ko, *Inch'on Kim Sŏngsujŏn*, p. 379.

72. Ch'oe Hyoŏnbae, "Inch'on ŭl urŭm" (Weeping for Kim Sŏngsu), *Tonga Ilbo*, February 25, 1955.

73. The date and source of the picture vary according to Japanese and Korean accounts. In this book, the information is based on the recollection of Chang Yongsŏ, a reporter for the social section of the *Tonga Ilbo* who handled the photograph (Kim, *Tonga Ilbo sasa*, 1: 364).

74. Ko, *Inch'on Kim Sŏngsujŏn*, p. 387.

75. Kim, *Tonga Ilbo sasa*, 1: 364–65.

76. Ibid., pp. 364–68.

77. Kohasŏnsaeng Chŏn'gi P'yŏnch'an Wiwŏnhoe, *Tongnip ŭl hyanghan chimnyŏm*, pp. 364–65.

78. This document was discovered in the Japanese Library of Congress by Ko Sŏkkyu in March 1994.

79. Ko, *Inch'on Kim Sŏngsujŏn*, pp. 411–14.

80. Ibid., pp. 414–15.

81. Kim, *Tonga Ilbo sasa*, 1: 384–85.

82. Ibid., pp. 385–86.

83. Ibid., pp. 387–88.

84. Ibid., p. 388.

85. Ibid., p. 389.

86. Ko, *Inch'on Kim Sŏngsujŏn*, p. 420.

87. Kim Hakjoon gives the detailed background of Song's assassination (Kim, *Koha Song Chinu p'yŏngjŏn*, pp. 346–78).

88. See Kim Sanggi, ed., *Tonga Ilbo sasa* (History of the *Tonga Ilbo*), vol. 3 (Seoul: Tonga Ilbosa, 1985).

5. The Establishment of Koryŏ (Korea) University for Higher Education

1. See Robinson, *Cultural Nationalism in Colonial Korea*, pp. 107–36.

2. Ko, *Inch'on Kim Sŏngsujŏn*, p. 339.

3. See Ch'ilsimnyŏn P'yŏnjipsil, *Koryŏ Taehakkyo ch'ilsimnyŏnji*; see also Hong Ilsik, ed., *Koryŏ Taehak ŭi saram tŭl: Kim Sŏngsu* (People of Korea University: Kim Sŏngsu) (Seoul: Minjokmunhwa Yŏn'guso, Korea University, 1986), 3: 127–59.

4. Ko, *Inch'on Kim Sŏngsujŏn*, pp. 341–42.

5. Ibid., pp. 342–43.

6. *Tonga Ilbo*, March 8, 1932.

7. Ko, *Inch'on Kim Sŏngsujŏn*, pp. 344–45.

8. Yu, *Yanghogi*, p. 9.

9. Ko, *Inch'on Kim Sŏngsujŏn*, p. 346.

10. Ibid., p. 359.

11. Ibid., pp. 355–57.

12. Ibid., p. 358.

13. Ibid., p. 358.

14. Robinson, *Cultural Nationalism in Colonial Korea*, p. 88.

15. Ko, *Inch'on Kim Sŏngsujŏn*, p. 359.

16. Ibid., pp. 362–64.

17. Ibid., p. 370.

18. Ibid., p. 369–70.

19. Paek Nakchun, "Inch'on Kim Sŏngsu wa minjok kyoyuk" (Kim Sŏngsu and national education), in *Inch'on Kim Sŏngsu ŭi aejok sasang kwa kŭ silch'ŏn* (The patriotism of Kim Sŏngsu in thought and deed), ed. Kwŏn Ogi, pp. 207–20 (Seoul: Tonga Ilbosa, 1982), pp. 219–20.

20. Kim, *Faithful Endurance*, p. 23.

21. Ibid., p. 24.

22. Ibid., pp. 24, 153n.38; and see also George Hicks, *The Comfort Women* (St. Leonards, Australia: Allen and Unwin, 1995); Chunghee Sarah Soh, "The Korean 'Comfort Women': Movement for Redress," *Asian Survey* 36 (1996): 1226–40.

23. Choong Soon Kim, *An Asian Anthropologist in the South: Blacks, Indians, and Whites* (Knoxville: University of Tennessee Press, 1977), p. 3.

24. Ko, *Inch'on Kim Sŏngsujŏn*, p. 408.

25. Ibid., p. 409.

26. Yu, *Yanghogi*, p. 81.

27. Ko, *Inch'on Kim Sŏngsujŏn*, pp. 409–10.

28. Yu, *Yanghogi*, p. 80.

29. Ko, *Inch'on Kim Sŏngsujŏn*, p. 409.

30. Dennis L. McNamara writes: "Pak [Hŭngsik] was born in South P'yŏngan Province near Chinamp'o in northwest Korea in 1903. He parlayed some family holdings into local printing and cotton investments. He moved to Seoul in 1926 and quickly established Sŏnil Paper Goods. The company's success led to a further investment in his famous and widely successful Hwasin Department Store on Chongno Avenue in Seoul. Pak organized firms for domestic wholesaling and retailing, trading ventures in China and Southeast Asia, and held minority shares in other joint-stock firms. He led the Hwasin chaebŏl through the liberation and the First Republic in the south under Syngman Rhee, specializing in trade and textile production" (McNamara, *The Colonial Origin of Korean Enterprise*, p. 180).

31. Eckert, *Offspring of Empire*, p. 333n.70.

32. Ko, *Inch'on Kim Sŏngsujŏn*, p. 410.

33. Eckert, *Offspring of Empire*, pp. 245–46.

34. Ibid., p. 247.

35. Ko, *Inch'on Kim Sŏngsujŏn*, p. 431.

36. Ibid.

37. Eckert quotes from and has appended the full text of the article in the November 6, 1943, issue of *Maeil Sinbo* (Eckert, *Offspring of Empire*, pp. 262–64).

38. See Ibid., p. 248.

39. Yu, *Yanghogi*, pp. 114–17.

40. Ko, *Inch'on Kim Sŏngsujŏn*, pp. 433–34.

41. Yu, *Yanghogi*, p. 115.

42. Ibid., pp. 115–16.

43. Bruce Cumings, *The Origins of the Korean War: Liberation and the Emergence of Separate Regimes, 1945–1947* (Princeton, N.J.: Princeton University Press, 1941), p. 148.

44. Yu, *Yanghogi*, pp. 115–16.

45. Personal interview with Yi Ch'ŏlsŭng on June 11, 1991, in his office in Seoul, Korea.

46. Ibid.

47. Yi Ch'ŏlsŭng, *Chŏn'guk hangnyŏn* (National student league) (Seoul: Chungang Ilbo and Tongyang Pangsong, 1976), pp. 20–21.

48. Yi Ch'ŏlsŭng, "Inch'on ŭl paro alja" (Let's understand Kim Sŏngsu correctly), *Tonga Ilbo*, July 15, 1989.

49. Eckert, *Offspring of Empire*, pp. 333–34n.70.

50. Sŏnggok Chŏn'gi Kanhaeng Wiwŏnhoe, *Pyŏlil ŏpche: Sŏnggok Kim Sŏnggon sŏnsaeng ilhwajip* (No special problem: A collection of Kim Sŏnggon's anecdotes) (Seoul: Korea Herald, 1988), 2: 73.

51. Ibid., passim.

6. Kim Sŏngsu and His Involvement in Politics

1. Ko, *Inch'on Kim Sŏngsujŏn*, pp. 478, 664.

2. Ibid., p. 765.

3. Kohasŏnsaeng Chŏn'gi P'yŏnch'an Wiwŏnhoe, *Tongnip ŭl hyanghan chimnyŏm*, pp. 425–27.

4. Ko, *Inch'on Kim Sŏngsujŏn*, p. 461.

5. Kohasŏnsaeng Chŏn'gi P'yŏnch'an Wiwŏnhoe, *Tongnip ŭl hyanghan chimnyŏm*, p. 428 cf. Bruce Cumings reports that the colonial authorities approached Song Chinu on August 9 at an unidentified Japanese home. See Cumings, *The Origins of the Korean War*, p. 70.

6. Kohasŏnsaeng Chŏn'gi P'yŏnch'an Wiwŏnhoe, *Tongnip ŭl hyanghan chimnyŏm*, p. 427.

7. Cumings, *The Origins of the Korean War*, p. 70.

8. Ko, *Inch'on Kim Sŏngsujŏn*, pp. 463–64.

9. Ibid.

10. Cumings, *The Origins of the Korean War*, pp. 474–75n.14.

11. Ibid., p. 71.

12. Ibid.

13. Ko, *Inch'on Kim Sŏngsujŏn*, pp. 465–66.

14. Ibid., p. 470; Kohasŏnsaeng Chŏn'gi P'yŏnch'an Wiwŏnhoe, *Tongnip ŭl hyanghan chimnyŏm*, p. 442.

15. Ko, *Inch'on Kim Sŏngsujŏn*, pp. 474–75; Kohasŏnsaeng Chŏn'gi P'yŏnch'an Wiwŏnhoe, *Tongnip ŭl hyanghan chimnyŏm*, pp. 449–51.

16. Cumings, *The Origins of the Korean War*, p. 84.

17. Yi Man'gyu, *Yŏ Unhyŏngsŏnsaeng t'ujaengsa* (History of Yŏ Unhyŏng's struggles) (Seoul: Minjumunhwasa, 1946), p. 260.

18. Eckert et al., *Korea Old and New*, p. 331.

19. Kohasŏnsaeng Chŏn'gi P'yŏnch'an Wiwŏnhoe, *Tongnip ŭl hyanghan chimnyŏm*, pp. 456–57.

20. Ibid., p. 458.

21. Cumings, *The Origins of the Korean War*, p. 96.

22. Ibid., p. 126.

23. Henderson, *Korea*, p. 121.

24. Ko, *Inch'on Kim Sŏngsujŏn*, p. 479.

25. Paek, "Inch'on Kim Sŏngsu wa minjok kyoyuk," pp. 216–17.

26. Ibid., pp. 217–18.

27. Ibid., p. 218.

28. Ko, *Inch'on Kim Sŏngsujŏn*, p. 479.

29. Cumings, *The Origins of the Korean War*, p. 147.

30. The date of the welcoming ceremony varies. While Cumings reports that it was on October 20 (ibid., 150), Song Chinu's biography dates it October 10 (Kohasŏnsaeng Chŏn'gi P'yŏnch'an Wiwŏnhoe, *Tongnip ŭl hyanghan chimnyŏm*, p. 465).

31. Cumings, *The Origins of the Korean War*, p. 150.

32. Kohasŏnsaeng Chŏn'gi P'yŏnch'an Wiwŏnhoe, *Tongnip ŭl hyanghan chimnyŏm*, p. 471.

33. Ko, *Inch'on Kim Sŏngsujŏn*, p. 485.

34. Ibid., pp. 485–86.

35. Han, *The History of Korea*, p. 500.

36. Kohasŏnsaeng Chŏn'gi P'yŏnch'an Wiwŏnhoe, *Tongnip ŭl hyanghan chimnyŏm*, pp. 482–84.

37. Ibid., p. 481.

38. Cumings, *The Origins of the Korean War*, p. 150.

39. Cumings reports that Song was assassinated two hours after the meeting that lasted until 4:00 A.M. (ibid., p. 219).

40. Ko, *Inch'on Kim Sŏngsujŏn*, p. 497.

41. Yi T'aekhwi, "Pulgap'i han sŏnt'aek: Chŏngch'i chidoja ŭi kil" (Unavoidable choice: The way of a political leader), in *P'yŏngjŏn Inch'on Kim Sŏngsu* (A critical biography of Kim Sŏngsu), ed. Sin Ilch'ŏl, pp. 339–421 (Seoul: Tonga Ilbosa, 1991), p. 370.

42. Ibid., p. 371.

43. Ibid., pp. 374–75.

44. Ko, *Inch'on Kim Sŏngsujŏn*, pp. 516–17.

45. Lee, *A New History of Korea*, p. 377.

46. Ko, *Inch'on Kim Sŏngsujŏn*, p. 506.

47. Ibid., pp. 530–31.

48. Yi Kyŏngnam, *Sŏlsan Chang Tŏksu* (Chang Tŏksu) (Seoul: Tonga Ilbosa, 1982).

49. Ko, *Inch'on Kim Sŏngsujŏn*, p. 532.

50. Yi, "Pulgap'i han sŏnt'aek," p. 384.

51. Ko, *Inch'on Kim Sŏngsujŏn*, pp. 538–39.

52. Ibid., pp. 542–43.

53. Yi, "Pulgap'i han sŏnt'aek," pp. 392–93.

54. Sim Chiyŏn, "Han'guk minjudang ŭi ch'angdang" (Establishment of the Korean Democratic Party), in *Han'guk ŭi chŏngdang* (Korean political party), vol. 1, ed. Yi Kiha, Sim Chiyŏn, Han Chŏngil, and Son Pongsuk (Seoul: Han'guk Ilbosa, 1987), pp. 192–93.

55. Ibid.

56. Cumings, *The Origins of the Korean War*, p. 235.

57. Yu, *Yanghogi*, p. 219.

58. Ibid., pp. 214–15.

59. Ibid., p. 218.

60. Ko, *Inch'on Kim Sŏngsujŏn*, p. 546.

61. Ibid., p. 547.

62. Yu, *Yanghogi*, p. 219.

63. Ibid.

64. Sim, "Han'guk minjudang ŭi ch'angdang," p. 195.

65. Yu, *Yanghogi*, pp. 218–19.

66. Ko, *Inch'on Kim Sŏngsujŏn*, p. 550.

67. Ibid., p. 553.

68. Personal interview with Yun T'aekchung, July 14, 1991, in Seoul, Korea.

69. Han Chŏngil reports that it was Chi Ch'ŏngch'on instead of Yi Ch'ŏngch'on. See Han Chŏngil, "Minju kungmindang ch'ulbŏm kwa 6.25 chŏn chŏnghwang" (The selling of the Democratic National Party and the political situation before June 25 [Korean War]), in *Han'guk ŭi chŏngdang* (Korean political party), vol. 1, ed. Yi Kiha, Sim Chiyŏn, Han Chŏngil, and Son Pongsuk (Seoul: Han'guk Ilbosa, 1987), p. 203.

70. Ko, *Inch'on Kim Sŏngsujŏn*, p. 574.

71. Ibid., p. 575.

72. Han reports that 201 seats were allocated for national assembly members (Han, "Minju kungmindang ch'ulbŏm kwa 6.25 chŏn chŏnghwang," 205). The correct number is 210.

73. Ko, *Inch'on Kim Sŏngsujŏn*, p. 576.

74. Ibid., p. 581.

75. The literature on the Korean War is relatively rich and is growing. A few important titles are: Roy E. Appleman, *United States Army in the Korean War: South to the Nakdong, North to the Yalu (June-November, 1950)* (Washington, D.C.: Office of the Chief of Military History, Department of the Army, 1961); Carl Berger, *The Korean Knot: A Military-Political History* (Philadelphia: University of Pennsylvania Press, 1957); Cumings, *The Origins of the Korean War*; Bruce Cumings, ed., *Child of Conflict: The Korean-American Relationship, 1943–1953* (Seattle: University of Washington Press, 1975);

Harold Joyce Noble, *Embassy at War* (Seattle: University of Washington Press, 1975); David Rees, *Korea: The Limited War* (New York: St. Martin's Press, 1964); John W. Riley and Wilbur Schramm, *The Reds Take a City: The Communist Occupation of Seoul, with Eyewitness Accounts* (New Brunswick, N.J.: Rutgers University Press, 1951); Michael C. Sandusky, *America's Parallel* (Alexandria, Va.: Old Dominion Press, 1983).

76. I. F. Stone, *The Hidden History of the Korean War* (New York: Monthly Review Press, 1953), p. 44.

77. Park Myung-Lim (Pak Myŏngrim), *Han'guk chŏnjaengŭi palbalgwa kiwŏn* (The Korean War: The outbreak and its origins), 2 vols. (Seoul: Nanam, 1996).

78. Ko, *Inch'on Kim Sŏngsujŏn*, pp. 586–93.

79. Kim, *Faithful Endurance*, p. 32.

80. Republic of Korea National Red Cross, *The Dispersed Families in Korea* (Seoul: Republic of Korea National Red Cross, 1977), pp. 74–76.

81. Ko, *Inch'on Kim Sŏngsujŏn*, p. 599.

82. It was accidental yet surprising for me to meet Yi Insu's surving son, Lee Sung-Il (Yi Sŏngil), who is an English professor at Yonsei University. While we were having an idle talk, Lee graciously gave me a copy of his book, which was a translation of several Korean poems into English and published in the United States. See Sung-Il Lee, *The Wind and the Waves: Four Modern Korean Poets* (Berkeley: Asian Humanities Press, 1989). As I was glancing over the book, I found that in the appendix of the book there were two of my second cousin's poems that were translated by Yi Insu (romanized as Lee Insoo). I found out that he was Yi Insu's son after all. I told him that I heard about his father because he happened to be my brother's favorate teacher at Chungang.

83. Allen S. Whiting, *China Cross the Yalu: The Decision to Enter the Korean War* (Stanford: Stanford University Press, 1969), p. 118.

84. John Millet, Jr., Owen J. Carroll, and Margaret E. Tackley, *Korea, 1951–1953* (Washington, D.C.: U.S. Government Printing Office, 1956), p. 4.

85. Eckert et al., *Korea Old and New*, p. 348.

86. Ko, *Inch'on Kim Sŏngsujŏn*, pp. 611–12.

87. Ibid., pp. 612–14.

88. Ibid., p. 614.

89. Ibid., p. 627.

90. Although the representative was de facto an ambassador, there were no normalized relationships between Korea and Japan after the war until 1965, during the military government of Park Chung Hee (Pak Chŏnghŭi).

91. Ko, *Inch'on Kim Sŏngsujŏn*, p. 622.

92. Ibid., p. 623.

93. A personal interview with Pae Sŏp, June 28, 1991, in Seoul, Korea.

94. This idea came from Chang Kyŏnggŭn at a strategy session in Yi Kibung's residence after the vote (Ko, *Inch'on Kim Sŏngsujŏn*, p. 672).

7. The Legacy of Kim Sŏngsu

1. The harshest biography was written by a former *Tonga Ilbo* employee, Wi Kibung, who sold his manuscript to *Chungang Ilbo* for 8,000,000 *wŏn*. When *Chungang Ilbo* withheld publication for seven years, Wi contributed the manuscript to *Mal* magazine in 1989. See Wi Kibung, "Kim Sŏngsu ilga *Tonga Ilbo* karoch'aetta" (The Kims stole the *Tonga Ilbo*), *Mal* (March 1989): 34–48; idem., *Tasissŭnŭn Tonga Ilbo sa* (Re-writing history of the *Tonga Ilbo*) (Seoul: Nokchin, 1991); see also Ch'oe Minji and Kim Minju, *Iljeha minjok ŏllonsaron* (History of the Korean press under Japanese imperialism) (Seoul: Ilwŏlsŏgak, 1977); Kang, *Ilje ŭi Han'guk ch'imnyak chŏngch'aeksa*.

2. Nancy Ablemann, "The Practice and Politics of History: A South Korean Tenant Farmers' Movement" (Ph.D. diss., University of California at Berkeley, 1990); idem., *Echoes of the Past, Epics of Descent: A South Korean Social Movement* (Berkeley: University of California Press, 1996).

3. See *Kodae Sinmun* (The Korea University Weekly), May 1, 1995; *Minju Kwangjang* (Public square for democracy), May 1 (1995): 22–26.

4. Chin, "Inch'on Kim Sŏngsu ŭi chŏngch'i inyŏme taehan sasangjŏk ihae," pp. 76–77.

5. Ibid., p. 106.

6. Hong, *Koryŏ Taehak ŭi saram tŭl*, p. 74.

7. Yu, *Yanghogi*, pp. 73–74.

8. Personal interview with Yi Sangdon on July 4, 1991, in Seoul, Korea.

9. Lee and De Vos, *Koreans in Japan*, p.29.

10. Eckert et al., *Korea Old and New*, p. 263.

11. Ko, *Inch'on Kim Sŏngsujŏn*, pp. 438–40.

12. Fukuzawa Yukichi (1835–1901) is one of the most respected educators of the mid-Meiji period.

13. Ko, *Inch'on Kim Sŏngsujŏn*, pp. 438–40.

14. Ibid.

15. Eckert, *Offspring of Empire*, p. 241.

16. Chin, "Inch'on Kim Sŏngsu ŭi chŏngch'i inyŏme taehan sasangjŏk ihae," 100–1.

17. Edward S. Mason, Mahn Je Kim, Dwight H. Perkins, Kwang Suk Kim, and David C. Cole, *The Economic and Social Modernization of the Republic of Korea* (Cambridge, Mass.: Council on East Asian Studies, Harvard University, 1980), p. 457.

18. Chin, "Inch'on Kim Sŏngsu ŭi chŏngch'i inyŏme taehan sansangjŏk ihae," pp. 110–11.

19. Ko, *Inch'on Kim Sŏngsujŏn*, p. 689.

20. Chin, "Inch'on Kim Sŏngsu ŭi chŏngch'i inyŏme taehan sansangjŏk ihae," pp. 110–11.

21. Eckert, *Offspring of Empire*, p. 241.

22. Yu Chino, "Inch'on ŭi munhwajŏk chokchŏk" (Cultural footprint of Kim Sŏngsu), *Tonga Ilbo*, February 24, 1955.

23. Chin, "Inch'on Kim Sŏngsu ŭi chŏngch'i inyŏme taehan sansangjŏk ihae," pp. 75–112.

24. Yu, *Yanghogi*, p. 6.

25. Young-Iob Chung, "Review of: *Offspring of Empire: The Koch'ang Kims and the Colonial Origins of Korean Capitalism, 1876–1945* by Carter J. Eckert (Seattle: University of Washington Press, 1991)," *Journal of Asian Studies* 51 (1992): 184–85.

26. A personal interview with Pae Sŏp, June 28, 1991, in Seoul, Korea.

BIBLIOGRAPHY

Daily, weekly, and monthly newspapers are not included.

Abelmann, Nancy. "The Practice and Politics of History: A South Korean Tenant Farmers' Movement." Ph.D. diss., University of California at Berkeley, 1990.

——. *Echoes of the Past, Epics of Descent: A South Korean Social Movement.* Berkeley: University of California Press, 1996.

An Kehyŏn. "Samil undong kwa pulgyoge" (The March First Movement and the Buddhist circles). In *Samil undong osipchunyŏn kinyŏm nonjip* (Collected essays for the 50th commemoration of the March First Movement), edited by Ko Chaeuk, 271–80. Seoul: Tonga Ilbosa, 1969.

Appleman, Roy E. *United States Army in the Korean War: South to the Nakdong, North to the Yalu (June–November, 1950).* Washington, D.C.: Office of the Chief of Military History, Department of the Army, 1961.

Baldwin, Frank Prentiss. "The March First Movement: Korean Challenge and Japanese Response." Ph.D. diss., Columbia University, New York, 1969.

Befu, Harumi. *Japan: An Anthropological Introduction.* New York: Thomas Y. Crowell, 1971.

Berger, Carl. *The Korean Knot: A Military-Political History.* Philadelphia: University of Pennsylvania Press, 1957.

Berry, Mary Elizabeth. *Hideyoshi.* Cambridge, Mass.: Harvard University Press, 1982.

211

Brandt, Vincent S. R. *A Korean Village: Between Farm and Sea.* Cambridge, Mass.: Harvard University Press, 1971.

Chandra, Vipan. *Imperialism, Resistance, and Reform in Late Nineteenth-Century Korea: Enlightenment and the Independence Club.* Berkeley: Institute of East Asian Studies, University of California at Berkeley, 1988.

Ch'ilsimnyŏn P'yŏnjipsil. *Koryŏ Taehakkyo ch'ilsimnyŏnji* (Seventy-year history of Korea University). Seoul: Korea University Press, 1978.

Chin Tŏkkyu. "Inch'on Kim Sŏngsu ŭi chŏngch'i inyŏme taehan sasangjŏk ihae" (An understanding of the conception of the political ideology of Kim Sŏngsu). In *P'yŏngjŏn Inch'on Kim Sŏngsu* (A critical biography of Kim Sŏngsu), edited by Sin Ilch'ŏl, 75–148. Seoul: Tonga Ilbosa, 1991.

Cho Chihun. *Han'guk munhwa sa taege* (A great heritage of Korean cultural history). Seoul: Minjokmunhwa Yŏn'guso, Korea University, 1970.

Cho Kijun. *Han'guk kiŏpkasa* (A history of Korean entrepreneurs). Seoul: Pagyongsa, 1983.

———. "Han'guk minjok kiŏp kŏnsŏl ŭi sasangjŏk paegyŏng: Inch'on Kim Sŏngsu ŭi minjok kiŏp hwaldong" (The intellectual background behind the establishment of Korean nationalist businesses: The nationalist business activities of Kim Sŏngsu). In *Inch'on Kim Sŏngsu ŭi aejok sasang kwa kŭ silch'ŏn* (The patriotism of Kim Sŏngsu in thought and deed), edited by Kwŏn Ogi, 85–155. Seoul: Tonga Ilbosa, 1982.

———. *Han'guk chabonjuŭi sŏngnipsaron* (Discourses on the formative history of Korean capitalism). Seoul: Taewangsa, 1977.

Ch'oe Chun. "Ilchŏngha ŭi minjokŏllon: *Tonga Ilbo* wa Inch'on" (The national press under Japanese rule: The *Tonga Ilbo* and Kim Sŏngsu). In *Inch'on Kim Sŏngsu ŭi aejok sasang kwa kŭ silch'ŏn* (The patriotism of Kim Sŏngsu in thought and deed), edited by Kwŏn Ogi, 156–203. Seoul: Tonga Ilbosa, 1982.

Ch'oe Hyŏngyŏn. "Samil undong kwa Chungang Hakkyo" (The March First Movement and Chungang School). In *Samil undong osipchunyŏn kinyŏm nonjip* (Collected essays for the 50th commemoration of the March First Movement), edited by Ko Chaeuk, 313–24. Seoul: Tonga Ilbosa, 1969.

Ch'oe Minji and Kim Minju. *Iljeha minjok ŏllonsaron* (History of the Korean press under Japanese imperialism). Seoul: Ilwolsogak, 1977.

Ch'oe Sijung. *Inch'on Kim Sŏngsu: Inch'on Kim Sŏngsu sasang kwa ilhwa* (Kim Sŏngsu: Thoughts and anecdotes). Seoul: Tonga Ilbosa, 1985.

Choi, Hochin. "The Process of Industrial Modernization in Korea." *Journal of Social Sciences and Humanities* 26 (1967): 1–33.

Chŏng Chinsŏk. "Ŏllonin Inch'on Kim Sŏngsu" (Journalist Kim Sŏngsu). In *P'yŏngjŏn Inch'on Kim Sŏngsu* (A critical biography of Kim Sŏngsu), edited by Sin Ilch'ŏl, 309–38. Seoul: Tonga Ilbosa, 1991.

————. *Han'guk hyŏndae ŏllonsa* (History of the modern Korean press). Seoul: Chŏnyaewŏn, 1985.

Chŏng Sehyŏn. "6.10 manse undong" (The June Tenth Independence Movement). In *Han'guk kundaesaron* (Discussions of modern Korean history), edited by Yun Pyŏngsŏk, Sin Yongha, and An Pyŏngjik, 2: 401–38. Seoul: Chisik Sanŏpsa, 1977.

Chŏng Yosŏp. "Samil undong kwa yŏsŏng" (The March First Movement and women). In *Samil undong osipchunyŏn kinyŏm nonjip* (Collected essays for the 50th commemoration of the March First Movement), edited by Ko Chaeuk, 335–44. Seoul: Tonga Ilbosa, 1969.

Chu Yohan. *Andosan chŏnsŏ* (The complete book on An Ch'angho). Seoul: Samjung-dang, 1963.

Chung, Young-Iob. "Review of: Offspring of Empire: The Koch'ang Kims and the Colonial Origins of Korean Capitalism, 1876–1945, by Carter J. Eckert." *Journal of Asian Studies* 51 (1992): 184–85.

Chungang Kyouhoe, ed. *Chungang yuksimnyŏnsa* (Sixty-year history of Chungang School). Seoul: Chungang Kyouhoe, 1969.

Cole, Robert E. *Japanese Blue Collar: The Changing Tradition*. Berkeley: University of California Press, 1971.

Cook, Harold. "Pak Yong-hyo: Background and Early Years." *Journal of Social Sciences and Humanities* 31 (1969): 11–24.

Cumings, Bruce. *The Origins of the Korean War: Liberation and the Emergence of Separate Regimes, 1945–1947*. Princeton, N.J.: Princeton University Press, 1981.

————, ed. *Child of Conflict: The Korean-American Relationship, 1943–1953*. Seattle: University of Washington Press, 1975.

Deuchler, Martina. *Confucian Gentlemen and Barbarian Envoys: The Opening of Korea, 1875–1885*. Seattle: University of Washington Press, 1977.

————. *The Confucian Transformation of Korea: A Study of Society and Ideology*. Cambridge, Mass.: Council on East Asian Studies, Harvard University, 1992.

Deutsch, Karl. *Nationalism and Social Communication*. Cambridge, Mass.: MIT Press, 1953.

Durkheim, Émile. *The Division of Labor in Society*. Glencoe, Ill.: Free Press, 1947.

Eckert, Carter J. *Offspring of Empire: The Koch'ang Kims and the Colonial Origins of Korean Capitalism 1876–1945*. Seattle: University of Washington Press, 1991.

————. "The Colonial Origins of Korean Capitalism: The Koch'ang Kims and the Kyŏngsŏng Spinning and Weaving Company, 1876–1945." Ph.D. diss., University of Washington, Seattle, 1986.

Eckert, Carter J., Ki-baik Lee, Young Ick Lew, Michael Robinson, and Edward W. Wagner. *Korea Old and New: A History*. Seoul: Ilchokak, 1990.

Eisenstadt, S. N. *Modernization: Protest and Change.* Englewood Cliffs, N.J.: Prentice-Hall, 1966.

Fairbank, John K., Edwin O. Reischauer, and Albert M. Craig. *East Asia: The Modern Transformation: A History of East Asian Civilization.* Vol. 2. Boston: Houghton Mifflin, 1965.

Han Chŏngil. "Minju kungmindang ch'ulbŏm kwa 6.25 chŏn chŏnghwang" (The sailing of the Democratic National Party and the political situation before June 25 [Korean War]). In *Han'guk ŭi chŏngdang* (Korean political party), edited by Yi Kiha, Sim Chiyŏn, Han Chŏngil, and Son Pongsuk, 1: 202–36. Seoul: Han'guk Ilbosa, 1987.

Han Man Nyun (Manyŏn). *Irŏp ilsaeng* (Only one job for a lifetime). Expanded 2nd ed. Seoul: Ilchokak, 1994.

Han, Woo-keun. *The History of Korea.* Seoul: Eul-Yoo, 1981.

Han'gŭl Hakhoe. *Han'gŭl hakhoe osimnyŏnsa* (Fifty-year history of the Korean Language Society). Seoul: Han'gŭl Hakhoe, 1971.

Hatada, Takashi. *A History of Korea.* Edited and translated by W. W. Smith, Jr., and B. H. Hazard. Santa Barbara, Calif.: American Biographic Center, 1969.

Hayes, Carlton. *The Historical Evolution of Modern Nationalism.* New York: Macmillan, 1967.

Henderson, Gregory. *Korea: The Politics of the Vortex.* Cambridge, Mass.: Harvard University Press, 1968.

Hicks, George. *The Comfort Women.* St. Leonards, Australia: Allen and Unwin.

Hŏ Sŏndo. "Samil undong kwa yugyo" (The March First Movement and the Confucianist circles). In *Samil undong osipchunyŏn kinyŏm nonjip* (Collected essays for the 50th commemoration of the March First Movement), edited by Ko Chaeuk, 281–300. Seoul: Tonga Ilbosa, 1969.

Hong Ilsik, ed. *Koryŏ Taehak ŭi saram tŭl: Kim Sŏngsu* (People of Korea University: Kim Sŏngsu). Vol. 3. Seoul: Minjokmunhwa Yŏn'guso, Korea University, 1986.

Hwang Myŏngsu. "Inch'on Kim Sŏngsu ŭi kiŏp hwaldong kwa kyŏngyŏnginyŏm" (Business activity and management ideology of Kim Sŏngsu). In *P'yŏngjŏn Inch'on Kim Sŏngsu* (A critical biography of Kim Sŏngsu), edited by Sin Ilch'ŏl, 267–308. Seoul: Tonga Ilbosa, 1991.

Hyŏn Kyuwhan. *Han'guk yuiminsa* (A hisory of Korean wanderers and emigrants). 2 vols. Seoul: Ŏmungak, 1967.

Hyŏn Sangyun. "Samil undong palbal ŭi kaeyo" (Summary of the outbreak of the March First Movement). *Sasangge* (March 1963): 44–49.

Jacobs, Norman. *The Korean Road to Modernization and Development.* Urbana: University of Illinois Press, 1985.

Juhn, Daniel S. "Nationalism and Korean Businessmen." In *Korea's Response to Japan: The Colonial Period, 1910–1945,* edited by C. I. Eugene Kim and Doreth E. Mortimore, Korean Studies Series no. 5, 45–52. Kalamazoo: Center for Korean Studies, Western Michigan University, 1977.

Kang Chaeŏn. *Sinp'yŏn Han'guk kŭndaesa yŏn'gu* (Newly edited studies of modern Korean history). Seoul: Hanul, 1986.

Kang Chujin. "Inch'on ŭi tongnip sasang kwa nosŏn" (Kim Sŏngsu's thought and direction for Korean independence). In *Inch'on Kim Sŏngsu ŭi aejok sasang kwa kŭ silch'ŏn* (The patriotism of Kim Sŏngsu in thought and deed), edited by Kwŏn Ogi, 15–84. Seoul: Tonga Ilbosa, 1982.

Kang Tongjin. *Ilcheŭi Han'guk ch'imnyak chŏngch'aeksa* (History of the Japanese imperial policy of aggression in Korea). Seoul: Han'gilsa, 1980.

Kedourie, Elie. *Nationalism*. London: Hutchinson, 1960.

Keishōhokudō Keisatsubu. *Kōtō keisatsu yoshi: Bōtoshi henshū shiryo* (A major history of the Higher Police: The editorial materials for the history of rioters). Keijō: Keishōhokudō Keisatsubū, 1934.

Kim, Choong Soon. *The Culture of Korean Industry: An Ethnography of Poongsan Corporation*. Tucson: University of Arizona Press, 1992.

———. *Faithful Endurance: An Ethnography of Korean Family Dispersal*. Tucson: University of Arizona Press, 1988.

———. *An Asian Anthropologist in the South: Field Experiences with Blacks,Indians, and Whites*. Knoxville: University of Tennessee Press, 1977.

Kim Hakjoon (Hakchun). *Koha Song Chinu p'yŏngjŏn: Minjokchuŭi ŏllonin. Chŏngch'iga ŭi saengae* (A critical biography of Song Chinu: A journalist and a statesman: The life and times of a Korean nationalist democrat). Seoul: Tonga Ilbosa, 1990.

Kim Hwangjung, ed. *Ulsan Kimssi chokpo* (The Ulsan Kim genealogy). 3 vols. Changsŏng, Korea: Kim Hwangjung, 1977.

Kim Sanggi, ed. *Tonga Ilbo sasa* (History of the *Tonga Ilbo*). Vol. 3. Seoul: Tonga Ilbosa, 1985.

Kim Sangha, ed. *Sudang Kim Yŏnsu* (Kim Yŏnsu). Seoul: Samyangsa, 1985.

Kim Sangman, ed. *Tonga Ilbo sasa* (History of the *Tonga Ilbo*). Vol. 1. Seoul: Tonga Ilbosa, 1975.

———. *Tonga Ilbo osimnyŏnsa* (Fifty-year history of the *Tonga Ilbo*). Seoul: Tonga Ilbosa, 1975.

Kim Sŏngsu. "Ōkuma Shigenobu wa Chosŏn yuhaksaeng" (Ōkuma Shigenobu and Korean students in Japan. *Samch'ŏlli* 6 (1934): 96–99.

———. "Nan'gwan ŭn tugaji" (Two obstacles). *Pyŏlgŏngon* (February 1927): 12.

Kim Taesang. "Samil undong kwa haksaengch'ŭng" (The March First Movement and student circles). In *Samil undong osipchunyon kinyom nonjip* (Collected essays for the 50th commemoration of the March First Movement), edited by Ko Chaeuk, 301–11. Seoul: Tonga Ilbosa, 1969.

Kim Yongsŏp. *Han'guk kŭnhyŏndae nongŏpsa yŏn'gu: Hanmal-ilcheha ŭi chijuje wa nongŏp munje* (Studies in the agrarian history of twentieth-century Korea: Landlordism and agrarian conflicts in modern Korea). Seoul: Ilchokak, 1992.

Ko Chaeuk, ed. *Inch'on Kim Sŏngsujŏn* (The biography of Kim Sŏngsu). Seoul: Inch'on Kinyŏmhoe, 1976.

Kohasŏnsaeng Chŏn'gi P'yŏnch'an Wiwŏnhoe. *Tongnip ŭl hyanghan chimnyŏm: Koha Song Chinu Chŏn'gi* (The will to national liberation: A portrait of Song Chinu). Seoul: Tonga Ilbosa, 1990.

Kohn, Hahn. *The Idea of Nationalism.* New York: Macmillan, 1967.

Kuksa P'yŏnch'an Wiwŏnhoe, ed. *Han'guk tongnip undong saryo* (Historical documents on Korean independence movement). Vol. 4. Seoul: Kuksa P'yŏnch'an Wiwŏnhoe, 1968.

Kuno, S. Yoshi. *Japanese Expression on the Asiatic Continent.* 2 vols. Berkeley: University of California Press, 1937.

Kwŏn Ogi, ed. *Inch'on Kim Sŏngsu ŭi aejok sasang kwa kŭ silch'ŏn* (The patriotism of Kim Sŏngsu in thought and deed). Seoul: Tonga Ilbosa, 1982.

Kwŏn, T'aeŏk. *Han'guk kŭndae myŏnŏpsa yŏn'gu* (A study of the history of the modern Korean cotton industry). Seoul: Ilchokak, 1989.

Langness, L. L. *The Life History in Anthropological Science.* New York: Holt, Rinehart and Winston, 1965.

Lee, Changsoo, and George De Vos. *Koreans in Japan: Ethnic Conflict and Accommodation.* Berkeley: University of California Press, 1981.

Lee, Chŏng-sik. *Politics of Korean Nationalism.* Berkeley: University of California Press, 1964.

Lee, Ki-baik (Yi Kibaek). *A New History of Korea.* Translated by Edward W. Wagner, with Edward J. Schultz. Seoul: Ilchokak, 1984.

Lee Kwangrin (Yi Kwangrin). *Han'guk kaehwasa yŏn'gu* (A study in the history of enlightenment in Korea). Seoul: Ilchokak, 1993.

Lee, Sung-Il. *The Wind and the Waves: Four Modern Korean Poets.* Berkeley, Calif.: Asian Humanities Press, 1989.

Levy, Marion J., Jr. *Modernization and Structure of Society.* Princeton, N.J.: Princeton University Press, 1966.

Lew Young Ick (Yu Yŏngik). *Kabo kyŏngjang yŏn'gu* (Studies on the *Kabo* reform movement). Seoul: Ilchokak, 1990.

Maine, Henry Sumner. *Ancient Law.* New York: Dutton, 1965.

Mason, Edward S., Mahn Je Kim, Dwight H. Perkins, Kwang Suk Kim, and David C. Cole. *The Economic and Social Modernization of the Republic of Korea.* Cambridge, Mass.: Council on East Asian Studies, Harvard University, 1980.

McCune, Shannon. *Korea: The Land of Broken Calm.* New York: D. Van Nostrand, 1966.

McNamara, Dennis L. *The Colonial Origins of Korean Enterprise, 1910–1945*. New York: Cambridge University Press, 1990.

———. "The Keishō and the Korean Business Elite." *Journal of Asian Studies* 48 (1989): 310–23.

———. "Entrepreneurship in Colonial Korea: Kim Youn-su," *Modern Asian Studies* 22 (1988): 165–77.

Millet, John, Jr., Owen J. Caroll, and Margaret E. Tackley. *Korea, 1951–1953*. Washington, D.C.: Government Printing Office, 1956.

Noble, Harold Joyce. *Embassy at War*. Seattle: University of Washington Press, 1975.

Osgood, Cornelius. *The Koreans and Their Culture*. New York: Ronald Press, 1951.

Pak Inhwan. *Kyŏngbang yuksimnyŏn* (Sixty years of Kyŏngbang). Seoul: Kyŏngbang, 1980.

Pak Kyŏngsik. *Ilbon chegukchuŭi Chosŏn chibae* (Japanese imperial control over Korea). Seoul: Ch'ŏnga Ch'ulp'ansa, 1986.

Paek Nakchun (George Paik). "Inch'on Kim Sŏngsu wa minjok kyoyuk" (Kim Sŏngsu and national education)." In *Inch'on Kim Sŏngsu ŭi aejok sasang kwa kŭ silch'ŏn* (The patriotism of Kim Sŏngsu in thought and deed), edited by Kwŏn Ogi, 207–20. Seoul: Tonga Ilbosa, 1982.

Park Myung-Lim (Pak Myŏngrim). *Han'guk chŏnjaengŭi palbalgwa kiwŏn* (The Korean War: The outbreak and its origins). 2 vols. Seoul: Nanam, 1996.

Pelto, Petti J. *Anthropological Research: The Structure of Inquiry*. New York: Harper and Row, 1970.

Redfield, Robert. "The Folk Society." *American Journal of Sociology* 52 (1947): 293–308.

Rees, David. *Korea: The Limited War*. New York: St. Martin's Press, 1964.

Republic of Korea National Red Cross. *The Dispersed Families in Korea*. Seoul: Republic of Korea National Red Cross, 1977.

Riley, John W., and Wilbur Schramm. *The Reds Take a City: The Communist Occupation of Seoul, with Eyewitness Accounts*. New Brunswick, N.J.: Rutgers University Press, 1951.

Robinson, Michael E. *Cultural Nationalism in Colonial Korea, 1920–1925*. Seattle: University of Washington Press, 1988.

Sandusky, Michael C. *America's Parallel*. Alexandria, Va.: Old Dominion Press, 1983.

Sim Chiyŏn. "Han'guk minjudang ŭi ch'angdang" (Establishment of the Korean Democratic Party). In *Han'guk ŭi chŏngdang* (Korean political party), edited by Yi Kiha, Sim Chiyŏn, Han Chŏngil, and Son Pongsuk, 1: 143–99. Seoul: Han'guk Ilbosa, 1987.

Sin Ilch'ŏl, ed. *P'yŏngjŏn Inch'on Kim Sŏngsu* (A critical biography of Kim Sŏngsu). Seoul: Tonga Ilbosa, 1991.

————. "Han'guk kŭndaehwa ŭi sŏn'gakcha Inch'on Kim Sŏngsu ŭi saengae" (Kim Sŏngsu's career as a leader of Korean modernization). In *P'yŏngjŏn Inch'on Kim Sŏngsu* (A critical biography of Kim Sŏngsu), edited by Sin Ilch'ŏl, 15–73. Seoul: Tonga Ilbosa, 1991.

Sin Yongha. "Iljeha Inch'on ŭi minjok kyoyuk hwaldong" (Activities of Kim Sŏngsu for national education under Japanese colonization). In *P'yŏngjŏn Inch'on Kim Sŏngsu* (A critical biography of Kim Sŏngsu), edited by Sin Ilch'ŏl, 237–66. Seoul: Tonga Ilbosa, 1991.

Smith, Anthony. *Theories of Nationalism.* New York: Holmes and Meier, 1983.

Soh, Chunghee Sarah. "The Korean 'Comfort Women': Movement for Redress." *Asian Survey* 36 (1996): 1226–40.

Sŏnggok Chŏn'gi Kanhaeng Wiwŏnhoe, ed. *Pyŏlil ŏpche: Sŏnggok sŏnsaeng ilhwajip* (No special problem: A collection of Kim Sŏnggon's anecdotes). 2 vols. Seoul: Korea Herald, 1988.

Stands-IN-Timber, John, and Margot Liverty. *Cheyenne Memories.* New Haven, Conn.: Yale University Press, 1967.

Steers, Richard M., Shin Yoo Keun, and Gerardo R. Ungson. *The Chaebol: Korea's New Industrial Might.* New York: Harper and Row, 1989.

Stone, I. F. *The Hidden History of the Korean War.* New York: Monthly Review Press, 1953.

Suh, Dae-sook. *The Korean Communist Movement, 1918–1948.* Princeton, N.J.: Princeton University Press, 1967.

Suh, Sang-chul. *Growth and Structural Changes in the Korean Economy, 1910–1940.* Cambridge, Mass.: Council on East Asian Studies, Harvard University, 1978.

Tünnies, Ferdinand. *Community and Society.* Edited and translated by Charles P. Loomis. New York: Harper and Row, 1963.

Wagner, Edward W. *The Korean Minority in Japan: 1904–1950.* New York: Institute of Pacific Relations, 1951.

Waldron, Arthur N. "Theories of Nationalism." *World Politics* 37 (1985): 416–31.

Weber, Max. *The Theory of Social and Economic Organization.* Translated by A. H. Henderson and Talcott Parsons. New York: Free Press, 1957.

Whiting, Allen. *China Crosses the Yalu: The Decision to Enter the Korean War.* Stanford, Calif.: Stanford University Press, 1969.

Wi Kibung. "Kim Sŏngsu ilga *Tonga Ilbo karoch'aetta*" (The Kims stole the *Tonga Ilbo*). *Mal* (March 1989): 34–48.

————. *Tasissŭnŭn Tonga Ilbo sa* (Re-writing history of *Tonga Ilbo*). Seoul: Nokchin, 1991.

Yi Ch'ŏlsŭng. *Chŏn'guk hangnyŏn* (National student league). Seoul: Chungang Ilbo and Tongyang Pangsong, 1976.

Yi Hyŏnhŭi. "Samil undong kwa Inch'on Kim Sŏngsu" (The March First Movement and Kim Sŏngsu). In *P'yŏngjŏn Inch'on Kim Sŏngsu* (A critical biography of Kim Sŏngsu), edited by Sin Ilch'ŏl, 197–236. Seoul: Tonga Ilbosa, 1991.

———, ed. *Tonghak sasang kwa Tonghak hyŏngmyŏng* (The thought of Tonghak and Tonghak revolution). Seoul: Ch'ŏnga Ch'ulp'ansa, 1984.

Yi Kwangsu. "Kim Sŏngsuron" (Discussions on Kim Sŏngsu). *Saebyŏk* (May 1955): 81–82.

———. "Minjok kaejoron" (Treatise on the reconstruction of the nation). *Kaebyŏk* 3 (1922): 18–72.

Yi Kyŏngnam. *Sŏlsan Chang Tŏksu* (Chang Tŏksu). Seoul: Tonga Ilbosa, 1982.

Yi Man'gyu. *Yŏ Unhyŏngsŏnsaeng t'ujaengsa* (History of Yŏ Unhyŏng's struggles). Seoul: Minjumunhwasa, 1946.

Yi Pyŏnghŏn. "Naegabon samil undong ŭi ildanmyŏn" (A slice of the March First Movement that I saw). In *Samil undong osipchunyŏn kinyŏm nonjip* (Collected essays for the 50th commemoration of the March First Movement), edited by Ko Chaeuk, 407–11. Seoul: Tonga Ilbosa, 1969.

Yi T'aekhwi. "Pulgap'i han sŏnt'aek: Chŏngch'i chidoja ŭi kil" (Unavoidable choice: The way of a political leader). In *P'yŏngjŏn Inch'on Kim Sŏngsu* (A critical biography of Kim Sŏngsu), edited by Sin Ilch'ŏl, 339–421. Seoul: Tonga Ilbosa, 1991.

Yoshino, Kosaku. *Cultural Nationalism in Contemporary Japan: A Sociological Inquiry*. London: Routledge, 1992.

Yu Chino. *Yanghogi* (Teaching at Korea University). Seoul: Korea University Press, 1977.

Yu Kwangyŏl. *Kija pansegi* (As a reporter for half a century). Seoul: Sŏmundang, 1970.

Yun Chaegŭn. *Kŭnch'on Paek Kwansu* (Paek Kwansu). Seoul: Tonga Ilbosa, 1996.

ABOUT THE AUTHOR

CHOONG SOON KIM, University Faculty Scholar and professor of anthropology, has taught at the University of Tennessee at Martin since 1971. From 1981 to 1991, he was chairman of the Department of Sociology and Anthropology.

In 1993–94, Dr. Kim taught business and industrial anthropology at Yonsei University in Seoul, Korea, as a senior Fulbright scholar. He also has been a senior Fulbright researcher at Seoul National University in Korea, a visiting professor at Hirosaki University in Japan, and a Rockefeller Foundation scholar-in-residence at the Bellagio Study Center in Italy.

Dr. Kim is the author of several books, including *Japanese Industry in the American South* (1995), *The Culture of Korean Industry: An Ethnography of Poongsan Corporation* (1992), *Faithful Endurance: An Ethnography of Korean Family Dispersal* (1988), and *An Asian Anthropologist in the South: Field Experiences with Blacks, Indians, and Whites* (1977). In addition, articles by Dr. Kim have been published in scholarly journals, including *American Anthropologist* and *Current Anthropology,* as well as in various monographs and collections.

He is currently at work on a new book, *Cyberia in Asia: An Anthropological Perspective on the New Cultural Hegemony.*

INDEX